RIDE
THE
WAVE

Praise for *Ride the Wave*

"Still bruised by the lumps you took when the stock market bubble burst? Battered by a never-ending barrage of information? Why not nurse yourself back to financial health with the help of Sherry Cooper's ambitious look at the forces pummeling the New Economy into shape. A great aid to identifying the trends and innovations that will shape the winning investments and strategies of the future. And a fact-filled, interesting read!"

—Kathleen Hays, Economics Editor, CNBC

Sherry Cooper's *Ride the Wave* is a much-needed "time out" for investors and business executives grappling with today's frenetic and fast-paced New Economy. She presents a well-reasoned, commonsense approach that will help you plan effectively in the challenging years ahead.

—Susie Gharib, Co-Anchor, PBS's *Nightly Business Report*

"Dr. Cooper is a rarity—she demystifies, deconstructs and delights as she explains the forces shaping our fast-moving world."

—Donald Coxe, Chairman and Chief Strategist, Harris Bank

"Sherry Cooper has done a remarkable job defining a new age, where speed is a constant but timing and direction are often uncertain."

—Erich Almasy, Vice President and Director,
The Boston Consulting Group of Canada Limited

"It is always a pleasure, and an insightful one, to read the work of Sherry Cooper. Her newest book, *Ride the Wave*, is no exception. We strongly recommend *Ride the Wave* to both the most sophisticated investors and to initiates ... and we cannot do this strongly enough."

—Dennis Gartman, Editor/Publisher, *The Gartman Letter*, L.C.

"A story that needs to be told. The world has changed dramatically and we all need to understand it — NOW! Thank you, Sherry!"

—Steve Slifer, Chief U.S. Economist, Lehman Brothers

"Sherry Cooper's keen insight will help you ride the rocky shoals of change."

—Edward Yardeni, Chief Investment Strategist, Deutsche Banc Alex. Brown

"Sherry Cooper is a gifted interpreter of complex technical, social, and economic issues and their impact on our futures. *Ride the Wave* left me better informed and hopeful about the New Economy, despite the current turmoil of world markets."

—Margaret Barrett, CEO Merrill Lynch HSBC

"This book should be required reading for those interested in their personal and financial success. Sherry does an excellent job outlining the key drivers of the new economy and pointing out which strategies work best. I highly recommend this book."

—Professor Karl Moore, McGill University,
author of *Foundations of Corporate Empire*

RIDE
THE
WAVE

SHERRY COOPER

A Pearson Company
London · New York · San Francisco · Toronto · Sydney · Tokyo · Singapore · Hong Kong
Cape Town · Madrid · Paris · Milan · Munich · Amsterdam

FINANCIAL TIMES

Prentice Hall

A Pearson Company

© 2001 Sherry S. Cooper
Foreword © 2001 Don Tapscott

IN THE UNITED STATES

ISBN 0-13-067086-3 *Ride the Wave: Taking Control in a Turbulent Financial Age*

The publisher offers discounts on this book when ordered in bulk quantities. For more information, contact: Corporate Sales Department, Phone: 800-382-3419; Fax: 201-236-7141; Email: corpsales@prenhall.com; or write: Prentice Hall PTR, Corp. Sales Dept., One Lake Street, Upper Saddle River, NJ 07458.

IN CANADA

ISBN 0-13-031104-9 *Ride the Wave: Take Control in the Acceleration Age*

Books are available at quantity discounts with bulk purchase for educational, business, or sales promotional use. For information, please email or write to: Pearson PTR Canada, Special Sales, PTR Division, 26 Prince Andrew Place, Don Mills, Ontario, M3C 2T8. Email ss.corp@pearsoned.com. Please supply: title of book, ISBN, quantity, how the book will be used, date needed.

This publication contains the opinions and ideas of its author and is designed to provide useful advice in regard to the subject matter covered. The author and publisher are not engaged in rendering legal, accounting, or other professional services in this publication. This publication is not intended to provide a basis for action in particular circumstances without consideration by a competent professional. The author and publisher expressly disclaim any responsibility for any liability, loss, or risk, personal or otherwise, which is incurred as a consequence, directly or indirectly, of the use and application of any of the contents of this book.

Prentice-Hall International (UK) Limited, *London*
Prentice-Hall of Austraila Pty. Limited, *Sydney*
Prentice-Hall Canada, Inc., *Toronto*
Prentice-Hall Hispanoamericana, S.A., *Mexico*
Prentice-Hall of Indi Private Limited, *New Delhi*
Prentice-Hall of Japan, Inc., *Tokyo*
Pearson Education Asia Pte., Ltd.
Editora Prentice-Hall do Brasil, Ltda., *Rio de Janeiro*

National Library of Canada Cataloguing in Publication Data

Cooper, Sherry S.
    Ride the wave : take control in the acceleration age

ISBN 0-13-062278-8 (Can. ed.).—ISBN 0-13-067086-3 (US ed.)

1. Economic forecasting. I. Title.

HC59.15.C66 2001   330'.01'12   C2001-901232-2

1 2 3 4 5   FR   05 04 03 02 01

Printed and bound in Canada.

This book is dedicated to Vilma Liedman, Peter Cooper, and Stefan Atkinson—three generations, three pillars of my life.

Acknowledgments

No book is ever written alone, and this one is no exception. Many of the people I would like to thank I will never meet—the scholars and thinkers on whose shoulders I stand. Many, but not all, are listed in the notes and bibliography.

My greatest debt of gratitude goes to my husband, Peter Cooper, who accepts and endures my arduous work, travel, and writing schedule—not to mention mood swings—with unflagging support and encouragement. Peter read several drafts of the manuscript and provided incisive critiques. He is my sounding board and devil's advocate. A brilliant business strategist and active participant in the dot-com sector, Peter gives me invaluable insight and real-world expertise in our rapidly changing economic environment. Peter, you are my best friend.

To my son, Stefan Atkinson, I owe my sense of purpose, drive, and enthusiasm. In an interesting twist of role reversal, my son is my mentor and shining model. There is no height to which he will not aspire. I admire his courage, perseverance, and dedication to excellence. Stefan, you are the best. Thank you for bringing so much joy to my life; I bask in your reflection.

To my mother, Vilma Liedman, you will always be my rock-solid foundation. How can I thank a person for providing the emotional support through a lifetime to make me believe that I can do anything I set my mind to? The self-appointed president of my fan club, my mom read an early draft of this book and provided helpful comments.

My family extends beyond the bounds of blood and relation. It includes the many people who support me at home and at work. A very special and private thanks to Thelma Flores and Carmen Grant; without you two, this could never have been possible. Much appreciation, as well, to Caitlin MacNamara and Dia-Lynn Wear. Your support in organization, management, and creativity has been invaluable.

In addition, I owe a huge debt of gratitude to Jennifer Lee, who flexed her enormous skills in research and fact checking (and re-checking). Jennifer, thank you for your unstinting support, great sense of humor, and positive attitude. Our flurry of weekend e-mails often kept me going.

Daniel Jankowski provided meaningful technical and research support. Thanks also to the many people who read and contributed to early drafts of the manuscript. These include Donald Coxe, Michael Galper, Megan Gwin, Jennifer Lee, Caitlin MacNamara, Kerry Mosher, Douglas Porter, Russell Sheldon, and Dia-Lynn Wear.

I am indebted to Professor Charles L. Jones, Senior Fellow in Sociology, Massey College of the University of Toronto, for his excellent review and assistance on the sections regarding the sex ratio and its implications for social change. The views and opinions expressed in these sections are, however, my own and cannot be attributed to Professor Jones.

Thanks as well to Andrea Crozier, Editorial Director at Pearson PTR Canada. Your unfailing enthusiasm and support from the earliest days of this project have been extremely valuable and reassuring. Lisa Berland has provided able editorial assistance and has markedly contributed to the book's flow and readability.

I am also grateful for the ongoing support of the senior executives of the Bank of Montreal group of companies who never questioned my ability to complete this project while carrying out my responsibilities in the organization. Special thanks go to Tony Comper, William Downe, and Gilles Ouellette for their continuing support.

To all of these people and the many I may have forgotten, thank you. The errors and omissions remain my own, but the successes I share with them.

Contents

Foreword

By Don Tapscott

T his is a time of great confusion in business. During the latter part of the 1990s, corporate imagination was swept away by the dot-com wave. The obvious revolutionary power of the Internet was channelled primarily into myriad start-ups that seemingly challenged incumbents in every industry from bookselling to banking. Venture capitalist financing flowed fast and freely, and many people forgot (assuming they ever knew) about business fundamentals. Momentum investing set in. Alan Greenspan's admonishment of "irrational exuberance" was an understatement. And in early 2000 the bubble burst.

Having been reminded that the laws of business gravity continue to apply, many managers have wisely returned to the fundamentals. They are focusing on customer value, creating viable business models and strategies, and achieving operational efficiencies.

But a return to the fundamentals in itself is insufficient to ensure business success. We cannot just turn back the clock. Many executives I work with still believe the Internet has revolutionary significance, which it does. And where will the turmoil in capital markets lead? Must we go through a recession? Business leaders need to understand the new business context before they can develop effective strategies. This is the importance of Sherry Cooper's book. She has few rivals in articulating the big picture within which we must all operate.

My view is that we are not at the end of profound change. We are just beginning. For decades, the starting point for strategic thinking has been the standalone vertically integrated corporation. These powerful companies do everything from soup to nuts and dominate the competitive landscape. We think of them as intrinsic to the economy and they provide the context for theories about competitive strategy.

Internally these corporations have always operated more as planned economies rather than efficient marketplaces, and we are now beginning to appreciate that they were actually clumsy, costly, and inefficient. (Dilbert captures this well.) But during the last century such companies prospered because they were superior to any other model of production. It was cheaper and simpler for companies to perform the maximum number of functions in-house, rather than incurring the high cost, hassle, and risk of constantly searching, contracting, understanding, collaborating, and executing transactions with outside partners.

This is no longer the case. Because of the Internet, a new business architecture is rising to challenge the industrial-age corporation. My colleagues and I call it the "business web," or "b-web," and we define it as any system—of suppliers, distributors, service providers, infrastructure providers, and customers—that uses the Internet as the basis for business communications and transactions. In the most successful business webs, each constituent focuses on its core competence. We have studied hundreds of examples of b-webs, and in industry after industry, these new vehicles for value creation are proving more supple, cost-efficient, and innovative than their traditional competitors.

Because of this, myriad new models have emerged that are different from the industrial age template. Hundreds of successful examples show that companies can now focus on their core capabilities and partner for the rest. Siebel Systems, for example, one of the fastest-growing companies in America, has established a vast partner network to deliver a unique assemblage of customer, supplier, and employee relationship software. Tom Siebel argues that its b-web is the most important element is his company's success, saying, "We only have 8000 people on our payroll, but more than 30,000 people work for us." The relatively small core company creates software products and orchestrates an extensive b-web comprising consultants, technology providers, implementers, suppliers, and vendors that take its products to the global marketplace. The result: 1400 percent growth in the past three years.

The CEO of Boeing says his company is a systems integrator, not an aircraft manufacturer. Dell shifted from classic mass production to a shop production model, introducing entirely new business concepts like the demand chain. LEGO through its Mindstorm robot products brings customers into its business web, enabling them to co-create products. Schwab moved from being a tightly integrated financial services provider to an Internet-based aggregator of financial services and stole huge market share. IBM is a computer company that doesn't manufacture computers—its partners do.

Simply deploying Intranets within corporate walls fails to capture b-web power because they fail to capture the tonic of the marketplace. Most of what companies do is not based on their core competencies. They attempt to build up and "make do" with design, manufacturing, marketing, and other capabilities that are often not best of breed in the open market. Now with the Net, business functions or large projects can be reduced to smaller components and farmed out (often simultaneously) to more specialized companies around the world with virtually no transaction costs.

This harnesses the enormous benefits of the competitive environment. Suppliers strive to reduce costs and increase quality and innovation. They know there are other specialized workers and companies around the world keen to do the work.

By contrast, insisting a project stay in-house often means it is comparatively more difficult to mobilize resources, even with a high-performance Intranet. Employees are pressed into jobs unrelated to their skills, as managers try to "make do" with the workers on hand. Alternately, adding new employees to the payroll is time-consuming and costly. Approvals must be sought, reporting structures developed, workspace arranged, and so on. Every manager knows these internal rigidities increase corporate costs and stifle innovation.

To prosper in today's economy the business strategist needs new tools—including strategic concepts and analytical methods—to comprehend and exploit the unprecedented business architectures suddenly available. This was almost a non-issue when the superiority of the industrial corporation was taken for granted. It was just assumed, for example, that most resources would be internal to the company. A business' human resources strategy dealt with people on the payroll.

Simple. But in the Internet era firms can profit enormously from resources that don't belong to them.

Issues such as partnering, corporate boundaries, distribution channels, industry restructuring, and strategic repositioning are suddenly much more complex. The b-school case studies of five or ten years ago no longer apply. This is why *Ride the Wave* is such a solid contribution to understanding the new economic context. In the increasingly inter-networked world, business leaders require a firm grip on the total environment in which they are operating. Read and prosper.

Don Tapscott
Co-founder of Digital 4Sight and
co-author of *Digital Capital: Harnessing the Power of Business Webs*

Introduction

We are in the midst of a truly revolutionary period in the development of humankind. Everyday acts of many ordinary people are changing the world. More and more, we will live our lives in real time—in motion—spontaneous, immediate, always connected. This is a time of increasing complexity, of an overabundant data and sensory onslaught. Technology is enabling and empowering, but it is also inhibiting for those individuals and businesses (even governments) that get it wrong—that misstep in the rapidly changing world of the Digital Revolution.

The Internet is the most powerful communication medium the world has ever known and it has been adopted more quickly than any other new technology in history. The Internet is open, immediate, non-hierarchical, and democratic. It is impacting whole sectors, industries, countries, and societies. The Net is one of those inventions that can truly shake institutions to their core. In the next five years or so, the Net will be pervasive and nearly invisible. Almost everything—virtually all devices, appliances, and manufactured products—will become intelligent, interconnected, and mobile. The Internet will be always "on" and ubiquitous.

We will soon see the merging of the digital world with the life sciences, as biological systems become the model for information systems. Already, rapid advances in information technology have enabled scientists to begin to unlock the secrets of living organisms. Very soon, biology itself will revolutionize information and communications technology. Scientists and researchers are even now building computers and machines that mimic molecular structures and biological systems.

Things will happen faster than ever before in this, the Acceleration Age. The key to empowerment is understanding and flexibility. As Charles Darwin said, "It is not the strongest of the species that survive, nor the most intelligent, but the one most responsive to change."

A PERIOD OF IMMENSE AND RAPID CHANGE

I have spent most of my adult life studying the economy and financial markets and I cannot help but be struck by the forces shaping the landscape today. The level of volatility is without precedent, while the pace of change has never been greater. The markets respond to incoming data, political developments, and even analysts' comments with lightning speed. Often the responses are precipitous and exaggerated. The media play an increasing role in impacting, even determining, household and business psychology. And psychology crucially affects spending and investment decisions. We live in a financial and economic world that never sleeps. With the popularity of twenty-four-hour news coverage and financial-news broadcasting, public sentiment is subject more than ever to a herd mentality. So we see the rush to believe one year that the bull market in Internet stocks will never end and, the next year, that the Internet is a fad and a passé one at that. Neither extreme is correct.

But volatility is inherent in the speed at which the world is now changing—technological advance and societal acceptance of these advances have never been swifter. As knowledge increases, response times shorten. Consumers, spooked by the collapse in the Nasdaq and the surge in heating bills in 2000, rapidly revised down their spending plans. Businesses, aware of these downward revisions more promptly than ever before—thanks to advanced inventory-monitoring systems— accelerated the pace of response. Production was aggressively slashed, workers were laid off, and capital spending plans were shelved. The decline in business investment in technology was all the more pronounced because of the massive overinvestment that had occurred in 1999 and early 2000 when capital was cheap and readily available. The economy tumbled. In the space of a few months, sentiment shifted from euphoria to gloom. Predictions of recession came fast and furiously and many suggested the recession would be long and severe. Stocks plummeted, particularly the once-lauded technology stocks, and consumer sentiment sank further. All this just a few months after the Fed and market pundits were hailing the longest expansion in American history.

In April 2000, a bond fund manager berated me during a very rowdy after-dinner speech for predicting that the U.S. economy would be slowing. I remember the heat I felt as many in the audience espoused the view that the economy would continue to surprise on the up side, as it had for more than four years. The dot-com bubble was in the process of bursting, but no one in the room saw it as more than a temporary correction. Inflation, according to many, was the real concern. The Fed concurred, as it raised interest rates for the sixth and final time (that tightening cycle) in May 2000. By October, someone had seemingly turned the lights out. The downturn was fully in train and sentiment rapidly shifted.

THE ACCELERATION AGE

Welcome to the Acceleration Age. Things happen faster and more aggressively than ever before. Information is communicated more rapidly and more completely, allowing for the shortening of response times. Stability and predictability become increasingly rare. Stocks might have posted an average annual return of around 12 percent over the past thirty years, but the average rate of increase masks stunning gains and gut-wrenching losses, and the volatility will only rise. Get caught in the losses column early in retirement and your plans can be devastated.

People are often unnerved by these changes. Even when the economy was booming and jobs were easy to get, feelings of job insecurity continued to run rampant. Fully one-third of surveyed workers in the United States during the late-1990s economic boom reported that they regularly feared losing their job. Many feared skill obsolescence, a reasonable concern during a period of immense and rapid technological change. Business consolidation, restructuring, and downsizing also contribute to the unease. Wall Street rewards the companies that cut costs, which often means cutting bodies. CEOs, themselves, are increasingly on the chopping block if earnings disappoint. Businesses that have a leading edge one day might find themselves in serious trouble the next. The list of such fallen angels increased explosively in 2001—Lucent, Xerox, Kodak, and TWA, among many others.

The human toll from this uncertainty is meaningful. Feelings of insecurity are discomforting. But this acceleration in the pace of change is not new; it is a process that has been in train for some time. Alvin Toffler, in his landmark book *Future Shock*, wrote about it in 1970.[1] Even then people were feeling overwhelmed by the pace of change, the transience of society and the workplace, and the impermanence of institutions and relationships. He asserted that most people were grotesquely unprepared to cope with it.[2] Toffler's book has sold more than five million copies, testimony to the nerve he touched, the social and personal upset the rapidly transforming "disposable" economy has caused. If anything, since 1970, the pace of change has accelerated.

Gone are the days of guaranteed lifetime employment with one company—the single-stream career where you could confidently set your sights at graduation on a predestined future. Gone are the five-year business plans and a stable environment that all but assured that the behemoths today would be the giants of tomorrow. But in its place is a time of innovation, transformation, and high energy. Frightening as the volatility might be, it is also laden with opportunity and excitement. New fortunes will be built by people who understand and harness these forces and successfully ride the rocky waves of change. The ride is dangerous but thrilling, and there are ways to prepare for it. That is what this book is about—understanding and taking control of the dynamism of today's economic and financial milieu. Historical perspective is essential in this task, but it is not sufficient.

Also necessary in the Acceleration Age is foresight and adaptation. Knowing that the world will continue to change rapidly and anticipating the direction is a daunting but imperative endeavor. Careers and businesses must be dynamic, not static; they must anticipate and respond to the forces at work. Winners will win big, but market leadership is difficult to sustain. There are always new rivals poised to emerge—new, agile, and innovative competition. Key to continuing success is ongoing innovation. Anticipation, calculated risk-taking, and cunning are crucial elements of the New Economy—an information-based world where the most successful products are, in essence, congealed knowledge.

Knowledge, ideas, and innovation create value in the New Economy. Global competitive forces have never been greater and global capitalism has grown rapidly in recent years with the demise of communism. Countries, like companies, face the mounting challenge of competition and change. Some will prosper in an atmosphere of flexibility and adaptation, and others will languish—mired by bureaucracy, rigidity, and an environment that does not foster change.

MY U.S.–CANADA EXPERIENCE

I have seen this rapid change from the perspective of two countries—two very different responses to the forces at hand. My career straddles both the United States and Canada. I was born and educated in the United States. I majored in economics at Goucher College in Baltimore, Maryland, in the early 1970s; at the time, majoring in economics was a somewhat unusual thing for a young woman to do. Goucher, back then, was a small liberal arts college for women. In 1987, like most other schools of its genre, it started admitting men. The most popular majors were psychology and elementary education. There were only four economics majors in my year. Hard to believe today, when economics is among the most popular majors at most universities. I went on to graduate school at the University of Pittsburgh and, upon completion of my Ph.D., I joined the Federal Reserve Board in Washington, D.C., as a staff economist in the research department.

Those were the days of sky-high inflation and stagnation. The world was still reeling from the OPEC energy crises in the 1970s and the Iranian hostage affair, and we were about to embark upon the disastrous credit-control period of President Jimmy Carter. The Fed was in a period of tremendous flux. I started there in 1977 at the tail end of the Arthur Burns era. The brief but rather inauspicious reign of Fed Chairman G. William Miller—the former CEO of Textron who had little knowledge of economics or financial markets—did nothing to break the mounting inflation pressure. The Fed under Miller attempted to follow a gradualist policy of monetary tightening through very modest increases in the federal funds rate—the overnight interest rate banks pay to borrow money from one another.

When Mr. Miller was appointed treasury secretary, in came Paul Volcker, the towering, cigar-smoking, former president of the New York Federal Reserve Bank—a veteran market watcher and financial guru. Many of the young economists on the staff, including myself, quaked in his presence, as his devil's advocate style was daunting to all but the most experienced. Volcker's tenure at the Fed was marked by radical change. He recognized that inflation reduction would require a new approach. The Miller experience had proved that small, gradual interest rate hikes would not be sufficient to crush inflation. In an unprecedented Saturday press conference in October 1979, Chairman Volcker shifted away from traditional interest-rate targeting to monetarism, a policy of targeting the growth of the money supply, allowing interest rates to be determined by the forces of the supply and the demand for money. Monetarism provided the political cover to allow the Fed to hike rates more dramatically. But even we would not have imagined that the federal fund rate would rise to the stratospheric levels we actually saw at its peak in 1981—levels over a stunning 20 percent.

Precipitating the extent of the rate rise were the newly introduced changes in the structure of deposit rates at the financial institutions. The Fed along with the Federal Home Loan Bank Board, the regulator of the savings and loan (S&L) industry, had linked deposit rates to Treasury bill rates. Each time the Fed tightened monetary policy, deposit rates rose and money came pouring into the financial institutions. But as long as money was flowing into the banks and S&Ls, mortgage money flowed out to prospective homebuyers, albeit at ever-rising interest rates. It turned out that price rationing—through higher mortgage rates—was far less effective than credit rationing. It wasn't until mortgage rates rose to the ozone that the housing market really collapsed. And collapse it ultimately did, taking with it the economy, but not until after President Carter tried his ill-fated credit controls in 1980.

The controls were a disaster, as people misunderstood the rules on credit card usage and spending stopped dead in its tracks, causing a mini-recession in early 1980. A widening variety of disgruntled borrowers, strangled by the punitive interest rates, suffered enormous pain, and demonstrators burned Paul Volcker in effigy outside his office window on Constitution Avenue. One irate homebuilder even stormed the Fed's boardroom armed with a machete, in search of the chairman. Needless to say, metal detectors and much more stringent security measures were immediately installed at the entrance to the building on C Street.

In the midst of this turmoil, I was appointed Special Assistant to the Chairman, largely to respond to the mounting barrage of hate mail—talk about a terrible job. I think my senior colleagues gave me this assignment because I was five months pregnant and so knew it would be temporary. Maternity leave was my reprieve. The deluge came from desperate farmers, builders, automakers, and ordinary citizens shattered by the dramatic surge in interest rates. It included bags and bags of profanity-laden blocks of two-by-fours from the home-building industry. Consumers begged for relief, concerned that the next step would be foreclosure and bankruptcy. Some of the toughest letters to answer were from Capitol Hill, where congressmen, especially from the House Banking Committee, were particularly upset about the torrent of angry letters they were receiving from constituents. The only supporters of the policy were retirees living on fixed-income investments. I remember many handwritten letters from elderly coupon clippers grateful for the opportunity to earn 15 percent or more on their Treasury bonds.

Finally, by 1982, the economy had weakened enough to bring inflation down; but the real impetus for the ultimate easing in monetary policy was the Mexican debt crisis, which threatened the stability of many banks around the world. I moved on to the Federal National Mortgage Association for a brief stint as Director of Financial Economics. But I wasn't to stay there for long.

BAY STREET BECKONS

Thanks to the wild gyrations in interest rates, unprecedented in American financial history, and to the fixation on weekly money supply data, Fed economists became a hot ticket on Wall Street. Formerly among the most stable of employees, key Fed staffers were suddenly bombarded with job offers that doubled or tripled their measly government salaries. Many were lured away.

I followed a somewhat different route; I went to the Canadian financial world of Bay Street—rather than Wall Street—mainly for family reasons. I was then married to a Canadian who was offered a great job in Toronto. Our son was just turning two and we thought that Toronto would be a bit more family-friendly than New York for a traveling working couple with very demanding jobs. That was 1983, and I have been headquartered in Toronto ever since.

I am now chief economist of BMO Nesbitt Burns, a large, Canadian investment dealer, and Global Economic Strategist for our parent, the Bank of Montreal in Toronto and for the Harris Bank in Chicago (which is wholly owned by the Bank of Montreal). I spend my time roughly evenly divided between the U.S. and Canada, with trips to Europe and the Far East thrown in as well. Studying and forecasting both the U.S. and Canadian economies so intensively for nearly twenty years has given me a unique perspective. I see the profound role the U.S. plays in the global economy and financial markets and analyze daily the impact of the U.S. on its number-one trading partner, Canada. But I also follow the U.S. in great depth with, hopefully, a somewhat broader perspective.

From the vantage point of where I sit, it has been evident over the past two decades that much of what has happened in the U.S. has been extremely positive. The policy shifts that began in the early 1980s with the Reagan Administration set the stage for the economic boom of the 1990s. While the economy has slumped sharply since then, U.S. leadership in the technology revolution is firmly entrenched and, in my view, without rival. What the U.S. did right in the '80s is in stark contrast, for example, to what Canada did wrong. Even today, Canada is still paying the price. This has important implications for Germany, Japan, and economies all over the world.

THE ANGLO-WORLD DICHOTOMIES

While President Ronald Reagan was busily slashing U.S. taxes in the early 1980s, Margaret Thatcher was doing the same in Britain. In dramatic contrast, Pierre Trudeau was hard at work creating an ever-growing government social safety net in Canada that ultimately led to a dramatic ratcheting up of all tax rates—business, personal, and capital gains. At the same time, Trudeau bucked the pro-business trends of U.S. and U.K. leaders by clamping down on the energy industry and discouraging foreign (read American) direct investment in Canada.

Businesses throughout the United States and Britain were deregulated and privatized, while Canada continued with foreign-content limits and enormous provincial and federal regulatory restrictions, many of which remain today. While Reagan took on the air traffic controllers, and Thatcher took on the coal miners, unions in Canada became ever more powerful and disruptive. The Canadian economy, a global growth leader in the thirty years following World War II, began to underperform, and government budget deficits exploded.

Budget deficits grew in the U.S. as well, but they were mainly the result of the huge increase in defense spending that accompanied the tax cuts. This spending ultimately broke the back of the Soviet Union and led to the 1989 end of the Cold War. In contrast, in Canada, much of the government money was spent to subsidize declining industries. Canada, a leader in agribusiness, fisheries, forest products, mining, and energy, suffered from the global decline in many of these sectors. Government dollars were poured into decrepit pulp mills and fisheries with no fish. In contrast, steel mills, coal mines, and other basic manufacturing businesses were shut down all over the U.S. as the rust belt embarked on a mammoth renovation.

Economic restructuring proceeded at a rapid pace in the States and Britain, spurred by the need to become competitive with the growing economic power of Japan and Germany. Canadian business was slow to adjust, relying instead on an ever falling Canadian dollar to render their products competitive in the all-important U.S. market.

Never was the contrast between Canada and the U.S. greater than during the first half of the 1990s. The U.S. was poised for the take-off of the New Economy, while Canada was still mired in the Old. Following the brief Gulf War-related U.S. recession in 1991, the transformation of the American economy became spectacularly evident. What started as the jobless recovery eventually morphed into the tightest labor markets in American history. Capital in the U.S. was cheap and readily available as venture capital companies boomed and the stock market fueled an ever-growing number of initial public offerings (IPOs). Britain was also doing well. Although lagging the U.S. in the tech world, the U.K. jobless rate fell below even the rock-bottom levels in the United States.

Canada, on the other hand, continued to suffer high unemployment and lagging growth. The early-1990s recession was much deeper and longer than in the U.S. Household balance sheets deteriorated as living standards fell. Families went increasingly into debt as they attempted, usually in vain, to maintain their living standards as purchasing power waned—felled by the combined plunge in the value of the Canadian dollar, rising tax burdens, and lower wage rates. The Canada-U.S. gap became increasingly obvious: American household wealth surged, thanks to the booming stock market, and personal income growth strengthened as jobs became easier and easier to get. Debt-to-net-worth ratios fell in the U.S. to record lows, even though household debt increased, while Canadian household balance sheets continued to deteriorate.

The number-one-selling car in the mid-1990s in Canada was the Honda Civic, compared to the much-more-expensive Toyota Camry in the U.S. Canada had Wal-Mart, while the U.S. had Nordstrom's, Saks, and Bloomingdales—retailers that chose not to come to Canada even when the long-standing Eaton's department store chain went bust and their real estate was available for a song. The Americans wore cashmere, while the Canadians made do with something less.

Boosted finally by booming exports to the U.S.—mostly Ford, Chrysler, and GM Canada automobiles (which are cheaper to produce north of the border) along with forest products and oil and gas—the Canadian economy belatedly took off in 1996. But the currency continued to underperform and the catch-up was slow to spread to the domestic economy, still stifled by enormous tax burdens. The Asian crisis and subsequent Russian default in 1998 exacerbated the situation, as capital moved increasingly to the U.S. and the Canadian dollar hit a record low.

CANADA TURNS THE CORNER

Productivity growth, a hallmark of the New Economy, boomed in the U.S., ratcheting upward in the late '90s thanks to business investment in technology. While Canada is now showing great progress on that score, it is still playing catch-up. The good news is, the Canadian economy strengthened markedly, outpacing the U.S. in the second half of 2000 and early 2001.

I wrote my first book, *The Cooper Files: A Practical Guide to Your Financial Future*,[3] in the early days of the New Economy transformation. It describes the necessary steps that Canada needed to take to regain its global growth leadership. I am happy to say that some of those steps have been taken; the process has begun. Personal, corporate, and capital gains tax rates were reduced beginning in 2000 by the Liberal government of Jean Chrétien, and the process continues. Even so, this is just a start—the job is far from over—particularly given the further tax reductions in the U.S. legislated in 2001. Tax cuts are now supported at the grass-roots level in Canada and some regulatory restrictions are under review. Deregulation has begun in the financial services industry and, hopefully, more is in store. The Canadian stock market was boosted in 2000–2001 by the oil and gas sector. With its own New Economy champions—such as Nortel and JDS Uniphase—the Canadian stock market also experienced the surge of the late 1990s and the subsequent sickening plunge as the U.S. economy faltered and fell.

YOU TOO CAN TAKE CONTROL IN THE ACCELERATION AGE

Even with the dramatic slowdown in economic activity, technology growth in the next decade will remain a strong underpinning for economic expansion. Innovation will continue at a breakneck gait and the pace of change will remain rapid. The economy, in this environment, is prone to excesses of the kind that caused the 2001 downturn. Herd mentality contributes to the swings. It is a reflection of human nature influenced so significantly by mass media. The outright gloom of the first half of 2001 was no less an example of this than the elation of the late 1990s. We must temper our responses, see the facts for what they are, and refrain from knee-jerk reactions. This book is intended to help you do that. I will help you see and understand the ever-changing landscape—developing a road map to the future that will avoid the potholes and blind alleys and show you the way to business and financial success. It is not an easy road, however; it requires hard work, flexibility, self-discipline, and a willingness to take personal responsibility.

While the Fed attempts to steer the economy through rough waters, the rest of us must manage our businesses, careers, and investments. I believe that even with the risk and volatility, growth and opportunity will abound. We are in the early days of a technology revolution that is led by the Internet and breakthroughs in the life sciences, miniature computers, and alternative energy sources. It is a very positive story, although sometimes it won't seem so. I wrote this book to empower you to understand the tremendous opportunities that lie before you and your children. You can take control and prosper in the Acceleration Age. Brace yourself, however—it will not be a smooth, easy ride. The pace will be hectic but exhilarating for those who understand what's coming.

One

Spiral Up
Spiral
Down

1

Old and New
Economy Distinctions
Blur

T oday we take for granted that progress, innovation, and growth are the standard rather than the exception. Yet for most of human history, this was not the case. Growth in global output per capita was negligible for centuries, averaging little more than 0.1 percent per year from the Middle Ages until the American Revolution. That is not to say that there weren't important advances: they included the increasingly sophisticated use of tools and the harnessing of animal, wind, and rudimentary water power; the development of land and sea transport; the improvement in agricultural techniques; and the invention of the clock, eyeglasses, and the printing press. Art, music, theology, philosophy, and literature flourished long before the Industrial Revolution. These developments and more were seminal and important, but they led to only a modest rise in life expectancy and the standard of living. And the pace of change from generation to generation was much slower than today. It was not until the late eighteenth century that per capita growth accelerated, and it has averaged 1.2 percent per year ever since.

This acceleration was the result of an outburst of technological innovation—the application of human knowledge to products and processes. In the past two hundred years we have experienced five main waves of innovation. The first was the Industrial Revolution in Britain beginning in the 1780s, fueled by water power and the cotton gin. The second was triggered by the invention of the railway in the middle 1800s. The third began at the turn of the last century with the introduction of electricity, the radio, and the automobile. And the fourth commenced in the 1950s with the jet engine, electronics, and television. Today we are in the fifth such wave, the Information Age, with breakthrough technological advances that include the Internet, the application of digital technology to the life sciences (biotechnology, the building of miniature machines atom by atom), nanotechnology, and the development of the fuel cell and other alternative energy sources.

The pace of change has been accelerating. More innovation has occurred in the past two centuries than in the previous ten. Clearly, innovation is key to the growth process, but it has gotten short shrift until recently in most of our postwar economics textbooks. Somehow in the 1950s, '60s, and '70s the great works of many earlier economists were forgotten—such as the analysis of Joseph Schumpeter, an Austrian-American economist at Harvard University in the prewar period who focused on the importance of the innovator in the growth process. His ideas are now back in vogue. But many of us who studied economics in high school or college learned 1950s-style traditional growth theory that focused on the three basic "factors of production"—land, labor, and capital—and largely ignored innovation. Land included natural resources, and capital consisted of durable produced goods that were used to make other goods.[1] Technological innovation or knowledge was not seen as an intrinsic factor contributing to growth. To the extent it was emphasized at all, it was viewed as an exogenous force that rained down like manna from heaven.

But the technology revolution of the 1990s finally pierced the psyche of modern academic economists, and a new body of growth theory is evolving that places innovation and knowledge creation at the heart of economic progress, no longer as simply an appendage. This research, sometimes called the "New Growth Theory," focuses on the *sources* of technological change—the importance of a flexible, ever-changing marketplace; the links between business, government, and universities; and the protection of intellectual property rights.[2] This book emphasizes the sources of innovation as well, because they are the wellspring of success and value creation in today's economy.

THE IMPORTANCE OF KNOWLEDGE

The reason that we are so much wealthier today than ever before is knowledge—human know-how applied to our day-to-day lives, the functioning of our businesses, and the health and well-being of the population. It is not because of the physical assets in the global economy. The natural resources that made up these physical assets existed all along. As Paul Romer, a leading New-Growth theorist and economics professor at Stanford University Graduate School of Business, puts it: "The total physical mass here on earth is the same that it's ever been."[3] But the number of people who divide this physical mass has grown over time. The reason we are wealthier is because of the knowledge we have applied to these limited assets to leverage their value. And the reason that the pace of change is accelerating is because knowledge builds on itself, creating a virtuous circle—the more you know, the more you can know.

No longer do we imply that only land, labor, and capital generate economic growth. Instead, we have increasingly come to realize that ideas, formulas, and new ways of doing things are the key contributors to the rise in living standards. Growth takes place when individuals and businesses *perceive* and *apply* new formulas, instructions, and recipes. Both parts of this are important—the discovery of new ways of doing things, as well as the implementation.

Increasingly in today's world, wealth is created in the discovery process rather than the implementation process. Not surprisingly, therefore, more people than ever before are working as innovators rather than as copiers or executors. This is very different from earlier eras. The New Economy is all about innovation. From information technology to financial services, the pharmaceutical industry to the entertainment business, the real value is in creation or discovery. While implementation and replication are important, they do not provide the foundation for sustained growth and outperformance.

The same is true for countries. The innovating countries produce the highest standards of living. To be such a country requires a well-educated, technically literate workforce. This provides the recipe for growth in the emerging world—education is the essential ingredient for rapid ascension to developed-world status. The East Asian Tigers—Hong Kong, Singapore, Taiwan, and South Korea—prove this point. For all countries, knowledge creation is the key to economic leadership. So growth and wealth today are all about innovation and knowledge.

WHAT IS THE NEW ECONOMY?

The New Economy is one where ideas dominate, where talent and knowledge create competitive advantage, not natural resources or industrial plants. In the New Economy, intangible assets such as knowledge, speed, intellectual capital, innovative business models, and proprietary technology are the fundamental underpinnings for value creation—the most important forms of capital. In the Old Economy, the physical assets of the economy were seen as the predominant form of value creation—the natural resources, real estate, industrial capacity, and bricks-and-mortar presence. But even well before the computer, technology as applied to physical assets was the key to growth. The distinctions between Old and New Economies can be misleading. Even in the past, growth depended on more than just the physical fitness of an economy. While for the thirty years following World War II, industrial and resource production often contributed meaningfully to the wealth and growth of a country's economy, the global growth leaders were not just those countries that best exploited their hefty physical advantages.

Countries like Japan, England, and Germany had little in the way of natural resource endowment, but they were still able to engage in human capital and physical capital development. For Britain in an earlier era, the then-unique advantages of private property, democracy, and relative social equality allowed them to lead the early Industrial Revolution. The British form of legal organization allowed the private sector to respond best to the innovations that dominate growth. In the postwar period,

Japan's form of social organization and emphasis on education and discipline (if not uniformity) fostered an environment of rapid industrial growth. Ditto for Germany, as innovation and precision manufacturing were huge competitive advantages over the period.

Canada, rich in physical assets, was also a global growth leader in the postwar period. It benefited from the worldwide growth in the demand for oil and gas, forest products, and metals and minerals; at the same time, a skilled population base, rapid pace of research and development (R&D), stable democracy, and proximity to the United States contributed to the growth of basic industries. Russia, on the other hand, had huge physical-endowment advantages, but lacked the legal and social "software" needed to compete on a sustainable basis.

The distinctions between Old and New are rapidly waning as so-called Old Economy companies use technology to innovate, consolidate, and change. Traditional businesses have increasingly gone online to deal with their competitors, suppliers, and customers. The dramatic growth of business-to-business (B2B) websites that streamline the supply chain and markedly reduce the costs of production are now prevalent in such Old Economy sectors as agriculture, metals and mining, aerospace, chemicals, building supplies, and more. Traditional retailers are using the Net to educate, inform, communicate, and market with the proliferation of business-to-consumer (B2C) sites of formerly offline-only businesses. Digital technology of all forms is used today for oil exploration, automobile design, and tree harvesting. Increasingly, the New Economy is today's economy—getting closer and closer to the entire economy.

Moreover, the New Economy is not new; it is a continuation of a process kicked off at the start of the Industrial Revolution. Even then, knowledge creation began to revolutionize the way the economy operated. Information technology (IT) is the next step on the continuum, rather than a break from the past. The New Economy is undeniably global. National economic boundaries blur as they become more and more porous. Most big businesses are multinational and the Internet knows no home base. Any company with a website becomes, in essence, a multinational company.

Most important in today's economy is talent. Talent is not body count; it is the relatively small proportion of the labor force that creates inordinate value. Talent is scarce, and the market for talent is global. Businesses buy other businesses for their talent, not for their factories, physical resources, or real estate. The owners of talent, the innovators and creators of ideas and processes, will garner inordinate returns in the marketplace. For businesses to maintain an edge, they must promote flexible minds that can see the future, recognize the dizzying pace of change, and go with the flow. The waves of change can be extremely volatile, but the innovators will see the breaks, understand the turmoil, and take control.

INCREASING RETURNS

Knowledge is key to growth and success and it is a unique element in the production process. It is not an exhaustible resource. Knowledge begets knowledge. Sir Isaac Newton, arguably the greatest physicist of all time (no offense to Albert Einstein), understood this. It is what he meant when he wrote to a colleague that he "stood on the shoulders of giants." The pace of innovation today does not just seem faster, it is faster. It is claimed, strikingly, that more than 75 percent of all the scientists who have ever lived are alive today.

Knowledge yields increasing returns. This is the cornerstone of the Acceleration Age. Economists have had trouble dealing with knowledge in their models because it seems to defy the basic law of economic scarcity. When a physical object is sold, the seller ceases to own it. But when an idea is sold, the seller often still possesses it and can sell it over and over again. Regardless of how much knowledge is used, it is never used up. There is not a finite and fixed supply. The generation of knowledge is ongoing and constant. Knowledge can be used by more than one person at a time. We keep building on the knowledge developed in the past. Breakthroughs in one field open doors in many others.

Our ability to disseminate knowledge has also increased dramatically. So scientists and researchers today in every field can share their work on the Internet and put it through the tests of colleague critique and examination, multiplying each others' discoveries more rapidly than ever before.

Traditional models of economic growth operated according to the law of diminishing returns, which stated that the more you already use a physical asset—such as land, labor, or machines—the less you gain from added increments. Put one apple picker on a hundred-square-foot plot of trees and you might pick ten bushels of apples per hour. Add another and the marginal product might rise—assuming two are more efficient than one; but add twenty more pickers and the last one could well reduce the hourly per capita output as too many of them bump into each other. Diminishing returns can also reflect the limited supply of some physical assets. It is generally more costly to extract each additional barrel of oil or ton of ore the more that has already been extracted. Conventional theory assumes that most industries experience diminishing returns at some point, so unit costs start to rise. In this world, no one firm can corner the market.

Intangible assets, however, behave quite differently. It might have cost Sun Microsystems $200 million to develop Java, for example, but once the software was created, it cost next to nothing to replicate it. Indeed, it can be downloaded from the Internet, which means there are no additional distribution or production costs at all. Once the initial investment is made, returns increase, rather than diminish, as each copy is sold. Information is expensive to produce, but cheap to reproduce. This applies to an increasing number of information products, such as software, books, bioengineered drugs, movies, financial services, and websites. High fixed costs and negligible variable costs give these industries vast potential economies of scale.

There is also nothing new about increasing returns and economies of scale. Alfred Marshall, a British economist, discussed them at length in the late 1800s. Railroads, autos, and electricity were subject to increasing returns long before the Information Age. These new technologies were very expensive to develop and initially the costs were prohibitive. But as efficiencies were exploited and innovation in production continued, the price of cars, electricity, and train rides became accessible to the mass market. It took far longer for this to happen then, however, than it does now. Personal computer (PC) ownership and Internet usage, for example, spread to a critical mass of households in the U.S., Canada, and Scandinavia in record time.

Though they are not new, increasing returns are more prevalent today than ever—especially in information goods and services—not only because of their production cost structure, but also because of the nature of the demand for these products. Early innovators in the information world can enjoy the positive force of "network effects." If, for example, Java, Microsoft Windows, or America Online are early into the market and become widely adopted, then network effects set in: As more people use the technology, the likelihood increases that others will also use it. So there are increasing returns on the demand side as well. The bandwagon effect can be huge and it applies to everything from fax machines to e-mail; their value increases the more people use them. Customers value the Microsoft Windows operating system in part because so many people use it.

We have seen these effects so vividly on the Internet; the benefit of being online increases exponentially with the number of connections. According to *Metcalfe's Law*—attributed to Robert Metcalfe, a pioneer of computer networking—the value of a network grows roughly in line with the square of the number of users. Network effects give rise to an important virtuous circle on the Web. Better content attracts more users, and more users attract better content. That is why the three busiest consumer websites—Yahoo!, AOL, and MSN—have increased their lead over the rest during the past three years. Firms compete intensely to have their unique technology adopted and become the industry standard.

"Groove-in" or "lock-in" effects further augment this tendency. The more you use a product, the more convenient and easy to use it becomes. If you are accustomed to Microsoft Word, for example, you will be reluctant to go through the hassle of learning a new program, even if you hear there are better ones out there.

Michael Porter, business professor and strategist at Harvard Business School, has pointed out that for these network effects to present a sustainable advantage, they have to be proprietary to one company. He suggests that the openness of the Internet, with its common protocols, standards, and ease of use, makes it difficult for a single company to capture the benefits of network effects. He suggests that America Online is the exception rather than the rule.[4] Evidence to date, however, suggests otherwise, although monopoly power may well be fleeting.

MONOPOLY POWER

Taken together, increasing returns, network effects, and groove-in effects mean that companies and technologies that gain a dominant position early tend to increase their domination of the market, at least for a while. These forces govern the markets for computer operating systems and Internet browsers. The ability to extract monopoly benefits, however briefly, is key to assuring the innovation process continues. If the stakes weren't so great, few companies would take the risks necessary for the creation process.

This calls into question the U.S. Justice Department's clamp-down on Microsoft. True, Microsoft could use its monopoly power to thwart upstart competitors, like Netscape, and this has to be regulated; and Gates-like returns are not necessarily needed to encourage innovation. But without the potential for at least temporarily outsized gains, the initial risks and research investments might never be taken. The payoff in this game can be huge, but so is the downside, as we have seen with so many failed endeavors. Without the enormous potential returns, the gamble might not be worth taking, stifling future innovation.

What's more, these monopoly powers can be quite fleeting. In the Information Age, the game keeps changing. New technology evolves, rapidly shifting the leading edge. No one company can maintain a competitive advantage indefinitely. The Internet tends to change industry structures in ways that dampen profitability and it has an equalizing effect on business practices, which reduces the ability of any company to establish an eternal operational advantage. Some have misinterpreted this phenomenon as evidence that the technology revolution is all hype— citing examples of fallen giants, of which there were many in 2001. Instead, the truth is that the beauty of the tech revolution is that it is in a state of perpetual innovation and reinvention. The winners win big, but their positions are always endangered, requiring constant modification. As we saw in the 1990s, as long as capital is cheap and readily available to finance new entrants, even the giants in today's economy are vulnerable to losing their edge.

ECONOMY IN TRANSITION

We have moved rapidly from a mass-production, commodity-manufacturing economy in the U.S. to something that is information based, digital, high tech. Every fifty years or so (since the first Industrial Revolution in the eighteenth century) the economy goes through a shift like this, involving deep structural changes. The economy changes its character and the basic rules of operation appear to change as well. While some rules are still immutable, like the rules of supply and demand and of human nature, many of the underlying assumptions must change.

In the tech-driven world of today, the marginal costs of computation and communication are nearly zero. The academic community in economics now generally accepts that high-tech markets operate under increasing, rather than diminishing, returns, thanks to economists such as W. Brian Arthur, Citibank Professor at the Santa Fe Institute.[5] Not long ago that view was seen as heresy—like Galileo's assertion that the world was round.

In the high-tech world, in contrast, the more you get ahead the more advantage you have in getting further ahead. However, it works the other way too. One misstep is all it takes and you go spiraling downward. Incorrectly predict a change in technology or consumer habits and today's winner becomes tomorrow's loser. Some companies are agile enough to rebound and others are not. This dramatically changes the economic model and adds to the volatility of the system. Markets become very unstable. There are many examples of companies with a huge leading edge miscalculating the next new thing and losing to a competitor.

Apple Computer, for example, was an early leader in the PC market, making big inroads in households and businesses that were too small for IBM's mainframe systems. Early on, IBM seemed entrenched in the world of mainframes; but as PC demand began to take off, IBM—rapidly losing market share—woke up. It reinvented itself as an innovator in the PC market. It stalled Apple's penetration into business computing. And by 1988, Apple's retreat turned into a rout as IBM PCs and their clones, coupled with Microsoft's Windows operating system, had taken much of the household market as well. Apple has attempted to make a comeback.

It might once again find its niche, with style and image as its product. The new Macintosh computers are all the rage among the under-thirty set.

CHANGE IS CONSTANT

The New Economy has only one pace—hectic. The rewards of creativity go to the swiftest. Change is rapid and risks are high. Revolutions are, by definition, marked by volatility, surprises, and reversals. Luck, no doubt, plays a role. The ultimate form of the products and services that will be spawned is yet unclear and will likely be ever changing. Competitive pressures continue to intensify as technology spreads across sectors and regions.

The New Economy is not just about technological innovation—it is about financial innovation as well. In particular, the easy availability of venture capital and IPO stock market financing in the late 1990s— especially in the United States—greatly accelerated the speed at which new technology leapt from the planning stages into the marketplace. The combination of financial and technological innovation dramatically changed the competitive landscape. Once the cheap capital dried up, as we saw so vividly in late 2000 and 2001, the engine of business capital spending—so crucial to the productivity boom—ground to a screeching halt. It even moved into reverse, as businesses recognized that they had overinvested in technology, spurred by an unrealistic sense of euphoria and a seemingly bottomless pool of capital. When the stock market collapsed and the capital dried up, the economy tanked—responding faster to the decline in corporate earnings than ever before. The business cycle, therefore, certainly has not been repealed. As we grope our way through this next phase of the Acceleration Age, we know that volatility will remain, but so will the dynamism of this era.

BUILDING ON THE PAST, BUT IN A UNIQUE WAY

As we have seen, it is always very dangerous to believe that this time is different. History does have a way of repeating itself. However, there are numerous ways in which this technology revolution truly is unique. For one, the costs of computers and wireless devices for Internet usage have fallen precipitously, far faster than the costs of the breakthrough technologies of the past, explaining the rapid adoption rates. For example, it took 35 years from the time the first Model T rolled off the assembly line until a critical mass of U.S. households owned a car. The time frame was about the same for the telephone. In contrast, in a mere seven years, more than a third of American families were accessing the World Wide Web at home. Today that ratio stands at more than 55 percent.

IT is pervasive: it can boost productivity in almost everything a business does, from design to marketing, in every sector of the economy. This is the first tech revolution to boost productivity in services, from health care to finance. And services account for over half of the U.S. economy. It is true that steam, electricity, and railways also increased productivity growth, but mainly in the manufacture and distribution of goods. To be fair, however, railways did provide the foundation for personal travel, including commuting; and electricity formed the basis for the massive increase in communications during the twentieth century.

By increasing access to information, IT helps to make markets work more efficiently. Thanks to the Internet, far more information is available. Consumers can more easily comparison shop and businesses can deal with a greater number of competitive suppliers. Inventories can be kept at rock-bottom lows as information travels seamlessly from consumer to retailer to supplier and through the production process. The Net also reduces transaction costs and helps remove barriers to entry—anyone can set up a website. In some ways, this accessibility and seamlessness moves part of the New Economy closer to Adam Smith's traditional model of perfect competition, which assumes abundant information, many buyers and sellers, zero transaction costs, and no barriers to entry. At the same time, monopoly power increases in some sectors, owing to still-high initial R&D costs and increasing returns, coupled with network and groove-in effects. This seeming paradox is reflected in how fleeting any competitive advantage might be.

Today's IT revolution is building on the breakthrough technologies of the past to make the New Economy more global than ever before. By further reducing the cost of communication, today's technology revolution has helped to globalize production and capital markets. In turn, globalization enhances competition and hence innovation as it accelerates the diffusion of new technology through trade and investment. The very nature of today's tech revolution is self-reinforcing. Digital technology speeds up innovation itself as processing large amounts of data becomes cheaper and easier, reducing the time it takes to create new products and services.

All of this contributes to the unpredictability. W. Brian Arthur likens the New Economy to a casino where the business leaders must decide not just how much money to bet, but also which games to play. Microsoft's Bill Gates, Intel's Andy Grove, Nortel's John Roth, and the rest must choose between blackjack and roulette and the yet-to-be-created game in the next room. To extend this analogy, economists are applying Monte Carlo theory—advanced probability models—to the economy and the stock market with great insight.

Getting there first can be a key advantage, and often the winner takes all; but make the wrong move and you lose everything. Second movers can learn from others' mistakes, but they also run the risk of missing the early advantages. The talent shifts to the next big thing and so does the money as the game keeps changing and the rules evolve. New Economy winners must be agile and daring. The competition is intense and the upstart of today can be the blockbuster of tomorrow. Scientific knowledge expands at a pace never before seen. Perpetual R&D is essential, but expensive. Keeping on top of what everyone else is doing, thinking, and planning is crucial. Flexibility and adaptability are key in business and in financial markets.

2

Shock Treatment
The Stock Market Collapse

he dramatic slowdown in economic activity beginning in late 2000
and continuing into 2001 led to a sharp reduction in business capital spending, which markedly reduced the revenue and earnings
outlook for the technology sector. I will discuss this slowdown in detail
in Chapter 7. But even before the cyclical decline in stocks began, there
was considerable churning in the equity market and a significant rotation
of winners and losers within the technology sector itself. Even when the
markets were euphoric, some companies were slipping while others were
gaining ground. This process is an inherent characteristic of the
Acceleration Age; it will continue after the cyclical rebound in the economy begins.

In addition, the mass media hype surrounding the Internet stocks—
the dot-coms in particular—contributed to the volatility. I will examine
why the bubble swelled so dramatically in the first place, and why it
burst, in Chapter 6. But the process of change is what is of interest here.
All periods of rapid technological change are fraught with great volatility.
In the early days of an innovation upwave, we are in uncharted waters.
The forces of change are strong and, in many ways, innately

unpredictable. Volatility surged to record levels in 2000 and 2001 and is likely to remain a feature of the evolving economic landscape.

The dramatic stock market corrections—gut-wrenching plunges in the dot-com stocks and then in technology generally—led many to suggest that the New Economy was dead. This is tantamount to suggesting that the Industrial Revolution was over in the early 1800s because textile manufacturers were going broke in Manchester. The very essence of the New Economy is rapid innovation and change; volatility is endemic to this environment. We have seen that the speed of change is accelerating. Even without a cyclical slowdown in the economy, winners cannot be guaranteed their continued competitive advantage when the incentive for new players to enter their sectors remains so extraordinarily high. Speed is crucial, yet the most successful companies risk being hampered by their own success. The larger they are, the less agile and responsive to developing market trends they risk becoming. So even before the general economic slowdown began in late 2000 and intensified in 2001, the stock market was vulnerable to shifts in leaders and laggards that had nothing to do with the general state of the economy but instead with the nature of technological innovation.

CREATIVE DESTRUCTION

Joseph Schumpeter, the patron saint of the New Economy thinkers, first described the forces of *"creative destruction"* more than fifty years ago, and the term has now become a part of the lexicon.[1] Creative destruction is the process by which new replaces old. It is the churning in a rapidly changing economy. This churning is a necessary and healthy reflection of innovation. Capitalism is a process of perpetual creative destruction, where winners can quickly become losers and then, maybe, winners again. The stock market gyrations mirror the forces of change. They do not signal the demise of the technology revolution.

The New Economy—the economy that is driven by productivity-enhancing technological change—is far from dead. It moved into a cyclical downturn in late 2000–2001, but from that it will recover. The intensification of global competition has made raising prices all the more difficult for many businesses, even when energy or labor costs rise. And even for those that can—such as the airlines and delivery services—they cannot fully recoup the rising costs. So they respond aggressively by cutting other costs, such as payrolls and capital spending plans, at least temporarily. The New Economy is more dynamic than the Old because business leaders are increasingly compensated through stock holdings. Even in cyclical upturns, Wall Street dictates that streamlining and innovation be continual to ensure that productivity grows and markets expand.

This is a great deal to ask on an enduring basis. Profit growth, the fundamental factor of stock market performance, is difficult if not impossible to sustain at the breakneck pace recorded by the market leaders in the technology sector in the second half of the 1990s. Intense competition—the perfectly competitive model in the economics textbooks—generates, according to the theory, only modest, marginal profitability. If any company is too profitable in the perfectly competitive world, new businesses spring up to grab market share. There are few barriers to entry in this world as long as capital is available for initial R&D efforts. The only path to higher profits and sustainable competitive advantage is through constant innovation, which is very expensive. It requires leading-edge talent, an extremely flexible organization, the willingness to take risk, and capital. Often, the giants in an industry found it necessary to buy their upstart competition because that was more cost effective than trying to build the capability on their own. It is also true that smaller firms can be more innovative. As long as a company's stock is highly valued, it can be used as currency to buy other businesses. But the process, while self-reinforcing on the upside, is similarly self-reinforcing on the downside. If, for whatever reason, the stock value slips—because, for example, the firm is losing its technological lead—buying the promising new businesses is that much more expensive and therefore more difficult. Keeping its own talent is also that much more difficult. So, once again, we see the spiral up and the spiral down.

First-mover advantage is great, but it is often not enduring. Visionaries aren't always good managers, and the much-heralded first movers can lose out to companies that get the bugs out of great ideas. Timing, execution, and having the right fundamental approach are key. It is rare for the first entrant into a new sector to get all of those elements right initially. More often, a later arrival is the one that thrives. Jeff Bezos, founder of Amazon.com, suggests that even though his company is expected to post sales of around $3.5 billion in 2001, it isn't yet a lasting company—and may never become one. The track record for innovators is not good.

FALLEN GIANTS

Investors have painfully learned that even well-managed, innovative companies have trouble maintaining their lead indefinitely. Indeed, the innovative company in the early days of product acceptance rides a huge upward trajectory, but as the company hits the top tier of the market it ultimately finds that insufficient volume exists to sustain growth. This is what Clayton Christensen, professor of business administration at the Harvard Business School, calls the *innovator's dilemma*.[2] It is very difficult for mature, successful businesses to sustain their innovative edge by introducing disruptive technologies—those that create major new growth in the industries they penetrate—because in the short run it is not in their best interests to do so. Their client base is generally not interested in new, innovative, low-end products and their own bureaucratic management structures increasingly preclude that kind of initiative. Such technologies are often relatively unprofitable to start and their ultimate market potential is very difficult to predict.

But what we have seen in the past decade is that the U.S. economy has significantly outperformed others around the world because it has been able to repeat the "cycle of disruption."[3] When U.S. companies are perceived to have peaked, ambitious entrepreneurial employees leave. They find venture capital on the way out—often from their former colleagues and customers—and start new disruptive companies of their own.

A vivid example of this occurred in 1985 in the last technology meltdown, a period that became known as the "technology recession." The dynamics of the electronics and computer industry back then were remarkably similar to what we are seeing today. The personal computer was the revolutionary product that spawned thousands of start-ups and drew worldwide interest, similar to the Internet today. Some thirty PC companies battled for market share and many failed. Inventories of chips were in enormous excess supply and job losses were counted in the thousands. Computer companies were dying in the mid-1980s at the pace that dot-com companies expired in 2000 and 2001. Both the PC and the Internet were disruptive technological advances that helped form new industries and damaged established companies. Both have become essential tools of business, government, and education and have changed the lives of millions.

It should not be forgotten that the last tech downturn was followed quickly by the entrance of newcomers with breakthrough technologies. Newspapers around the world gave little coverage to Microsoft's plans to launch a public stock offering in 1986. It was seen as part of a resurgence in initial public offerings by high-tech companies following the cooling of this market in the previous year. At the proposed offering price, Microsoft had a total market capitalization of about $400 million—small potatoes, even then. It is worth remembering, as well, that John Chambers was the head of U.S. operations at the soon-to-be-bankrupt Wang Laboratories before he turned Cisco into the growth stock of the '90s. Adobe Systems and Oracle also had blockbuster IPOs in 1986. Who knows how many Microsofts and Ciscos now wait in the wings.

This constant weaning and replacement does not happen in most other developed countries. Take Japan as an example. A global growth leader from the 1960s through the mid-1980s, Japan's economic fortunes have reversed. Many of their leading companies faltered because they were, in effect, so well managed, so process oriented, so linked to their customer base. The Japanese economic structure is too inflexible, its labor and capital markets too stagnant, to encourage the process of *creative disruption*.[4] In consequence, for more than a decade, the Japanese stock market has languished. Creative disruption is critical to economic growth leadership in the New Economy. But the very nature of disruption is characteristic of the Acceleration Age—rapid change, uncertainty, and volatility.

Look at Cisco, the once invincible tech giant that watched its market value plunge in 2000, despite sky-high earnings growth. It felt real competitive pressure from upstart Juniper Networks in the high-end router market—the system that directs traffic on the Net. Juniper's share value surged in 2000 as many worried that Cisco might be getting too big to move fast. For the first time in the history of the company, Cisco senior executives began to jump ship voluntarily. With a fall in the value of its stock, Cisco's ability to continue to buy leading-edge technologies through the purchase of other companies was called into question.

A decline in one tech leader sets off a chain reaction. When many feared that Cisco sales would slow, stock prices of the makers of chips and components nose-dived. PMC-Sierra, Applied Micro Circuits Corp., and Broadcom Corp. all dropped on concern that Cisco might reduce its inventory of their products as orders from providers of phone and Internet services slowed. The euphoria of earlier years, when tech could do no wrong, turned into the enormous pessimism of late 2000. Even stellar earnings, stronger than analyst expectations, weren't enough to assuage mounting fears. And when those earnings plunged in 2001 with the dramatic downturn in the economy, the one-time stars of the technology constellation went into free fall.

Lucent was another example of an early fallen giant. Having posted disappointing earnings for more than a year, by 2000 the company was no longer seen as invincible. Lucent was bested by its archrival Nortel Networks in the key market for optical switches. Once upon a time, Nortel was seen as the industry dog and Lucent was the winner. Nortel made a bet in 1995, however, to build network gear that would zap data at speeds of 10 billion bits per second through a single strand of optical fiber. By mid-2000, Nortel had 45 percent of the exploding optical equipment market, compared to Lucent's 15 percent. Lucent decided in 1996 to develop a slower switch because its customers weren't asking for anything faster. Nortel, instead, anticipated customer needs.

Lucent learned this lesson the hard way. As its share price plummeted, it reportedly suffered more than a 20 percent turnover of key senior talent. Increasingly it became the subject of takeover rumors. At the end of the day, Lucent was too slow and bureaucratic to excel (or maybe even survive) in the torrential, creative-destructive world of the New Economy.

Nortel had its own problems as well, but they were cyclical rather than structural. Its shares were pummeled in October 2000, causing the biggest single-day point drop ever in the Toronto Stock Exchange (an index that it still dominates) after it reported slower-than-expected sales growth. Slow, in this case, still meant an impressive 42 percent. At the worst of it in late 2000, Nortel's share price plunged a sickening 62 percent from its then 52-week high. The rout intensified in 2001 as the economy slowed and businesses dramatically cut back their capital spending plans. Nortel repeatedly announced weaker-than-expected revenues and earnings for the year as a whole and its stock tanked once again. Other tech leaders endured a similar fate, thanks to an ever more skeptical marketplace and a weakening economy. Included in the list of tech companies that lost nearly 50 percent of their market value in 2000 are Dell Computer, JDS Uniphase, Research In Motion, Micron Technology, Motorola, Novell, Gateway, Xerox, and Yahoo!, to name just a few. They also suffered substantial further declines in the first half of 2001 as the economy continued to slow. But even without the economic slowdown, volatility in the tech sector would still have been evident.

Moreover, the techs weren't the only casualties in 2000. Earnings disappointments wreaked havoc on many sectors. Hard hit as well were Bausch & Lomb, Caterpillar, Carnival Corp., Campbell Soup, Clorox, Circuit City, DaimlerChrysler, Dole Food, DuPont, Gap Inc., Goodyear, Home Depot, Inco, International Paper, Nike, Office Depot, Rite Aid, Safeco, UAL, and Whirlpool. Clearly the stock market euphoria of earlier years had dissipated.

A RUDE AWAKENING

Throughout the late 1990s, investors were increasingly convinced that a few innovators, mostly in the technology sector, could enjoy sustainable, rapid earnings growth. It was believed, or at least hoped, that they would continue to do so by exploiting their proprietary technologies and first-mover advantage. More and more, their stocks were priced for perfection—for perpetual profit growth and head-spinning revenue gains. Valuations of these companies' stocks rose to unprecedented levels, only to be surpassed by the surge in stock prices of the dot-coms—Internet retailers and service providers—that in the main had no profits, only losses.

The dramatic nosedive in the technology stocks in 2000—before the economic rout took hold—taught an important lesson. Even the best-managed companies are not likely to meet straight-line forecasts of extraordinary growth month after month. With the rapid pace of technological change, even the best business leaders can misstep. Prolonged success often creates complacency or hubris, which sets the stage for a setback. The larger and more successful an organization, the greater the difficulty in recognizing a shift in the marketplace that requires rapid and often dramatic change. A long list of faltering behemoths—such as Xerox, Kodak, AT&T, Lucent, and Apple—are all examples of creative destruction at work. Some will reinvent themselves, like Corning—once a glassware manufacturer and now the number-one supplier of optical fiber—or General Electric, Texas Instruments, or Hewlett-Packard, all branching out, with varying degrees of success, from their traditional roots.

The economic slowdown will mortally wound the weakest among them. The strong ones, however, will use it as a time to build capabilities and pick up talent and enterprises on the cheap. General Electric, for example, has always had a policy of expanding in a downturn. JDS Uniphase is still buying companies, while those like Lucent are selling once-lucrative pieces of their operations. But the longer the downturn lasts, the tougher it becomes. Capital has dried up for all but the most creditworthy, and that does not include many tech companies. But well-managed companies with deep pockets use this time to scoop the competition.

THE DOT-COM DOMINOES

The one sector that got hit first and hardest in the 2000 rout was the dot-coms. Many have disappeared and all have felt the pinch of rapidly diminishing capital. We will look at the specifics of this sector—its demise and its prospects for the future—in later chapters, but first let's use it as an excellent example of the interconnectedness in the economy. The decline in one sector—indeed a relatively small one, never representing any more than roughly 9 percent of the Internet economy and a miniscule proportion of the economy at large—can have devastating effects on many others as well. Indeed, the dot-com demise could well have triggered the global economic slowdown of 2001.

The list of dot-com fatalities is now legion. The fallout has been pervasive, sending shock waves through the Internet world that have reverberated well beyond. The venture capital (VC) firms were devastated by many of their ill-advised forays into this space. The Internet incubators—early investors like CMGI and Idealab—were also decimated. Disenchanted investors confronted the established VC firms, such as Hicks, Muse, Tate & Furst, as well as Kleiner Perkins Caufield & Byers. Capital dried up—a huge problem because capital was the lifeblood of the dot-com mania. Without it, the rapid cash-burn rates forced many to close. Dot-com heaven is well populated by the likes of Pets.com, Garden.com, and hundreds of others for which the plug was mercifully pulled. The majority of the rest were forced to substantially downsize—announcing layoffs, slashing spending plans, and raising prices to improve margins and quicken their race to profitability.

Consumers, leery that the e-tailers might shut down before items could be shipped, shifted increasingly to the click-and-mortar retailers for their online purchases. Reaping the online benefits, according to market researcher PC Data Online, were traditional retailers such as Sears, Wal-Mart, Nordstrom, and Barnes & Noble. Some consumers likely ditched the idea of online shopping altogether; although revenue in the B2C space continued to grow rapidly, even with the economic slowdown, some consumers were no doubt spooked by the bad press, rising prices, and service problems online.

Dot-com spending in the euphoric early days had also fueled the growth of online advertising companies like DoubleClick and Engage. As the taps were turned off, those companies suffered a gut-wrenching plunge in their stock values. In some cases, prices fell by more than 90 percent. The damage spread from the B2C firms to B2B companies. Failure rates in that once overfunded sector exploded.

The carnage did not stop there. The people who built the dot-com websites were ravaged as well, along with Internet market research companies and consultants. Who could afford those expensive Internet research services? And, what's more, who needed them? Personal services companies of all sorts were impacted—lawyers, accountants, and investment bankers, along with consultants, had ridden the dot-com gravy train and the train had just derailed. Analysts and investment bankers who had specialized in the sector saw their stock and human-capital values plunge. Many of the most well-known promoters of the dot-com hype fell into disrepute as IPOs and other investment banking deals dried up. The once red-hot consulting industry fell on hard times and many began to quietly reduce their payrolls through attrition and reduced hiring. Eventually, many firms expanded the layoffs to include partners and senior producers. This was particularly painful for the laid-off dot-comers who often desired to return to the safe haven of the professional-services sector.

Next on the chopping block were the infrastructure builders. Companies like Dell, Oracle, Cisco, Sun, SAP, and Lucent were also dangerously exposed to the dot-com capital expenditure crunch. Lucent, for example, made more than $7 billion in financing available to customers. The company lowered its earnings estimates in late 2000 in part because it feared it might not collect on some of that revenue. Credit extensions and direct investments in the e-tailers were once a lucrative component of the balance sheets of many of the giants. When the dot-coms imploded, the sucking sound could be heard far and wide.

Even dead dot-coms still wreaked havoc with a glut of used Internet gear coming onto the market from fire sales at so many bankrupt e-businesses. High-tech equipment makers like Cisco and Sun Microsystems and their distributors, already struggling to reduce inventories and cope with evaporating customer demand, were forced to deal with a deluge of nearly new and untouched equipment for networking, computing, and telecommunications that was auctioned at rock-bottom prices.

Next in the downslide were the application-service providers (ASPs), companies that basically rented the dot-com software over the Net. With so many of them closing, the ASP market was crunched—a market that accounted for a fast-growing portion of Cisco and Sun's gear sales. A study from AMR Research Inc. of Boston predicted that 40 percent of enterprise ASPs and 60 percent of the broader ASP market would either fail or be bought out.[5] The failing ASPs also flooded the market with relatively new equipment. Sun Microsystems has actually had a deal with auction site eBay since late 1999 to help it unload surplus equipment.

And the dot-coms were not alone in the 2000 collapse. Just as hard hit were the small telecom upstarts in the U.S. known as competitive local exchange carriers (CLECs). They also began defaulting en masse in 2001, triggering many of the same negative side effects and dislocations as the dot-com bankruptcies.

Did this mean the technology revolution was over, victim of sudden infant death syndrome so early in life? No—it meant that new life forms would evolve, new business models would spring up, and the evolution of the Net would proceed. Capital markets painfully relearned the lesson that earnings do indeed matter. Cheap capital would no longer be available for companies with little more than a concept. The remaining dot-coms would have to work that much harder and faster to achieve profitability, and new entrants to the marketplace could no longer count on the VC and IPO gravy to grease their early days. The Net, however, was far from dead. Even B2C business would find new life, but often from traditional businesses.

Two

Technology Explosion

3

The Internet Revolution

It Is Still Early Days

The growth in the Internet has been explosive. It is estimated that Internet traffic doubles every one hundred days.[1] Never before has a new technology been adopted so quickly by the mainstream population. In 1992, relatively few people used e-mail, less than a thousand web pages existed, and no one had ever heard of a dot-com. The World Wide Web didn't open for commercial use until the introduction of the first popular browser in 1993.[2] Yet by 1997, roughly one-third of households in the U.S., Canada, and Australia, and even more in Scandinavia, were regularly accessing the Net at home. Today, in the U.S., that ratio stands at over 55 percent of all households and over 65 percent of households with children. According to Jupiter Media Metrix, the number of U.S. wireless Web users is projected to soar from 1 million in 2000 to more than 80 million in 2005, despite the economic downturn.

E-MAIL AMPLIFIES THE NET'S GROWTH

E-mail remains the Internet's killer application, with more than 6.1 billion messages sent each day. Not only has e-mail opened a whole new medium for personal correspondence, it has also launched the modern corporation into the Internet Age. It is simple and unglamorous, but e-mail meets a critical set of human needs. In business settings, it allows people to communicate quickly, efficiently, and inexpensively—whenever and wherever they desire. It is a great leveling agent, as it is status-blind, democratizing business communication. It allows an instant exchange of ideas unimpeded by gatekeepers and protocols. E-mail overload hits everyone, from the CEO to the lowliest stock clerk alike.

In the personal environment, e-mail has taken on a life of its own. It is tremendously popular, boosted by instant messaging from AOL and others. E-mail dating is now far from rare. Virtual sex via e-mail has been cited in divorce cases. Kids and teens are writing to their friends rather than just talking on the telephone. A whole new lexicon and writing style is developing around e-mail. Friends and family dispersed all over the world communicate instantaneously and at zero marginal cost—without the intrusiveness of phone calls. E-mails are a more passive medium. You respond when you want to, and only once you know the content of the message. Telephones, even with voice mail and caller identification, are more meddlesome and invasive. Ask anyone who gets phone solicitations during dinner. The societal implications of so many people being a mere mouse click away keep growing all of the time.

E-mail and e-commerce are synergistic. E-tailers use e-mail to market their wares, communicate with customers, and survey needs. Customers use it to file complaints, track deliveries, and make queries. As more and more people carry around mobile e-mail tracking devices like the Blackberry pager and Palm VII, e-mail's popularity will grow. I can get my e-mails through my Blackberry—no bigger than the palm of my hand—in places where I can't easily listen to my phone messages, such as in a meeting. I can even unobtrusively respond to e-mails. I've been told that some Wall Street investment firms ban Blackberries in meetings because they are so distracting. I know I can reach people out of the office far more easily by e-mail than by phone because they are glued to their

Blackberries. The device has been dubbed "the Crackberry," as it is truly addictive.

THE INTERNET IS A BREAKTHROUGH TECHNOLOGY

The Internet has already transformed the economy and revolutionized the business model in North America, Europe, and Asia. It has contributed to a dramatic streamlining of economic activity and accelerated the globalization of virtually every sector. The Net's expansion led to an unprecedented rise in global competitive pressure, increased productivity, and sharply accelerated economic growth. The Internet, in its early days, was a huge engine for change and prosperity. And much, much more is yet to come. Paul Saffo, the head of the Institute for the Future— a California think tank whose clients include Nokia, Coca-Cola, and the U.S. Postal Service—believes that the IT revolution has only just begun, both in terms of innovation and the adoption of new technologies.[3]

With Internet usage growing so rapidly, the one thing that Net users want is faster access. This is where fiber optics—the transmission of messages or information by light pulses along very thin strands of glass—is important. By using optical fibers instead of traditional copper wires, we can now send more information more quickly than ever before, broadening "bandwidth" or communication capacity. Unlike existing copper wires, which use electrons to carry bits, fiber uses laser light, which is inherently faster. One strand of fiber can carry about fifty times more traffic than today's copper wire, and it can carry it roughly one hundred times further. But fiber optic networks have not yet reached their full potential—a lot of copper networks are still in use—which means that photons need to be converted to electrons and then back, slowing the process down. In the U.S. today, fewer than 10 percent of homes have high-speed access to the Net, but the demand is growing rapidly and so is the technological capability.

High-speed Net access through "infinite bandwidth" or *broadband* will dramatically accelerate the use of the Net. Broadband is synonymous with fat bits (expansive, data-rich communications) and rich multimedia, but maybe even more importantly, it is *"always on."* Broadband allows you to change the way you use the Net, shifting it from a cool medium (receiving data and text-only communication) to a hot one—with video streaming allowing for TV-quality transmission of everything from movies to rock concerts. The Net is no longer tied to just the PC; as with the Blackberry and the Palm VII, we will be tapping into the Net through wireless devices of every imaginable sort as well as through Web-enabled television. Internet cafes are already around, and high-speed connections are increasingly available in other public places such as airports and hotels. Rare is the business conference now where Web access is not available. As the medium becomes ubiquitous, the commercial usage will increase dramatically.

HYPERGROWTH BY 2003

The growth we have seen to date in the Internet-related world will pale in comparison to the growth over the next decade. And the gyrations in stocks, productivity, and economic expansion will also be as gut-wrenching. We have yet to hit the period of hypergrowth. A study by Forrester Research asserts that a building period of twelve to eighteen months precedes e-commerce hypergrowth, reflecting the time it takes for consumers to become comfortable with a new channel.[4] Based on their analysis of conditions in fifty-two countries, they project that the global economy entered this critical first stage in 2001, although different countries continue to move at different speeds.

By the year 2004, Forrester Research estimates that global Internet trade will reach $6.8 trillion, representing 8.6 percent of all global sales of goods and services. Business-to-consumer revenues on the Web are a drop in the bucket compared to those of business-to-business. B2B revenues are a whopping five times bigger than B2C, and they are growing even more rapidly. The expansion, however, will be highly concentrated, with twelve countries representing 85 percent of the activity. North America will command half of all e-commerce in 2004, as the U.S. will remain the leader with $3.2 trillion that year. Asia will account for $1.6 trillion and Western European e-commerce will hit

$1.5 trillion. North American dominance of worldwide Net commerce will likely begin to fade after 2004, once Asian and Western European countries hit their stride.

Even with the slowdown in the economy in 2000–2001, the growth in e-commerce remained strong. World online sales over Christmas 2000, which was one of the worst holiday seasons in recent years for American retailers, were still up by more than 60 percent over the previous year. And, even now, only a small fraction of the world's population is online. The potential growth in coming years is immense.

In addition, pure online stores crushed the sites of their bricks-and-mortar competitors when it came to customer satisfaction. According to a survey of 33,000 online shoppers by Nielsen/Net Ratings and Harris Interactive, reported in *Business Week*, seven out of the top ten sites were pure e-tailers.[5] These sites spent millions of dollars to improve the click stream and to add services. By contrast, sites of traditional retailers, such as Walmart.com, were struggling with online customer service. Heavy investments were being made to improve the sites, even with the economic slowdown. The survey also found that in-store sales were enhanced by the Web presence of traditional business. Consumers reported that they would go online to investigate the products they intended to buy in stores. Clearly, the Web has tremendous value for all retailers—on- and offline.

NEXT STAGE—THE MOBILE INTERNET

We are on the cusp of the next big wave of technological innovation. The Internet is going wireless, and video streaming and voice recognition will contribute to its value and ease of use. The key to the enhancements will be infinite bandwidth (broadband)—infinite communication capability. And broadband and wireless will grow side by side. The first programmable computers were built during World War II, but the IT revolution did not really get going until the mainframe became popular in the mid-1960s and the microprocessor was developed in 1971.[6] The growth since then has been described by Moore's Law, first stated by Gordon Moore, the co-founder of Intel. In 1965 he predicted that the processing power of a silicon chip would double every eighteen months. Indeed it has, and some computer scientists believe the pace could continue for another decade, although the physics of silicon technology is rapidly reaching its limits. (That is where nanotechnology comes in; more on that in Chapter 4.) But, according to Gilder's Law, bandwidth grows even more rapidly, at least three times faster than computer power.[7] In other words, George Gilder—well-known author and tech guru—believes that communication power doubles every six months.

By 2005, it is expected that more than one billion people on the planet will be regularly using the Internet—many through wireless devices. This explosion in Net usage is still in its infancy. In coming years, bandwidth, functionality, and access will mushroom dramatically.

Personal digital assistants—in the form of cellular phones, Blackberry pagers, Palm Pilots, and many more—will be available at near throwaway prices. These wireless devices will be connected to smart appliances in our homes, offices, and automobiles. The marriage of the two hottest tech trends—cell phones (or any handheld device) and the Web—is promising to create the "Mobile Net," an untethered communications and media web where e-mail and e-commerce travel in a billion pockets, purses, and glove compartments. It is capturing the imagination of consumers, telecommunications carriers, equipment manufacturers, and service providers. The Mobile Net will provide always-on communication with real-time streaming of video, audio, and text. Voice-recognition technology will allow you to communicate with devices too small for a keyboard. The systems will be "location sensitive," knowing where you are and servicing your needs accordingly. Imagine being on a business trip in Thailand. You need a restaurant recommendation, reservations, and directions. Your Web-enabled cell phone will provide all the help you need, including directions from your current locale to the restaurant you choose. Sound too good to be true? This kind of capability is already in the works.

Internet-enabled automobiles are already coming off the assembly lines. Voice-activated Internet is real and will be a huge step toward improving and broadening access and functionality. "Smart" cars—able to provide location and directions, maps to desired destinations, traffic reports, and weather conditions—are not the stuff of science fiction, but are increasingly available today, and the technology is dramatically improving. Imagine driving through a strange town in your rental car and knowing the exact route to the interstate highway, the closest clean restroom, and the best place to buy a cup of cappuccino. If your sense of direction is as bad as mine, you will find this useful even in your home town.

Don Tapscott, Internet visionary and author of many books about the Net, believes that the next phase of Internet development is more accurately described as the "hypernet." According to Tapscott, "Mobile computing devices, broadband access, wireless networks, and computing power imbedded in everything from bicycles to factory tools, are converging into a vast global network—a hypernet—that will fuel exponential change in business-model innovation."[8]

The hypernet will further expand the boundaries of the firm and change inextricably consumer and corporate behavior. The Internet of the future will be comprised of a billion net-connected mobile phones, networked game consoles, handhelds, toys, and information appliances. In this world, computing will be so readily available that the traditional computer will recede in importance. But wireless devices will not replace fiber optic networks; they are complementary, parallel systems. The mediums will be seamless and interconnected. Wireless is an extension of the Internet market. There will be an almost insatiable demand for bandwidth as well as mobility.

No sector of the economy will be left untouched. We are entering an era when getting customer attention will be ever more difficult. Consumers will use mobile devices to "pull" goods, services, or information from the Net whenever and wherever the impulse strikes. At the same time, they will be ever more bombarded by information "pushed" their way. Information overload will be an increasing problem.

THE CUSTOMER IS SOVEREIGN

Consumers will become increasingly demanding as online sophistication rises, expecting full customization and immediate gratification at rock-bottom prices. Online shoppers will actively research their purchases and use "robot" sites—like mySimon and BizRate—to search the Net for the cheapest prices for specified products. Consumers will no longer settle for the selection of jeans available on the store shelf. They will expect custom-made jeans, delivered to their door within a few days. And the same will be true for automobiles, furniture, and groceries. Online and offline capabilities will be integrated. A snowboarding enthusiast, for example, might want to use the Net to research the options, select a snowboard, compare prices, and buy the item—but choose to pick it up in two hours at the local ski shop.

Consumers will expect enhanced delivery of existing retailing capability and a broad array of new competencies. Retailers in all sectors will be markedly impacted. They will have to respond to growing consumer demands for service, value, and selection or go out of business. This will require a change in business culture and substantial investments in technology.

THE E-TAILING CHALLENGE

Innovative retailers will emerge to take advantage of the Net's infinite shelf space and rich customer data. They will anticipate shoppers' needs with widely expanded product assortment and provide widespread, multi-channel shopping access—shopping, for example, on the Net (through both wireless and wired devices), on interactive TV, through catalogs, and in the stores. In 1999, online sales were roughly $20 billion, by an estimated 17 million households. By 2004, it is estimated that nearly 50 million households in the U.S. will be doing some of their shopping on the Web. Kids today, so comfortable with the Net at an early age, will be the online shoppers of tomorrow.

With the burgeoning number of digitally savvy people under the age of twenty, the future of online retailing is bright, but it is fraught with risks and pitfalls as the 2000 dot-com meltdown illustrated. Providing all this extra service, value, and selection to ever-demanding consumers and delivering it to their doors is expensive. The new, single-purpose e-tailers of the earliest period did not have the correct business models to survive when the capital dried up. They were running at too high a "burn rate," losing money at a breakneck clip, with little prospect of future profitability in a time frame acceptable to investors.

The models will evolve—in many cases through the synergies of bricks and clicks. Traditional companies such as Wal-Mart and Home Depot have learned to maximize the profitability of their current floor space. Their sales-per-employee ratio is high. Inventories-to-sales ratios in retailing are higher than in other sectors of the economy as firms have learned to balance the tradeoff between high shipping costs and the cost of capital tied up in goods on the shelf. Sophisticated systems have allowed successful traditional retailers to stock sufficient quantities of the goods that will move and provide the optimal number of salespeople to help them move.

E-tailers face a different challenge. They do not need to stockpile goods to as large a degree, but their handling and shipping costs are much higher. Instead of consumers picking products off the shelves and taking them home, the e-tailers must individually fill each order and ship directly to the customer. This is a different model, requiring a different payment structure for the consumer. Business-to-consumer e-tailers are working hard to find a profitable model as market leaders like Amazon.com have increased prices and shipping charges. There is also a huge amount of "knowledge" imbedded in the e-tailing service—book reviews, music clips, and customer ratings in the case of Amazon.com, customized shoe selection in the case of Nordstrom.com. E-tailers ultimately will have to find a way to get paid for this knowledge, be it through enhanced volumes or revenues.

BACKLASH

Dot-com stock prices may have fallen, in some cases by as much as 100 percent, but the bricks-and-mortar world still feels threatened by the Internet's sting. As evidence, retailers, distributors, and other intermediaries are conducting fairly effective battles to block e-commerce. Most of it is behind the scenes. An early 2001 report by the Progressive Policy Institute, a Washington think tank, annotates how widespread the offline rush for protection has been in everything from wine to automobiles.[9] Optometrists are campaigning to make filling prescriptions online more difficult. The wine wholesalers are lobbying legislatures to stop wineries from selling their product on the Net. Radiologists are attempting to limit telemedicine, as the transmission and reading of X-rays online has become a relatively common occurrence.

Music retailers and realtors have also appealed to lawmakers and the courts to curb e-commerce. For example, the National Association of Recording Merchandisers has filed a suit against Sony for selling compact discs that, when played on a computer, can link users to a Sony-owned Web site where they can buy additional CDs. The recording industry obtained a court order to force Napster—the famous song-swap service—to remove copyrighted songs from distribution. Automobile dealers also feel threatened by the Net and are urging state legislatures to enforce laws that protect their industry.

This is nothing new. It has often been the case that industries threatened by technological change have sought protection from lawmakers. In the 1920s, the Horse Association of America lobbied to limit the number of cars and trucks parking on public roads. During the Depression, independent banks lobbied for a ban on branch banking. For decades thereafter, this was the foundation against nationwide branching in the U.S.

The Net is not without its champions, however. The nonpartisan Consumer Federation of America has produced a study showing that consumers are disadvantaged by state curbs on Net auto sales. The U.S. federal government, as well, is concerned about unfair practices against cyber-competitors. They are enhancing enforcement efforts to tackle retailers that collude against e-commerce companies.

THE NEW RETAILERS

The Internet provides a new platform for all retailers, enabling them to dramatically enhance their product scope. Retailing will be increasingly unshackled from the limits of the physical bricks-and-mortar world. Unlimited shelf space allows for much broader product range while reducing the need for expensive printed brochures and catalogs. Site offerings can be changed easily and kept up-to-date in real time. With the proper tracking devices, retailers will capitalize on a wealth of customer information and preferences. Portals like AOL and Yahoo! are an important source of customer information. These data will allow the New Retailers to anticipate what people will be buying next; merchandising will be based on consumer analysis, fully exploiting the plethora of information available from Net-based transactions.

In the future, the Net will not be dominated by start-ups. Everyone will be involved—including the big companies. Capital will be crucial to survival. One legacy of the dot-com debacle may be that the days of starting a company on a shoestring are over. Although the Net does enable the small unit to compete with the giant, even the small unit will need some funding. To be successful, firms will have to spend more and more on technology. The Net allows them to get closer to their customers. Feedback—both positive and negative—now arrives in real time. Click-stream analysis—tracking the movement of customers online—helps companies to understand customers' thought patterns as never before. That makes it imperative for a business to put this knowledge to work, fast. If they don't, their competitors will.

Another legacy of the dot-com meltdown is that growth and profits matter. A good business is a good business. Forget looking at just the number of hits or potential revenue. The bottom line is what counts. In the future, there will be no such thing as a purely electronic business. From the start, all companies will operate in both the electronic and the physical worlds. Positive experiences will get results. E-tailers have to entertain shoppers. Give customers something they cannot get elsewhere. Force them to alter the way they think about retailing.

Inventories will be kept as low as possible, further streamlining the production-to-consumer process. However, this will require that the sources of merchandise are plentiful and reliable. New synergies between wholesalers and retailers are developing and some e-tailers, like Amazon.com, are finding it necessary to build their own warehouse systems. Many of the dot-com calamities of 2000 lay in the delivery; insufficient inventories meant delays in shipping and long waits for fulfillment. Today's consumer is impatient and unforgiving. Traditional retailers have the advantage of ready-made inventories and a site for returns and exchanges.

The New Retailers will target specific market segments with a wide array of customized products. There will be multiple points of sale—stores, websites, catalogs, interactive TV, kiosks. Consumers will be able to buy anytime, anywhere. A common infrastructure will support all channels.

Alliances are forming between retailing and service providers of all sorts. Companies will be part of interdependent "econets" or "business webs"—a loose network of partnerships. Shared websites for similar customer segments will evolve. Based on the demographics and psychographics of their customers, retailers will join forces and share data. A family buying designer luggage online likely has an interest in upscale travel, restaurant recommendations, fine wine, and high-end clothing. Luggage stores will partner with travel agents, restaurant reviewers, and specialty clothing retailers that can offer bathing suits for the beach and ski clothes for the slopes.

Retailers will share infrastructure to tie these alliances together and capitalize on economies of scale—common storefronts on the Net, centralized database management, and common customer service and fulfillment. Personalization of offerings across stores and lifestyle segments will be needed to meet the expectations of an ever more demanding customer base. Shoppers will be able to buy electronically at home, at work, and in the shopping malls. Online devices will be available in stores to widen the product array and satisfy unusual needs. No more problems finding your size or color preference.

Customers will use offline devices like bar code scanners to scan items such as groceries at home to automatically create a shopping list, which will then be submitted to online grocery stores. Services that remove the tedium of repetitive household tasks will be a big seller. Symbol Technologies embeds these bar code scanners in Cross pens and Palm handhelds.

Interactive TV will allow consumers to click and purchase the CD behind a music video or a product they see in a commercial. Already shoppers are flocking to the websites of popular TV shows to see and purchase the latest in fashion trends. These shows often actually set the trends.

Advertising will not be enough to build brand, as the big spenders on Super Bowl XXXIV advertising found out in 2000. The Net's best-known brands, such as Amazon.com, AOL, eBay, and Yahoo!, were all built by grassroots adoption and word of mouth. Advertising only reinforced that initial appeal to consumers. Internet companies that thought they could advertise their way to lasting success were just plain wrong.

TRADITIONAL RETAILERS COULD BE THE ONLINE WINNERS

In the earliest days of online shopping, the pure-play innovators like Amazon.com, Autobytel, and Priceline.com seemed to have the edge. The online auction site, eBay, certainly has made a splash with an innovative business model that brought liquidity to the market for countless items that were previously very difficult to buy or sell. By accessing the marketplace's supply and demand, eBay enables a buyer to be found for the outgrown bicycle or Aunt Jean's antique watch at a price that makes it worth selling, a true secondary market. This is one of the few dot-coms to turn a consistent profit.

For others, rivalry from traditional retailers is mounting. Online gift sites like Ashford and RedEnvelope are now face to face with Nordstrom and Saks. Barnes&Noble.com is now providing formidable competition for Amazon.com in the books space, and the online sites set up by the automobile dealers and the automakers themselves could put the pure-play online auto sites at a competitive disadvantage. Autobytel, the largest car-buying website, has responded by hooking up with General Motors for a pilot program. Under the deal, consumers using Autobytel.com to search for a GM brand will be given a list of inventory at local dealerships and a special "e-price" for the vehicle. Working on its own, Autobytel wouldn't have access to an inventory list, and GM benefits from the independence of a third-party website.

Traditional department stores could regain waning market share. Brand names like Macy's, Sears, and JCPenney create immediate customer recognition. They could easily extend their product lines, using their strong physical presence—stores in so many locations—to complement their online businesses, making delivery and exchanges easy. They could partner with boutiques as well to significantly improve their product lines.

Supermarket chains are gobbling up online grocers. So far, Webvan—the largest online grocer—is the only one that is not affiliated with a traditional retailer, and Webvan is having serious financial difficulties. Others have run for cover, which for them meant the arms of a traditional grocery chain. Jupiter Research expects that by 2005, the vast majority of online food sales will come from brick-and-mortar grocers. The fear of losing market share will drive them online. For example, Publix, a chain of more than 640 stores in the Southeast U.S., planned to launch PublixDirect in the summer of 2001 in Pompano Beach, Florida. It hoped to expand to Orlando in 2002. Not all traditional supermarkets have decided to take the leap, however. For example, Krogers, the largest chain in the U.S., is limiting its online shopping to an experimental service in Denver. And 1,000-store chain Winn-Dixie had no online plans as of early 2001.

There will be huge challenges for the New Retailers. Most importantly, they must effectively manage their databases, keeping track of all relevant information about shoppers. This would include lifestyle and demographic information, purchase history, direct-mail responses, and Web store click-stream data. Successful retailers will mine these data to determine their most profitable customer segments and to improve and adjust their product offerings to this group. These changes in retailing will encourage further consolidation for some. But the Net will also promote the boutique concept, allowing small to compete with big. Alliances will help the larger and smaller players alike, and many will develop the synergies quite effectively.

A REVOLUTION IN FINANCIAL SERVICES

New forms of money will proliferate, turning the financial services industry upside down. E-wallets and e-cash allow customers to pay for online purchases without the tedium and risk of providing credit card numbers and expiry dates. X.com's online service PayPal was started to make it easy for buyers and sellers on eBay to accept and make payment for their purchases. The system lets anyone with an e-mail address send, invoice, and accept credit card payments, even though they don't have a credit card merchant account. Anyone can send money this way to buy an auction item, for example, or to settle restaurant checks with friends or send money to kids at college. You just enter the recipient's e-mail address and the amount you wish to send is either charged to a credit card or to your checking account. The recipient gets an e-mail that says, "You've got Cash!" Recipients can then collect their money by clicking a link in the e-mail that takes them to PayPal.com, which credits their credit card or checking account. The service now has millions of customers and is growing at an astonishing rate.

Banks must respond to these challenges. They have a history of success in persuading consumers to adopt new technologies, particularly if they are more convenient. Automated teller machines (ATMs) were many people's first encounter with a computer. There are, however, wide divergences in consumer confidence levels. Early adopters demand the very latest in technological innovation—smart cards, online banking and investing, and wireless access to accounts—while others remain fearful of anything but face-to-face contact. Traditionalists are uncertain that new applications have been sufficiently tested and thus cling to the perceived security of the human contact with a teller or a stock broker.

The stock market decline in 2000 fed the fear of online trading and for many enhanced the value of personal advice and financial consultation. While the equity markets were running strong in the second half of the 1990s, pure-play online stock trading sites proliferated—E*Trade, Ameritrade, and Datek, to name a few. These e-brokers were sending shock waves through the industry and provided a huge wake-up call for mammoths like Merrill Lynch and Morgan Stanley. By March 2000, E*Trade Group's $9.4 billion market capitalization topped that of Bear Stearns Cos. The discount brokers like Schwab and TD Waterhouse caught on to the Internet craze and moved much of their business online. Schwab, at one time, had a larger market cap than Merrill Lynch. By 1999, the traditional giants in the industry were forced to respond, as Merrill Lynch did by launching an online discount service.

Online brokers and cheap trades were all the fashion when markets were rising; after all, everyone is a genius in a bull market. But with the Nasdaq crash, many exited stocks altogether or looked for an advisor, punishing discount brokers. They need transactions to survive. A painful shakeout among the 140 or so online brokers in the U.S. is in process. Consolidation will be evident. All of the big-name, full-service brokers have invested heavily in sophisticated online offerings. While Merrill's stock price hit a record high in early 2001, Schwab and the e-brokers' stock prices were languishing. Ameritrade laid off 14 percent of its workforce after announcing bigger-than-expected losses. Others followed.

The full-service investment dealers have the advantages of choice, scope of selection, and research. While many investors, badly burned by the Internet crash in 2000, have flocked back to the comfort of the full-service dealer, a market for online trading is clearly well entrenched and growing. Many consumers have both full-service and online accounts and some, though a declining number, still choose to deal offline via the telephone.

Wired consumers have discovered the value of the Internet as a financial partner. In addition to researching potential investments, they can chat with fellow investors and financial professionals in online forums (but watch out for the crackpots and outright embezzlers). Consumers can track stocks and bonds in real time, manage and monitor their portfolios, do sophisticated financial analysis and retirement planning, and conduct a wide array of financial transactions. These include stock and bond trading, transferring funds, applying for mortgages and other loans, bill paying, and more. T. Rowe Price and many others have built interactive planning tools on their websites. Morningstar and Globefund.com (in Canada) use search engines that comb through the universe of mutual funds for those that meet designated risk, return, and management styles.

Increasingly, financial institutions are expected to be at the cutting edge of technology while at the same time providing unmatched customer service. This is very expensive, and competition is intense. Pure-play businesses have proliferated, offering only one product—credit cards, high-yielding deposits, mortgages, or insurance—on terms more attractive than those provided by the full-service institutions. The Net may spur the breakup of companies into component parts, boutiques that provide better service and pricing. In addition, new financial intermediaries have come between customers and bankers, brokers, and insurers. America Online, for example, is a big player in online banking. AOL's Banking Center is partnered with many financial institutions, including Wells Fargo, Bank of America, Bank One, Chase Manhattan, and others. Each of these institutions has built a virtual branch accessible via AOL.

The transformation of all retailing and financial services is happening very quickly. In both the wired and wireless world, growth in e-commerce will accelerate as people become more comfortable with the Net. Privacy, security, and reliability issues are being hammered out now. These are still very early days and the growing pains are evident. Industry observers in Europe and Asia, however, estimate that by 2004, 40 percent of B2C e-commerce transactions in their regions will occur through portable wireless devices. In Finland, for example, kids already punch in a few numbers on their cell phone keypads to pay for a candy bar from a vending machine.

ALL BUSINESSES MOVE ONLINE

Most of the online commerce in the future will be in the business-to-business, B2B, space, growing to about $6 trillion by 2004—up from $215 million in 1999.[10] It will ultimately represent more than 80 percent of all e-commerce on a worldwide basis.

The Old Economy is rapidly morphing into the New through these B2B sites, enabling traditional business to cut costs, streamline the production process, and reduce friction in transactions. In their most developed form, B2B sites promote seamless, end-to-end, straight-through transactions and allow former cutthroat competitors to enjoy mutual synergies and economies of scale.

Procurement sites offer supply-chain management. Online marketplaces, such as MetalSpectrum, bring together the many institutional buyers and sellers in the metals industry. Farming, one of the world's oldest industries, is turning to the Web as well. Hit by the lowest commodity prices in many years, farmers increasingly looked to the Net to hike sales and cut costs. The Internet gave them a global marketplace in which to sell their products. By cutting out the intermediaries such as dealers and distributors, procurement sites like DirectAg, XSAg, and farmbid offer savings on everything from seed and fertilizer to crop-protection chemicals.

Oil companies are doing much the same. Chevron, the second largest integrated oil company in the United States, spends about $10 billion a year on materials and services. Until 1999, Chevron's buyers used more than seven different procurement systems and ordered materials and services from some 27,000 different suppliers. E-procurement allowed Chevron to cut dramatically the number of its suppliers and to simplify the process. Using Internet-based, standardized-buying systems, the company expects to save $200 million a year.

AUTOS—THE BIG EXAMPLE

In one of the most highly publicized moves, the automobile industry also joined the rush to the Net. The Big Three car companies—General Motors, DaimlerChrysler, and Ford—joined forces with Renault/Nissan, Commerce One, and Oracle to develop an online parts exchange called Covisint. It is expected to be the largest of the B2B exchanges, handling global purchasing of as much as $250 billion at the five automakers. Any auto parts manufacturers desiring to do business with these global giants must present their wares online and engage in an electronic auction process. The auto industry information hub connects the players in the procurement, product-design, and supply-management sides of the business. Detroit sees this exchange as the foundation of an Internet-based industry that designs and engineers cars faster and better, and that eventually will build them to order, delivering them directly to customers within a few days. It is estimated that this will reduce the cost of producing an automobile by nearly 15 percent. That is enormous savings for a highly regulated, capital-intensive, heavily unionized industry where companies fight and scrap for cost savings of just a few pennies on every dollar of sales.

Stage one was a parts exchange for everything that the automakers buy—from glass to gas tanks. This represented an unheard of level of cooperation among the Big Three. Suppliers were very reluctant at first. Their biggest fear was that with specifications and volume targets posted in plain view on the Web, car manufacturers would find it easier to drive down prices during the bidding process. What's more, about 20 percent of the transactions—mostly involving commodities—are made through online reverse auctions, which can drastically narrow margins. In a reverse auction, buyers post a request for an item or service and sellers bid their prices down to make a sale. Although it sounds somewhat convoluted, it's simple enough that it has caught on with a growing number of business and private-party auction sites. To make a reverse auction work requires the active participation of a large number of suppliers. The Covisint site certainly has that.

Communication between manufacturers and suppliers is now faster, cheaper, and simpler. Engineering changes, for example, which are at the heart of the vehicle development process, are sent instantaneously all the way down the line. (Firewalls between companies keep proprietary information under wraps.) Better, more complete information is available to suppliers, who historically have complained that manufacturers gave them overly rosy sales projections. As carmakers post their sales reports and production schedules on the Net, suppliers will have a clearer picture of actual customer behavior.

Auto Sales Will Move Online

Ultimately, the entire automobile industry could well be revolutionized by customized car manufacture. "Build-to-order" is the watchword, and it will mean the development of an enormous B2C sector. The existing system of car and truck manufacture, sale, and distribution is extremely wasteful. Since most buyers won't wait the six weeks or more it has historically taken to order a particular model from the factory, they choose from what is available in the dealer's lot. But that means that dealers are often caught out of stock on the hot new sports utility vehicles (until the industry responds with overproduction) and up to the gills on the turquoise sedans. Customers often find themselves waiting endlessly anyway and the duds are sold at fire-sale prices. In the meantime, huge sums are tied up in dealer inventories.

The shift to build-to-order is beginning. General Motors, Toyota, and Ford are starting with one or two models and will then convert the rest. General Motors plans to revamp all its factories in the U.S. to faster, more flexible production by 2003. This is more difficult than you might think. The actual manufacture of customized automobiles is extremely complex, involving far more possible permutations than, for example, made-to-order personal computers. While Dell might have to snap together a computer from a couple of dozen components, a special order for a vibrating seat in a Cadillac Eldorado could send shock waves all the way down the supply chain. Auto parts tend to be large and expensive, so it is costly to store inventories near assembly plants just in case they are needed. Suppliers are often hundreds of miles away, so a factory in Morganton, North Carolina, for example, ships anti-lock brake systems all over the Midwest, making it hard to place last-minute orders.

Distribution has been a nightmare. Railroads were often short of rail cars that can carry SUVs, pickups, and minivans, which can only be stacked two high, while cars can be three high. Sending them by truck, instead, can be prohibitively expensive. While overnight parcel services can track a package anywhere, carmakers often have little idea where their cars are, making it hard to reroute them. According to Daron Gifford, global automotive director at Deloitte & Touche, "They know the vehicle has left the plant and they know what dealership it's going to, but they don't know where it is during the 30 days or so in between."[11]

Automobile dealers will not disappear in the build-to-order world, but they will have to figure out how to add value. For eighty years, state franchise laws that prevent manufacturers from selling cars directly to customers have protected them. Competitive forces catalyzed by the Internet may finally revolutionize the system. Online car-buying services like CarsDirect.com, which act as brokers, have already started to change the system. These services could begin to buy dealerships and start selling directly to consumers. That would drastically alter the economics of the dealer business by lowering inventory costs and commissions. Estimates of the savings in advertising, sales support, and overhead exceed $1,000 per car. Conventional dealers would have to adapt or die. Used cars are already traded online. Many dealers will struggle to add value through enhanced car-maintenance and repair servicing and financing capabilities. They could act as manufacturers' reps by answering buyer questions, offering test drives, and marketing other auto-related products such as wireless Internet capability. The environment will be difficult, however, because independent maintenance firms will spring up, cutting the technical-capability gap. Also, financing will be easy online.

The Internet is changing the fundamental economics of the automobile business. The same is true for sector after sector around the world. Former vicious competitors will join forces to exploit economies of scale, network effects, and other synergies. Competition will increase as all prices become transparent, and waste and inefficiencies will be markedly reduced. Business-model innovation will be essential to capture the value created by new kinds of transactions. As the pace of change accelerates, obsolete businesses will disappear rapidly. We are in the early days of this hypergrowth phase in e-activity. The implications for the economy and financial markets are immense.

4

The Best Is
Yet to Come
The Knowledge Explosion

Not only in the world of the Internet will the growth be head-spinning. Technological developments throughout the economy are showing incredible potential. And thanks to increasing returns to knowledge, the speed of change and innovation will be faster than anyone might have predicted. Three areas that will have a meaningful impact on our lives and future well-being are nanotechnology, biotechnology, and the development of fuel cells and other alternative energy sources.

While many are legitimately concerned about the risks associated with the advance of human knowledge—particularly in the realm of artificial intelligence and genetic modification—I am excited about the opportunities. Sure there are risks and valid worries that must be addressed from a regulatory and legal standpoint, but scientific advance has always brought such risks. What could be more risky than nuclear reactors, the study of viruses, or even brain surgery? All technologies carry with them their inherent problems. In the Industrial Age, we were confronted by environmental degradation; in the IT world, issues of privacy and piracy. With biotech, we must deal with the safety, ethical, and moral issues surrounding bioengineered foods, eugenics, designer babies, and genetic patenting. Difficult as these issues will continue to be, they can be dealt with constructively.

As humans continue to stretch our knowledge base, we run the risk of scientific advances falling into the hands of those who intend to do harm rather than good. We could also inadvertently cause serious problems. But the answer to those risks is not to stop the research. I say we set up the systems to assess and manage the risks on a global basis, rather than try (in vain) to stem the tide of progress.

MINIATURE COMPUTERS— THE NANOTECH WORLD

Nanotechnology is the world of manufacturing in miniature. It is difficult to visualize just how small a nanometer is. It is a mere one-billionth of a meter—only three to five atoms across. Any technology done on a nanometer scale is nanotechnology. It is the production of miniature machines, molecule by molecule. It will revolutionize manufacturing, medicine, and many aspects of daily life. It is shining proof that "knowledge begets knowledge," as scientists apply breakthroughs in digital technology to the body of science in multiple fields, exploiting synergies and driving the way to innovation. Research in this area is taking place at the crossroads of physics, biology, chemistry, and electrical engineering. It is a relatively new field, but practical applications are already starting to surface.

You will be hearing more and more about nanotech as researchers around the world pore over their atomic force microscopes.[1] This is a device that has an extremely fine point, only a few atoms wide. When an electric charge is sent through the tip, the charge moves one or two atoms at a time. Human hand movements on a computer mouse can be translated to the level that pushes a single atom one way or the other. The microscope can also record an electronic image of the atoms, which can be blown up on computer for further analysis and manipulation. All of this sounds like science fiction, but work in this area has been progressing rapidly since 1989.

Microscopic machines are currently under development in laboratories in the U.S., Canada, Europe, China, and Japan. There are even nanotech start-up companies, such as Zyvex, which bills itself as the first molecular nanotechnology development company. Nanotech seed capital firms like Molecular Manufacturing Enterprises Inc. are also appearing. Heavyweight tech companies have entered the nano race as well, such as Hewlett-Packard, IBM, and Lucent.

Scientists are tearing down the walls between organic and inorganic chemistry, mining them for totally new structures. Tomorrow's substances will be tailor-made from scratch—molecule by molecule—to provide the precise properties needed for each application. Embedded in them will be tiny computers, allowing for the simulation of biological systems or the improving functionality of machines, automobiles, fiber optic networks, and countless other products. This is not new. In recent decades, inorganic chemists have concocted an impressive array of materials that allow for bigger, better buildings, bridges, and highways. Organic chemists, in the meantime, have created plastics, fertilizers, drugs, and all manner of synthetic products that have improved our lives and increased global productivity. The fusion of these sciences, along with the development of "internal intelligence"—digital reasoning capability—will dramatically open up new frontiers.

Over the next few years, a new breed of miniature machines called microelectromechanical systems (MEMS), currently in their earliest stages, will take the place of more expensive components in factories, computer hardware, automobile engines, and many other processes and products. MEMS combine sensors, motors, and digital capability on a single sliver of silicon. They open the way for the re-creation of human organs and the internal monitoring of blood counts, insulin levels, and organ functions. They could be the atomic-scale chips and memory of next-generation computers, thousands of times more powerful than those that run on today's silicon technology. They could be implanted into the material of tires, able to detect defects and act as tiny pressure gauges and pumps to assure that the tires are functioning properly. Wouldn't Firestone have loved to have had that technology?

Scientists at Cornell University are at the leading edge in creating molecular motors based on the structure of ribonucleic acid polymerase

(RNA), a biological enzyme that uses chemical reactions to propel itself from place to place. Scientists constructed a nanotech device that's part mechanical and part biological, with molecular-size rotors that can turn three to four revolutions per second—one of the world's first nanomotors. In a similar vein, Oxford University, along with Bell Labs, built a motor modeled after the molecular structure of DNA.

As the technology improves, scientists will eventually use these motors to power microscopic chemical plants. Injected into a human, the plants could be programmed to drive to the site of, for example, a cancerous tumor and prescribe and administer just the right treatment to kill the cancer, while protecting the healthy cells. The possibilities are breathtaking and endless. No industry or sector will be left untouched.

Optical Switching

One of the most exciting new applications for MEMS is in optical switches for the Internet. One historical problem with fiber optics is that the only way to switch incoming lines with outgoing lines is to turn the optical signals (wavelengths of light) into electrical signals so that computers can read them. Once the computer has made the switch, the electrical signals are turned back into optical signals and they are then sent on their way. This requirement markedly slows down the network. It is the equivalent of an airplane pilot having to land every 100 miles for refueling rather than carrying a tank big enough to make the full distance; it is inefficient and overly time consuming.

The answer is all-optical switching. It turns out that the only practical way this can be done is through MEMS that are arrays of movable mirrors cut from a wafer of silicon. Bell Labs, one of the innovators in this field, developed tiny lens-like machines that hold trampoline-like devices, each the size of a red blood cell. The trampolines can be bent into lens-like shapes that can modulate and switch a wavelength of light. Lucent put this technology to work in the much-ballyhooed LambdaRouter, the first optical switch of its kind. Global Crossing and other carriers are currently testing the switch. In March 2000, Nortel paid over $3.2 billion in stock for MEMS-maker Xros.

MEMS allow for far greater flexibility than electronic switches. They can switch signals in any format, wavelength, or speed. This is crucial in the rapidly changing world of the Net. When fiber channels commonly run at 40 billion bits per second in a couple of years—compared to 10 billion bits per second in 2000—only all-optical switches will be able to keep up. The market for switches based on nanodevices will exceed $1 billion by 2004, according to market researchers Cahners In-Stat Group. It will be nanotech's first real business. By 2004, the overall market for MEMS will be $7 billion strong.

MEMS in Medicine

Nanomedicine is the monitoring, repair, construction, and control of the human body at the molecular level, using nanodevices such as MEMS and nanostructures such as engineered enzymes. This is the stuff of science fiction books.

Once nanomachines are available, the ultimate dream of every healer, medicine man, and physician throughout recorded history will finally come to fruition. Imagine that programmable and controllable micro-scale robots will allow doctors to cure and reconstruct the human body at the cellular and molecular level. Think of it—today's surgery from the cell's point of view is pretty barbaric stuff. A huge blade cuts through a crowd of cells, killing thousands. A thick cable is dragged in to sew up the mess, leaving it up to the cells to abandon their dead and multiply so that healing can take place. The administration of a drug is no less brutal. The drug molecules bump aimlessly around until they fit into their target molecule.

Imagine, instead, a molecular machine that could sense, plan, and act. Repair machines the size of a bacterium will be built to enter and leave cells, destroy intruders in the blood, and even check the DNA itself for any errors. Pioneer K. Eric Drexler called these MEMS "engines of healing."[2]

Nanocomputing

In coming years, the transistors on computer chips will hit their limit in terms of size and speed. Nanotech might be the way to assure continued improvements in computing. A number of developments point the way. One is carbon nanotubes, first developed in Japan by electronics giant NEC in 1991. They are molecules of carbon, each 1.4 nanometers wide. Shaped like elbow macaroni, they conduct electricity and can modulate signals similar to a transistor. They are almost unbreakable and can bend and stick to surfaces like chewing gum.

Nanotubes might be the answer to the inevitable, looming limit to computer power. They could be the computer wires of the future. The more densely transistors are placed on a chip, the more powerful the computer becomes. But there are limits to how thin the already microscopic wires can get. They are already approaching the thickness of only a few hundred atoms. Once the wires get too fine—only several atoms thick—they blow up when you try to send electrical signals through them. Nanotubes are more resilient. IBM and others are hustling to use nanotubes to make the first carbon chips. These might be the next step beyond silicon.

Artificial Intelligence

All of this may seem like a pipe dream right now, but breakthroughs in artificial intelligence—the creation of "smart" computers—could dramatically speed progress in nanotech applications. Advancements in machine intelligence are now quite rapid. In its most rudimentary form, I have made my computer at home much "smarter" than my computer at the office (which is the same model) by diligently using the AutoCorrect function while writing this book. By telling the computer each time I make a mistake how I would like it corrected, it now "anticipates" the correction and makes it automatically. It is "learning" from my mistakes. This is a real time saver.

Researchers argue that computers can be made "smart" in a similar although more complex way, taking them well beyond mere calculating devices capable only of repetitive tasks. Computers are already beating chess grand masters, as they learn to "think" probabilistically. Machines with human-like ability to learn and organize knowledge will become more common, allowing for automated engineering, which will speed the development of newer MEMS faster than a human engineering team ever could.

Nanoterrorism—the Dark Side

As with all scientific endeavors, the potential to use innovations for evil and destructive purposes is real. Bill Joy, the top software architect for Sun Microsystems, has become a celebrity by talking about the dangers of runaway nanotechnology. He warns that if nano machines could be made to make other nano machines, they could take over the earth, choking out all life forms. Other risks abound. Molecular manufacturing will make it possible to produce extraordinarily lethal weapons at a much faster rate than ever before. Even more frightening is the development of dangerous, programmable germ nanomachines for warfare. The possibility of accidental world annihilation cannot be ignored. Indeed, nanotechnology in the wrong hands (or for that matter, any technology in the wrong hands) could have disastrous consequences. Even those responsible for its beneficial use must be wary of the potential dangers.

The human race, however, must not let potential destructive powers obliterate all that might be gained. While it might take a decade or two, nanotech will become a huge area of invention and commerce. In the meantime, the necessary safeguards and restrictions should be addressed and formulated.

THE BIOTECH REVOLUTION

Just as there is a dark side to nanotechnology, the current and potential breakthroughs in biotechnology are also of grave concern to many. Protesters throughout Europe have demanded the banning of genetically modified (GM) foods—"Frankenfoods," as they are called on placards and banners. More research is yet needed to understand what risks might be lurking in GM foods. Mad cow disease in Britain has sensitized Europeans to the risks associated with human intervention in feedstocks. In addition to health and environmental concerns, the possibility of genetic modification of animals and humans raises myriad ethical, moral, and legal questions. It doesn't take much to imagine the worst: Scientists run amok in an attempt to create a super-race of humans—the Masters—and a sub-par race of Servants; atrocities of cross-breeding and cloning; biological warfare; genetic mutations; and all manner of playing god with the human and animal species.

These are important and serious issues that global researchers and government bodies must address—issues that span the scope of regulation, laws, and societal mores. But as grave as these issues are, let's not forget the incredibly positive developments that genetic research does and will allow. Agritech has meaningfully increased the productivity of farmland, augmenting the global food supply and lowering food prices. Properly used, the new biotech crops have enormous potential to reduce pesticide use, improve human nutrition, and ease hunger in developing countries. In a world where many still go hungry, doesn't it make sense to continue this research, creating seed stocks that are impervious to pests and weather damage or crops that have higher nutritional value?

Examples of the tremendous opportunities to increase global food supply are upon us. Scientists sequenced the genetic code of rice in early 2001, opening the way for improvements in a food source that is the dietary staple of half the world's population. Decoding the rice genome makes it possible to create hardier crops, impervious to pests and unfavorable weather conditions. It also allows scientists to enhance the nutritional value of the rice crop, which would be a huge boon to the people of the poorer nations in Asia who rely so heavily on rice as their primary source of nutrition.

Precision farming will be common by 2005, and the farm will become a super-bioengineered place with multimillion-dollar manufacturing plants to augment the fields. Today's agricultural developments are the most important since hybrid corn, which led to the green revolution in the 1950s and 1960s—a period when crop yields soared and hundreds of millions of people were saved from starvation. Today, bioengineered milk, meat, and produce are already on our supermarket shelves, causing a good deal of consternation in some circles, especially in Europe. Numerous varieties of corn are biogenetically altered, although not without a stir. One study showed that pollen from some strains of altered corn killed the larva of the monarch butterfly. What a maelstrom that caused. Fears of Frankenfoods have caused enough furor to disrupt Monsanto's life-sciences strategy and help topple its CEO. Such incidents will certainly multiply.

Biotech has also significantly enhanced the supply and production of natural resources such as forest products, fossil fuels, and metals and minerals. Genetic engineers have created tree stocks that grow faster and stronger. Scientists at the University of Georgia are already developing wood pulp in the test tube. With today's environmental concerns, laboratory wood pulp is not such a bad idea. Global warming and greenhouse gases create a real threat to the future of the planet. And scientists have been able to produce fossil fuel substitutes such as ethanol from forest by-products and agricultural waste.

Beyond 2025, developments in the life sciences will spread to many seemingly unrelated sectors, just as the computer revolution impacted virtually all aspects of the manufacturing and service economy. For example, plants are under investigation for use in cleaning up sites polluted by heavy metals. Cadmium, copper, and mercury are poisonous to most creatures, but some plants have proteins called phytochelatins that bind them up and squirrel them away in places where they can do no environmental harm. The genes for the enzymes that make phytochelatins have now been identified, and researchers are working on transferring them into species that can be grown on the polluted ground and perhaps even harvested to recover the metals. Biotech is already in widespread use in the chemical industry, as DuPont has taken the lead in bacterial genomics research and its application to chemical production. For example, they have developed bacteria that can produce some of the necessary ingredients for nylon and polyester production.

Continuing developments in biotech will enhance the production of food, livestock, fish, and natural resources, increasing supplies and reducing costs. Safeguards must be established to deal with the health, moral, and legal issues; but they should not be so stringent that progress is stalled. The many benefits of continued productivity gains will outweigh the risks if they are carefully monitored and managed.

The Human Genome—Ahead of Schedule

In 1990, the National Institute of Health and the U.S. Energy Department launched the Human Genome Project in collaboration with the British government and a few private companies. The announced completion date was 2005, although they cautioned that this tremendous feat might take even longer. Instead, it was finished in early 2000, thanks largely to the influence of an independent scientist, J. Craig Venter, who capitalized on breakthroughs in digital technology.

Eight years after the official project began, Venter created a small company called Celera Genomics to develop its own program to map the human genome in direct competition with the government-sponsored project. Venter attracted the ire of the genomics community when he boasted he would complete his work by 2000 or 2001, well ahead of the government team. Celera took a computer-intensive approach that relied on sequencing techniques developed by its own scientists. Their speedier progress certainly lit a fire under the official researchers.

Celera was able to move so quickly by using three hundred high-speed DNA sequencers. This encouraged the public project also to buy these machines, and their progress sped up as well—only going to show that with the proper technology and incentives, developments can outpace even the most optimistic estimates. Clearly, the incentives created by the marketplace are essential to foster continued growth and innovation in this sector. Without the hope of commercial gain, Celera would never have undertaken the project. Pharmaceutical and biotech companies are racing to create pathbreaking drugs; but without sufficient patent protection and potential profits, the progress towards disease control and cure will be stunted.

As evidence of this, look at what happened to Celera's stock price. It surged to a record-high $276 in the first quarter of 2000 as news of their impending breakthroughs emerged. In early March, however, President Clinton and Prime Minister Blair announced that the results of the Human Genome Project would be public property. The stock market took this to mean that Celera could not capitalize on its database. The stock plunged, falling even further with the general stock market rout in 2000 to end the year at a mere $36. The Clinton-Blair announcement was somewhat misleading. Celera has sold the human genome database to many researchers in the medical field and they continue to decode the genome for other species—like those already completed for fruit flies, mice, and more—for commercial use. From a stock market perspective, however, volatility in this sector will continue to be immense. Risks are high and the proving grounds are fraught with land mines. The approval process can be relatively long and the political pressures are intense. The "excessive" profitability of drug companies was an election issue in 2000 and consumer groups will continue to pressure for government intervention in this space.

Immense Potential

The decoding of the human genome was only the first step. It is the beginning of what may well be the most important development of our time. Some researchers have suggested that deciphering the three to four billion data points now mapped for human DNA may take a decade or more. My guess is that the payoff will come much sooner. Thanks to increasing returns to knowledge, and a good dose of competitive spirit, the human genome project proceeded well ahead of schedule. Just as we exceeded all speed estimates there, we will also race to the discovery of specific genes and the proteins they produce, accelerating the development of novel drugs and therapies to combat, cure, and prevent disease.

The decoding of the genomes of mice and fruit flies has provided important information of relevance to human genomic research. By studying the progress of genetically related disease in these species, breakthroughs in the development of cures are already beginning. One genetic researcher recently told me that if you live ten more years, your average life expectancy would be nearly one hundred years. While some might suggest that this is overly optimistic, few would argue that life expectancy will rise sharply. And the last ten years of life will not be spent bedridden or in a wheelchair. Imagine what this will mean for the quality of life in our later years, what it will mean for the concept of retirement. How many of us will still want to retire at sixty-five, facing thirty-five years of relative inactivity? The implications for the economy, society, and the government pension systems like Social Security are enormous.

Scientists are now busily filling in the gaps and cataloging the variations in human DNA. They are working to find the genes and understand their functions. Researchers need to know which gene produces which proteins. Once this is determined, they will be able to investigate the role that proteins play in healthy humans and in different diseases. The hope is that the manipulation of those proteins may cure or even prevent the life-ending illnesses that have evaded medical research efforts for so long.

New revelations are uncovered almost daily. It was recently discovered that humans have fewer genes than once thought, which has plunged proteins onto the center stage of research. Proteomics, the large-scale study of proteins, is now believed to hold the secrets of human biology. Understanding how human proteins work is a massive undertaking. A new Human Proteome Organization has been formed, pulling together scientists from all over the world, similar to the Human Genome Project. Celera has said that it will do for proteins what it did for genes. This is a far more complex project, requiring enhanced digital capability.

As it turns out, mapping the human genome was comparatively straightforward because genes are fixed—people carry the same genes throughout life. Proteins, in contrast, are changeable, impacted by the environment, diet, and stress. It now appears that each gene may make several—or even several hundred—proteins, so the link between genes and disease is more tenuous than once thought. Proteins could well hold the key. The complexity of the endeavor is multiplied, however, by the fact that proteins interact with one another. Nevertheless, progress is being made. Although the term "proteomics" was coined less than a decade ago, strides in understanding have been meaningful. Scientists have already identified more than 30,000 proteins, compared to only 500 a few years ago.

Commercial Payoff

Biotech stocks are subject to enormous volatility. These stocks have a habit of surging and then collapsing as technical breakthroughs seem to trigger boom-bust cycles. Biotech stocks, for example, collapsed in

January 1992, following two years of strong performance. According to the American Stock Exchange Biotechnology Index, they didn't bottom until January 1995. They didn't regain old highs in a lasting way until December 1998. The stocks took off in October 1999, only to plunge once again starting in March 2000 with the Blair-Clinton genome announcement and the general rout in tech stocks. Biotech stocks are not for the faint of heart or for short-term investors. But over the next decade or so, they are likely to be among the big winners in the stock market.

The commercial payoff will go to the companies that use the research to develop products that find a market. R&D efforts are proceeding at a breakneck pace at the traditional pharmaceuticals companies, the biotech specialists, and in government and private research laboratories. These endeavors are spawning a growing number of ancillary industries. Examples are developers of the digital technology needed to unlock the genetic code, such as CRS Robotics Corporation and LJL BioSystems/ Molecular Devices, or outfits that create the analytical tools for drug discovery, such as the Applied Biosystems Group. Celera and Incyte Genomics catalog and store the data. We could well see an explosion in biotech-related companies similar to the dot-com frenzy in the 1990s. Many will fail or be swallowed up by the giants, but the winners will win big.

While the moral, ethical, and legal issues surrounding genetic research and modification will be thorny, it is easy to imagine the dramatic potential of these developments to benefit humankind—the end of cancer, diabetes, heart disease, Parkinson's, and Alzheimer's, just to name a few. We are in the early days of the biotech revolution, but the successes will be stunning and they will be here sooner than you think.

Medicine in the Twenty-First Century

Forecasting is never easy, but one forecast I am willing to make is that breakthroughs in the field of medicine in the next decade will be the most important and productive in history. I am betting that the average life expectancy does rise to nearly one hundred years for babies born in the next decade and for the population as a whole by 2030. That doesn't mean that you or I will be guaranteed to live to one hundred, but our life expectancy will rise and it could well change our focus and perspective on long-term financial and career planning. It will certainly change your children's perspective. While economists rarely get into the area of medical forecasting, and I will leave the science to others, these breakthroughs will be of tremendous relevance to the economy, financial markets, and your future.

The health-care model will be transformed from treatment of ailments to prediction and prevention. Computerized health care will be the norm within a decade, with all medical histories, genetic profiles, and test results moving online. Health care today is really sick care. Actually, it is now managed sick care. In the future, we will see a mammoth evolution from sick care to detection and prevention through genetic testing. Parents will be able to find out what diseases their children are susceptible to at birth and modify their lifestyle and medical treatment appropriately. The human genome and protein map will make miracle cures and prevention possible. The sick-care business model made money by filling doctor's offices, prescriptions, and hospital beds. Managed sick care tries to empty hospital beds but does little to actually prevent disease. In the next era of true health care, businesses will make money by helping people to prevent disease.

According to Marvin Cetron and Owen Davies, in their book *Probable Tomorrows*, four revolutions will transform medical treatment and markedly increase life expectancy for the population:[3]

- One we have already discussed is *gene therapy*. There are more than 4,000 known ailments caused by defective genes. Hundreds of breakthroughs in this area will obliterate many of these.

- A *cure for cancer* is also likely in the next decade. I won't get into the details of the science here, but suffice it to say that many researchers believe that the key will be to activate the human immune system to reject tumors and prevent cancers from growing.

- *Hormone replacement treatment* for the symptoms of aging will also extend the length and quality of life. Already in widespread use for women in menopause, many other hormones are now being used with tremendous success. These include human growth hormones, dehydroepiandrosterone or DHEA, melatonin, and others.

- *Cloned or artificial organ transplants* will be available to replace most body parts. Scientists will know enough about how to adjust the human immune system that transplants routinely will be rejection-free. Having alternatives to human organs will dramatically improve the long-term prognosis for recipients and reduce the donor problems.

Success in any one of these areas will be extremely beneficial. From a human perspective, the best is yet to come. The technology break-throughs that lie immediately before us will have enormous economic and societal benefit. We will see continued gains in technology-driven productivity coupled with rising life expectancies. There is a lot to look forward to.

FUEL-CELL TECHNOLOGY

The rapid development of clean energy sources is another strong positive for the future. Some would argue that fuel-cell technology deserves to be on the list of twenty-first century breakthroughs.[4] While I don't see this as having the same potential as the Internet or the breakthroughs in the life sciences, certainly it will be of enormous import for the environment and for manufacturing. Some believe the fuel cell, still in the developmental stage, will replace the internal combustion engine, first developed in Germany at the end of the nineteenth century. The heat and emissions generated by the engine commonly in use today are big problems. Moreover, the gasoline and other fossil fuels that usually run it are in limited supply.

Many see the fuel cell as an answer. It is not a new technology, having been invented even before the internal combustion engine by Sir William Grove in 1839. Fuel cells convert the chemical energy of fuels directly into electricity, without having to go through a combustion stage. Basically, a fuel cell is just like a battery, but it does not need to be recharged and its power doesn't run down. In the cell, hydrogen (the fuel) and oxygen (the oxidant) continuously pass over electrodes and produce a constant stream of electric current. The only byproduct is water, which has no negative environmental impact. NASA used hydrogen-powered fuel cells in spacecraft in the 1960s and 1970s, and they are still in use in the space shuttle program. They provide both electricity and drinking water.

Cost has been an issue—fuel cells are still too expensive for widespread application—but new technological developments are bringing the costs down. The other hitch is the source of the hydrogen itself, since the production of hydrogen can have its own deleterious environmental impact depending on what source is used. Hydrogen can come from hydrocarbons, such as gasoline, but that defeats the purpose. Another option is the use of renewable fuels such as methanol gas, which comes from decaying organic materials.

Millions of dollars are now pouring into fuel-cell research and development, and much of it is currently financed by the global automakers that see the potential for growing demand. The State of California, for example, has mandated that 2 percent of new cars offered for sale have zero emissions by 2003. The mandate will be gradually extended to include public buses. The leader in this technology for the auto sector is Ballard Power Systems Inc. of Vancouver, now partly owned by DaimlerChrysler and Ford. Ballard has successfully reduced the size of the fuel cell needed to run a small car from that of a refrigerator to that of a microwave. Ballard wants to be the Intel of fuel cells but the competition is stiff, as fuel-cell companies have sprung up all over the U.S. and around the world. Notable among them are Sure Power, Plug Power, and Global Thermoelectric. In response to the California electricity crisis in 2001, Ballard announced that it would be shipping fuel-cell-powered portable generators to the stores for Christmas 2001, as many consumers and businesses attempt to take control of their own power supplies.

DaimlerChrysler is slated to have a limited number of fuel-cell cars by 2004. The company has already spent $600 million on the technology and it expects to shell out another $900 million or so over the next decade to ensure its success. Honda, Toyota, and GM also say their fuel-cell cars will be ready by then, and others suggest they will follow.

Mass-market penetration will likely take longer. Fuel-cell technology still has problems such as sluggish engine start-up, as well as the availability of the fuel. A number of automakers and oil companies have jointly opened a hydrogen refueling station for their demo cars near

Sacramento, California. But a widespread infrastructure is needed to provide the source of hydrogen. Other than gasoline, no fuel supplies are readily available on a mass-market scale. Until it is possible to cleanly and safely produce, store, and use pure hydrogen, we will need to rely on gasoline or compressed natural gas, which are costly.

The car industry is firmly behind the new technology. Daimler's top researchers believe that in the next two decades, fuel cells will power perhaps 20 percent of all new passenger vehicles, and possibly all urban buses. Bill Ford, chairman of the Ford Motor company, recently stated: "I believe fuel cells will finally end the 100-year reign of the internal combustion engine."[5] Hiroshi Okuda, chairman of Toyota, is quoted as saying that he is betting the future on fuel cells and clean cars, but has no idea when his big bets will pay off.[6]

Fuel cells will ultimately power far more than just cars. Everything from home appliances to ski lifts could, in time, use this technology. Both stationary and mobile applications are in production. The U.S. Army plans to install hundreds of fuel-cell generators at military bases and Motorola is building cell phones that can run on methanol fuel cells. Japan has cancelled the construction of two nuclear power plants and instead will run the power generation using fuel cells.

Fuel-cell cars will likely begin to enter the mass market by 2005 and alternative energy sources will be widely used by 2009. Over the next twenty years, the electricity industry projects roughly an additional 10 trillion kilowatt-hours of new capacity will be needed around the world. The California electricity debacle of 2001 is testimony to the need. If fuel-cell costs drop to $500 per kilowatt, as expected after 2005, it could be competitive with coal- and gas-fueled generators. This is a slow build, but the industry has enormous potential.

THE FEAR OF CHANGE—POPULATION AND ENVIRONMENTAL FEARS

There are those who worry that rising life expectancies will drain our economic resources and put an undue burden on our future growth potential. The fear of the insatiable appetite of a fast-growing human population lies at the core of many people's worries about the environment and the prospects for growth. This fear is not new. The economic analysis of population dates back to the Reverend T. R. Malthus, whose bleak view of the future in the late eighteenth century caused economics to be dubbed "the dismal science" ever since.

Malthus wrote on the heels of another period of tremendous medical breakthrough that extended life expectancy—the period in the 1700s when public sanitation of urban areas was revealed as an important determinant of infant mortality and disease. The acknowledgment that bubonic and other plagues might have been carried and transmitted by rats exposed to human excrement led to the rudimentary development of public sewage systems in London. (Never mind that the Romans, Chinese, and Japanese understood this centuries earlier.) These and other improvements in medicine frightened Malthus because of the ensuing prospects for explosive population growth. His book, *An Essay on the Principle of Population*, was first published in 1798 and was an immediate bestseller.

Malthus postulated that the population, if left unchecked by rampant disease and limited food supply, would double every generation and ultimately become so large that we would, relatively quickly, run out of room for the amassing hordes. Along with this dismal prospect, he discharged the additional demon of *diminishing returns*. He argued that because land is fixed while the number of workers is growing, food supplies would never keep up with demand. Malthus gloomily concluded:

> As population doubles and redoubles, it is as if the globe were halving and halving again in size—until finally it has shrunk so much that the supply of food falls below the level necessary for life.

There is not a principles-of-economics student in the Western world who has not been exposed to the ideas of Malthus. He still makes it into every introductory textbook. And even though he was dead wrong, his specter still influences modern thought and, frighteningly, government policy.

His ideas were used to support a harsh modification of English poor laws. Under his influence, people argued that the poor should be left in abject misery so that high birth rates might be discouraged. The corollary to this was that trade unions, or other measures to improve the welfare of workers, would never succeed because higher wages would only lead to higher birth rates and ultimate starvation.

Even today, the shadow of Malthus appears and reappears in "doomsday" economic forecasts, such as the famous computer study called *The Limits of Growth* and its 1992 sequel, *Beyond the Limits.*[7] The predictions here were even more discouraging than their Malthusian roots:

> If present growth trends in world population, industrialization, pollution, food problems, and resource depletion continue unchanged, the limits to growth on this planet will be reached within the next one hundred years. The most probable results will be a rather sudden and uncontrollable decline in both population and industrial capacity.[8]

We see these same sentiments expressed by the anti-globalization movement, the radical environmentalists, and the neo-Luddites.[9] What they all have in common is the notion that growth, change, and technological development are frightening and dangerous. These include the people who most fear the biotech revolution, as well as those who believe the Internet is a fad, or simply a financial-market bubble, which will inevitably increase human alienation and augment the "digital divide" between rich and poor.

Erroneous Prognostications

Malthus's doomsday scenario did not anticipate the dramatic increase in productivity that would arise from technological innovation in agriculture and manufacturing. His emphasis on the diminishing returns of the fixed physical supply of land ignored the tremendous potential of knowledge that could be used to leverage its value. Malthus did not anticipate the economic miracle of the Industrial Revolution, although he lived in the midst of it, let alone the other technological breakthroughs since. He also failed to foresee the slowdown of growth in the population of most Western nations after roughly 1870, the period when real wages and living standards increased explosively, thanks to such innovations as the railroad, the steam engine, and the telegraph.

In the centuries following Malthus's strictures, technological change increased the growth of output at a rate far faster than the growth of the population, raising real wages and living standards. Nevertheless, his shadow remains. His concerns do hold grains of truth in countries with very low potential for technological advance owing to inadequate education systems, such as Ethiopia, Nigeria, and Bangladesh, where hunger continues to be a lingering problem and many barely survive at a subsistence level.

The Prospects for Growth in the Developing World

The pessimists point out that rich countries account for only 15 percent of the world's population but 90 percent of global technology spending and nearly that proportion of Internet usage. Much of the emerging world is too poor to buy computers or mobile phones. For example, according to *The Economist* magazine:

> In Bangladesh, a computer costs the equivalent of eight years' average pay. The 2 billion people living in low-income economies (with average incomes below $800 per head) have only 35 telephone lines and five personal computers for every 1,000 people, compared with 650 phone lines and 540 computers in America. One in two Americans is online, compared with only one in 250 Africans.[10]

But the prospects are that the diffusion of technology throughout the world, thanks to the Net, might actually benefit poor countries more than rich ones, especially if they can provide a base of educated workers. Some formerly emerging economies have been very successful in following this strategy—investing in education and technology—most notably the East Asian tigers. Mexico, India, and China are also following this prescription, with varying degrees of success. The Internet does make distance learning possible, and one Net connection can be shared by many. The African Virtual University, for example, which was partly funded by the World Bank, uses satellites to transmit televised courses to students in fifteen African countries.

Information technology is no cure-all for the world's ills, however, as we will see in Chapters 10 and 11. Other policies must be put in place for the potential benefits of IT to be realized. These include a stable government, an improving public education system, the rule of law, freer trade, the protection of intellectual property rights, and efficient financial markets. This is a tall order for the poorest countries, but progress is beginning in many parts of the world.

Environmental Concerns

There are many who are concerned that economic growth and industrialization lead us down the road to environmental ruin. Interestingly, however, the most serious pollution problems today are in the emerging world and the former Soviet bloc, as most of the richest countries have legislated and enforced at least some environmental protections. Data compiled by the World Bank show that the most consequential indicators of environmental degradation—such as poor sanitation and unsafe drinking water—are most likely to be found in the poorest countries.

Wilfred Beckerman, an Oxford University expert on the relationship between population, economic development, and pollution, concludes as follows:

> The important environmental problems for the 75% of the world's population that live in developing countries are local problems of access to safe drinking water or decent sanitation, and urban degradation. Furthermore, there is clear evidence that ... in the end the best—and probably the only—way to attain a decent environment in most countries is to become rich.[11]

The road to riches will continue to be strong growth generated by technological advance.

Without question, economic growth has generated a more intensive use of our natural resources and an increase in the emissions of air and water pollution. Industrial activity significantly changed the earth's climate and ecosystems. Today's environmental concerns are many. Among them are global warming, acid rain, the Antarctic "ozone hole" along with ozone depletion in temperate regions, deforestation, soil erosion, and species extinction. There is plenty to worry about. The pessimists are closely linked ideologically to Malthusian concerns of an earlier era. Whereas Malthus argued that production would be limited by finite land, today's growth pessimists hold that growth will be limited by the finite absorptive capacity of our environment. The need to reduce the use of fossil fuels could, according to this view, slow our long-term economic growth potential.

It is true that the quality of land and mineral resources has deteriorated over the past century. In the U.S., farming practices today have been far more beneficial to land quality than those prevalent in the 1930s. Even so, we are required to drill deeper for oil, use more marginal lands, and mine lower-grade mineral ores. Yet technological advance has, once again, more than offset these factors, driving down dramatically the inflation-adjusted price of natural resources in relation to labor. In fact, the real price of natural resources has been in secular decline for the better part of two hundred years. Surely oil and natural gas prices will continue to spike occasionally, usually in response to supply disruptions or war, but these moves are temporary. Even the tripling of the price of oil from 1998 to 2000 only took it to the average inflation-adjusted level of the past thirty years.

Amory Lovins, co-founder of the Rocky Mountain Institute—a natural-resources think tank—presciently predicted in the early 1970s, following the first oil-price shock, that improvements in energy efficiency would lead to a decoupling of economic growth and energy use. He was widely ridiculed at the time, but events have vindicated him.

In the past twenty years, as new environmentally friendly technologies have become increasingly important, many of the worst environmental abuses have been alleviated, at least in the developed world. Environmental constraints are costly, however, as argued by many emerging nations, and clearly countries such as the U.S. and others have paid a price to comply with them. Certainly, more needs to be done. Mr. Lovins in early 2001 made another prediction, that fuel cells would revolutionize the energy world, replacing the internal combustion engine the way the PC replaced the typewriter. Research in emission-free energy sources, like the fuel cell, is a major step that will help assure that growth will not be energy-bound.

But the most important fundamental to the positive outlook for growth is that it is coming, increasingly, from the knowledge-based sectors, where the use of fossil fuels is relatively small. Growth is no longer emanating primarily from the fuel-guzzling industrial world of the past, and even in those sectors proportional fuel consumption is down. Like Malthus, today's growth pessimists will prove to be dead wrong. We will continue to have our cyclical ups and downs, as the recent economic decline suggests, but the long-run potential for noninflationary global growth remains positive.

Three

The Information Age Economy

5

Creative
Synergies
The Amazing Expansion

The technological advances that we have seen in recent years have had a profound effect on the economy and on financial markets. And as the developments in the previous chapter highlight, much more is yet to come. A special wave of creative synergies in information and communications technology generated a confluence of very positive economic events in the 1990s. Microprocessors, computers, satellites, and the joining of laser and fiber optic technologies—and, of course, the Internet—triggered a flood of economic innovation. Information technology increased our ability to capture, analyze, and disseminate information. Real-time analysis became possible. Though information was not perfect, uncertainty and therefore risk could be reduced. Reaction times were shortened, as business became more flexible. The hope was that just-in-time management would dampen the swings in the business cycle.

The year 2000 was the turning point. Following nearly ten years of unprecedented economic well-being, the tide began to turn. The stock market plummeted, capital dried up for all but the most creditworthy borrowers, and consumer and business confidence waned. The ensuing economic slowdown, beginning in late-2000, led many to fear that the New Economy boom was permanently over—the good times were at an end. But before we analyze the turning point and its causes, let's look at the greatest expansion in American history.

THE POSITIVE POLITICAL ENVIRONMENT

By the mid-1980s, the Reagan measures to boost economic growth and assure American military superiority were coming to fruition. The tax cuts were paying off and the Soviet Union was finding it increasingly impossible to compete—either militarily or economically. Between 1985 and 1991, Soviet president Mikhail Gorbachev implemented a program of political and economic reform called *perestroika*—meaning "restructuring" in Russian. This was closely linked to his concept of *glasnost*, or openness and democratization. The Soviet satellite system in Eastern Europe collapsed, the highlight of which was the opening of the Berlin Wall in late 1989. East and West Germany were united in 1990. The forces of change led to the breakdown of the Communist system and the dissolution of the USSR in 1991.

End of the Cold War

The end of the Cold War helped to galvanize the positive effects of the surge in technology. Around the world, technological developments in the military sector were re-deployed for domestic use. Even the Internet itself went through this metamorphosis. It began life as ARPANET (Advanced Research Projects Agency Network), a defense communication system of the U.S. government. It was first conceived in 1962 and created in 1969 to ensure continued communication in the event of nuclear attack. With the end of the Cold War in 1989, the U.S. Congress decided to stop funding ARPANET. But its users in industry and the universities quickly made plans for its successor, the Internet.

Today, thanks to the demise of communism, five out of six people on the planet live in a market economy. The wide proliferation of international news networks like Sky TV and CNN, along with the Net, have dramatically increased access to information around the world. Globalization has flourished with the democratization of technology, financial markets, and information.[1] Global competitive pressures have never been greater. Markets have opened up as consumers in an increasing number of countries are ever hungrier for a widening variety of goods and services. A growing middle class in China, India, most of emerging Asia and Latin America, as well as in the former Soviet bloc, provided growing global demand for technology and consumer products. These same consumers also provided the labor so desperately needed by American companies, as labor shortages in the U.S. continued to mount in the late 1990s.

Freer Trade

Declining trade barriers also enhanced global competitive forces. Trade deals such as the European Union (EU) and the North American Free Trade Agreement (NAFTA) boosted global trade and broadened markets for all participants. These agreements reduced artificial impediments to efficiency, which helped to keep the lid on inflation. The more competition, the more difficult it is for any business to raise prices. Production shifted increasingly to the low-cost locale.

U.S. Fiscal Surpluses

Also contributing to the positive economic climate of the '90s was the political consensus in the U.S. that transformed a huge budget deficit into a surplus. As the defense demands of the Cold War waned, government expenditure growth slowed. Congress enacted controls on spending, helping to limit untoward increases. The dramatic decline in interest rates from peak levels in the early '80s reduced the cost of servicing the government debt, and the 1993 tax hikes augmented the flow of government revenues.

The surge in tax revenues was dramatic. In 2000, federal tax revenue as a percentage of the economy reached an historic peak—21 percent of gross domestic product (GDP), the total of all goods and services produced in the economy. An increasing chunk of that revenue came from personal income taxes, which rose to 10 percent of GDP compared to 7.7 percent in 1994. In 1997, the most recent year for which data are available, the average federal income tax rate was 15.3 percent—the highest level since the mid-1980s. Marginal tax rates climbed from the original Reagan tax program's percentages of 15-28-33 percent to the Clinton-tax-hike levels of 15-28-31-36-39.6 percent. The rise in wages and salaries coming from economic and productivity growth led to significant bracket creep, which also added to revenues, and many were pushed into paying the rather stiff Alternative Minimum Tax, once the domain of only the highest-income earners. Tax revenues grew faster than national income until the Bush tax cuts were implemented in 2001.

All of this increased revenue generated what were to be the largest federal budgetary surpluses in American history, approaching $300 billion in fiscal year 2001. In the words of Fed Chairman Alan Greenspan, these surpluses "helped fill the pool of saving that fed productivity-enhancing and cost-reducing capital formation."[2] The government surpluses were elemental in boosting national saving, keeping the cost of capital low, and quickening the pace of productivity growth. The ever-tightening fiscal policy also helped to keep inflation under wraps.

A BIRD'S-EYE VIEW OF THE 1990S

The decade of the 1990s brought the longest expansion in American history—an expansion that broke all the rules of the traditional economics textbooks (Figure 5.1). Growth accelerated without inflation. For a decade, the U.S. economy was the global growth leader. While the expansion began at a rather tepid pace—and was once called the "jobless recovery"—this was certainly to change. By the second half of the decade, the expansion took off. Growth was strong, inflation was low, and the stock markets were booming. The "Goldilocks" economy had been born.[3]

The Early Period Was Disappointing

From the end of the brief Gulf War recession in March 1991 until late 1992, economic growth averaged only 2.7 percent, despite repeated moves by the Federal Reserve to jump-start the economy.[4] The central bank eased

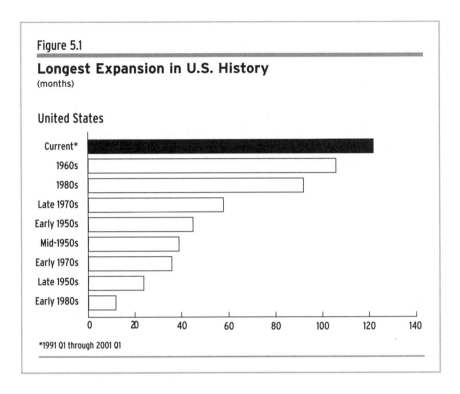

Figure 5.1

Longest Expansion in U.S. History
(months)

United States

Current*	
1960s	
1980s	
Late 1970s	
Early 1950s	
Mid-1950s	
Early 1970s	
Late 1950s	
Early 1980s	

0   20   40   60   80   100   120   140

*1991 Q1 through 2001 Q1

monetary policy eighteen times from July 1990 through September 1992, taking the federal funds rate down to a rock-bottom 3 percent. Yet the unemployment rate continued to edge higher as businesses, facing mounting competitive pressure, streamlined and restructured. Layoff announcements continued to be sizable, and by year-end 1992, the jobless rate had barely fallen, remaining well in excess of 7 percent.

President George Bush (Senior) lost the 1992 election to William Jefferson Clinton, despite the country's overwhelming support for the Gulf War. Clearly, Clinton hit the bull's eye with his campaign mantra—"It's the economy, stupid." Some in the Bush forces blamed Alan Greenspan for being too slow and begrudging in his efforts to reaccelerate the economy. Relations between Mr. Greenspan and the Bush Administration Secretary of the Treasury Nicholas Brady were cool at best. Bill Clinton, on the other hand, recognized the importance of the Fed, and Alan Greenspan in particular, to his political future. From the beginning, Clinton courted Greenspan, seeking his counsel and inviting him to sit next to Hillary at his first State of the Union address. Clinton's appointee to the Treasury, Robert Rubin, was a Wall Street heavyweight, a former chairman of Goldman Sachs. Rubin and his successor, Lawrence Summers, had a strong working relationship with Greenspan throughout the Clinton years.

Eventually, the Fed's easing did the trick. Things began to improve in 1993, as economic growth accelerated in the second half of the year and labor markets began to feel the effects of the recovery. The unemployment rate fell to 6.5 percent by year-end. Even at that level, some began to worry that inflation pressures might mount. Instead, year-over-year inflation fell to a mere 2.7 percent, its second-lowest reading in seven years, and bond yields dropped 100 basis points. The stock market caught the spark. The S&P 500 gained 10 percent that year, to be surpassed by the 17 percent rise in the Dow and the 15 percent jump in the Nasdaq.

By early 1994, it was finally evident that the economy was fully on the mend. Commodity prices increased sharply as global economic activity rebounded, leading many to forecast a significant rise in inflation. The Fed fell prey to this fear. Despite a jobless rate hovering around 6.5 percent, they embarked on an aggressive tightening cycle in February 1994. In a series of seven moves over the course of 1994 and early 1995, the Fed doubled the funds rate, taking it from 3 percent to 6 percent. The bond market reaction was ferocious. The long bond rose from a low of 6 percent to 8 percent in the course of a year. This wreaked havoc on the mortgage-backed securities market, creating enormous illiquidity and volatility. Some major players in that sector—such as Kidder Peabody and Askin Capital Management—were forced to shut their doors. The stock market felt the pain as well, showing virtually no net gain for the year 1994.

The economy lost momentum rapidly in the first half of 1995 and industrial prices cooled considerably, partly reflecting the impact of the sudden and dramatic Fed tightening and partly the steep recession in Mexico. Many have lauded the Fed for engineering a soft landing in 1994–95. Recognizing that they had stalled the economy enough, maybe even too much, by July 1995 Greenspan & Company reversed course, ultimately cutting interest rates three times.

The Expansion Shifts to High Gear

The Fed's easing had an immediate impact on business and consumer confidence and on the stock and bond markets. Bond yields resumed their decline and the economy—posting only 1.1 percent growth in the first half of 1995—rebounded to 3.2 percent in the second half. The stock market took off. The S&P 500 surged 37 percent that year, pacing the performance of the Dow, while the Nasdaq gained 40 percent. This was the start of what would be five consecutive years of greater-than-20 percent total returns. By late 1995, business investment ratcheted upward, posting double-digit growth for most of the rest of the decade. Companies across America were investing in technology to garner a competitive edge. Capital deepening—the rise in the capital-to-labor ratio, which meant in essence that employees had more IT—helped to increase worker productivity and real wages. Accompanying this was a surge in technological innovation—new and better processes, products, and services emerged, many of them related to the Internet. The technology boom had begun.

By the second quarter of 1996, the economy was roaring. The 6.8 percent growth in GDP was fueled by a 12 percent gain in investment in machinery and equipment—read computers—and consumers were also loosening their belts. Job growth was accelerating and the unemployment rate was finally below 5.5 percent. With inflation low, real wages were rising. And household wealth was increasing sharply as the stock market enjoyed another stellar year. While the Fed would not touch interest rates for the remainder of the year, Chairman Greenspan warned the markets about the dangers of "irrational exuberance" in his now-famous speech before the American Enterprise Institute on December 5, 1996.

The economy was on a roll. Growth was strong and the labor markets continued to tighten. The concern about impending inflation mounted as the jobless rate fell below 5 percent in early 1997. For years economists espoused the so-called "Phillips Curve" tradeoff, that falling unemployment always led to rising inflation. Many had believed that the natural rate of unemployment (the noninflationary floor) was 6 percent; when falling below that level didn't trigger inflation, they revised it down to a range of 5 to 5.5 percent. But, surely, at 4.5 percent unemployment, inflation would rear its ugly head. Instead, inflation fell sharply in 1997 and 1998—to a year-over-year low of 1.4 percent—as the Asian crisis slowed global growth, driving down commodity prices, especially oil. Contributing as well to the stellar inflation performance in the U.S. was the strengthening dollar, which ignited a decline in import prices, putting further downward pressure on domestic pricing power. The prices of technology products were also falling sharply.

In addition, despite the strength of the economy, businesses were not bumping up against capacity constraints because they had invested so heavily in plant and equipment. Supply-side constraints did not emerge. Vendor delivery delays and unfilled orders—indicators of bottlenecks in production—showed no signs of creating shortage-induced price gains. And, most importantly, business efficiency was improving. Technology was finally paying off as business and labor became more productive.

The Fed, however, was not convinced that inflation would remain at bay. Concerned about tightening labor market conditions and the booming stock market, they nudged the funds rate up 25 basis points in March 1997, taking it to 5.5 percent. To everyone's surprise, inflation remained remarkably muted.

The coming Asian crisis was to short-circuit any sustained period of tightening. In July 1997, Thailand devalued the baht and the Asian crisis began. Initially the turmoil had little direct impact on global markets, although the deepening recessions across the region put huge downward pressure on commodity prices, which helped to keep interest rates and inflation moving lower. As the problems spread to all emerging economies, however, financial markets worldwide were impacted. Fear was rampant and the flight to quality, meaning the flight to U.S. assets, was in full force. Stocks were rocked in late 1997 and then again in the summer of 1998, especially after Russia devalued the ruble in August and defaulted on some of its debt. Even so, stock market performance that year was still exceptional, posting gains of near 30 percent for the S&P 500 and 40 percent for the Nasdaq. The Dow lagged with an 18 percent total return as non-tech equities fell out of favor. Foreign money was pouring into U.S. stocks and bonds. By the end of the year, the long bond yield hit a cycle low of 5 percent.

The Russian moves eventually and indirectly led to the near-collapse in September 1998 of Long-Term Capital Management (LTCM)—the hedge fund run by John Meriwether, the former head of bond trading at Salomon Brothers, along with a slew of Nobel-Prize-winning economists and former Fed governors. LTCM had been lauded as one the world's greatest money managers, taking enormous leveraged positions in a whole host of high-risk securities, including Russian debt. They had among their clients a list of "who's who" in the world—including the central bank of Italy—and among their lenders, many of the largest banks and investment dealers. When the Fed discovered that LTCM was on the verge of going under, they blasted into action, fearing the systemic risk that would be generated by a default so large—bordering on $100 billion. In an unprecedented move, the Fed brokered a deal with Goldman Sachs, Merrill Lynch, J. P. Morgan, Chase, and others to keep LTCM afloat, at least temporarily. These were not altruistic actions on their part. Each of these institutions had meaningful exposure to LTCM and, therefore, a strong vested interest in protecting their investments.

With the risk of a Brazilian default and emerging markets everywhere in free fall, the Fed came to the rescue. Seeing itself as the lender of last resort for the world, the Fed began to re-liquefy the financial markets, taking the federal funds rate down in three consecutive moves to 4.75 percent by November 1998, its lowest reading since the fall of 1994.

Capital was now readily available and incredibly cheap. The burst of liquidity touched off a period of unprecedented stock market performance—at least in the growth stocks and most notably the techs— as well as tremendous economic expansion. In 1999, the Nasdaq rose an amazing 86 percent as the tech boom hit a crescendo. The gains in the S&P 500 and the Dow seemed paltry in comparison at 21 percent and 27 percent, respectively. The economy grew at 4.2 percent, posting the third consecutive year of greater-than-4-percent growth. The jobless rate fell to just above 4 percent, but wage inflation remained subdued, even retracing some of its earlier gains. By year-end 1999, the Employment Cost Index—a broad measure of labor compensation and benefits costs— had risen only 3.4 percent year over year. Over the same period, inflation was a mere 2.6 percent. No wonder consumer confidence hit a record high. Jobs were easy to get and real wages were rising.

Oil prices nearly tripled as global economic growth accelerated following the end of the Asian crisis. This increase in oil prices subsequently triggered a sharp rise in gasoline, heating oil, and electricity prices. Nevertheless, the impact on inflation was much more moderate than many had feared.

The Fed, however, wanted to take no chances. Alan Greenspan, though pleased with the surge in productivity growth since the mid-1990s, was concerned that the strength in consumer and business demand—running well in excess of the growth in supply—would eventually trigger a sustained bout of inflation. Even if it didn't, it would meaningfully reduce corporate earnings. The Fed began to raise interest rates in June 1999 and did not stop until May 2000, taking the fed funds rate to 6.5 percent, its highest level this cycle. In late 1999, however, the Fed reversed the tightening temporarily, pumping liquidity into the system by increasing the growth of the money supply, in preparation for potential Y2K disruptions. This, as we will see, turned out to be a big mistake. Y2K presented no significant problems and the infusion of liquidity in an already strong economy only further ignited euphoria and pumped more air into the Nasdaq bubble.

Finally, in the second half of 2000, the economy began to slow. Perhaps more importantly, the stock market tanked. Following five consecutive years of better than 20 percent total returns, the S&P 500 fell 9 percent in 2000 while the tech-heavy Nasdaq plunged. It was down a whopping 39 percent for the year, having fallen a gut-wrenching 51 percent from its March 10 high. The dot-com bubble had burst and the larger world of tech stocks hit the skids. Many fell 50 to 60 percent from their 52-week highs in 2000 and continued to slide another 20 percent or more in early 2001. The wealth effect, so crucial to the economic strength of the late '90s, would now be working in reverse.

The second half of the '90s was in many ways a period of unprecedented prosperity. GDP growth ran at an annual pace of 3.9 percent. Total annual returns in the S&P 500 averaged 28 percent over the period and the Nasdaq gained a whopping 42 percent on an average annual basis. Never before in modern American history had growth strengthened as the expansion lengthened. Defying virtually all economic forecasters, GDP growth surpassed expectations until the third quarter of 2000.

THE INFLATION SURPRISE

Even with the booming economy, however, inflation remained muted. Who would have imagined that with a tripling of energy prices and the tightest labor markets in history, inflation would have been so benign? Clearly, something had changed. The combination of productivity-enhancing technological changes, falling technology prices, worker insecurity, the Internet, growing competitive pressure, and a strong dollar kept the lid on inflation.

The Productivity Boom—The Late 1990s

For years economists at the Fed believed that growth above 2.5 percent would jeopardize price stability. Faster growth would surely trigger inflation. Yet, this time was different. The noninflationary "speed limit" appeared to have risen to 3 percent or maybe even 4 percent. The reason was the growth in productivity, the rate of return on labor and capital, which is crucially important. It is the key determinant of living standards—real income and consumption per capita. When productivity growth accelerates, companies can afford to pay workers more without reducing profits because they are worth more—their output per unit of time has gone up. So real (after-inflation) wage rates rise and, therefore, so do living standards.

Productivity growth increased over the second half of the decade. The tech spending boom was clearly the explanation. While IT represented less than 10 percent of the economy, it accounted for one-third of the growth in the U.S. from 1995 through 2000. Business investment surged, running at an 11 percent average annual pace in the second half of the decade. Firms in every sector were spending huge sums to upgrade systems, software, and networks. All the more so as the decline in computer prices accelerated.

In the early 1990s, Intel perceived a threat to its dominance of the semiconductor market. Understanding the importance of maintaining its first-mover advantage, Intel sent a new generation of faster and more powerful chips into the market at a dramatically quicker pace. The result was a sharp decline in computer prices beginning in early 1995. While prices fell about 20 percent annually between 1990 and 1995, they began declining at a 30 percent annual clip in the second half of the decade. The price decline unleashed an investment boom as both businesses and households purchased new equipment. Over the period, Internet usage in the home skyrocketed, as more than 50 percent of households bought home computers, and for many, more than one.[5]

The payoff for the investment in technology was immense. The efficiency of American workers shot up sharply (Figure 5.2). In the expansions of the '60s and '80s, productivity growth slowed as the expansion progressed—not so this time. Productivity growth accelerated in the second half of the '90s, and by mid-2000, workers produced close

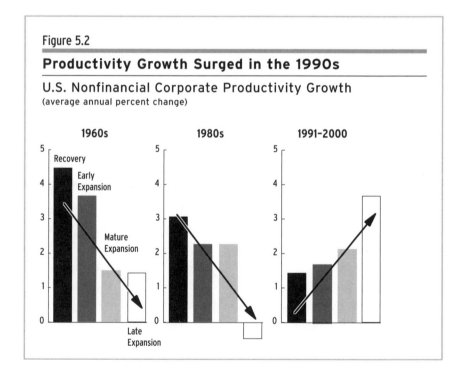

Figure 5.2

Productivity Growth Surged in the 1990s

U.S. Nonfinancial Corporate Productivity Growth
(average annual percent change)

to 5.5 percent more stuff per hour than they did the year before. That was the biggest annual productivity gain in nearly three decades.

As a result of this stellar growth in productivity, unit labor costs (the cost of workers' compensation per unit of output) fell by an annualized 0.4 percent in the second quarter of 2000. It was up less than 1 percent for the year as a whole, even though hourly pay rose by 3.7 percent. Soaring productivity growth more than made up for healthy pay increases and consumers enjoyed the benefits of rising real wages.

Many argued that the pace of productivity growth could never be sustained and, therefore, that inflation risk was right around the corner. To be sure, some of the rise in productivity was cyclical, the result of higher-than-expected output growth. When the economy grows unexpectedly rapidly, firms work their employees harder to keep up. Productivity growth did slow markedly in late 2000 and 2001 as the economy decelerated.

But there is also no doubt that a substantial portion of the stronger productivity growth was due to structural improvements in the U.S. economy. High rates of business investment in technology sharply increased business performance. Contributing further were improvements in the quality of the labor force, as on- and off-the-job training accelerated and many learned to use computers. In addition, gains in efficiency came from innovation and technological progress as well.

The productivity gains of the Information Age were real and sustainable, and Alan Greenspan understood that. The gains reflected everything from streamlined production processes to the automation of clerical functions. They were evident in every sector, not just in the production of tech goods themselves. Even in the service sector, where productivity is notoriously difficult to measure, Fed staff research suggested that efficiency gains were evident.[6]

Many, nevertheless, remained skeptical. While it was widely accepted that productivity growth had surged in the technology sector, some questioned whether it had spread beyond that domain. Helping to lay that view to rest was a study published in 2000 by Professor Dale Jorgenson of Harvard—a well-known productivity guru—and Kevin Stiroh of the Federal Reserve Bank of New York.[7] They find that productivity gains from technological progress were most definitely evident outside the tech sector. They conclude that "noninformation technology" industries contributed more to gains in productivity coming from technological progress than the computer industry itself. Their figures show that about 70 percent of the gain in this type of productivity comes from outside the sector.

They conclude that the noninflationary speed limit of the U.S. economy has indeed risen. As long as high-tech industries keep innovating, they say, the economy should be able to sustain the high rate of productivity growth and the "virtuous circle of an investment-led expansion will continue." Mr. Jorgenson has been quoted as saying that he "has become an enlistee in the army of people touting the New Economy."[8]

The crucial question for the future is, will high-tech industries keep innovating or will the stock market collapse and capital shortage in 2000–2001 stall the pace of advance? No doubt the plunge in capital spending in 2001 will continue to dampen the growth of productivity for a while. If it slows for too long, however, the Old Economy speed limit for growth could reemerge. It is more likely, instead, that the productivity growth slowdown will be a relatively short-term cyclical phenomenon that will not jeopardize the underlying momentum of secular productivity advance. The Fed's aggressive easing of monetary policy will eventually reignite the economy and the stock market and capital spending will once again take flight.

A Radical Change in Labor Markets

By the late 1990s, the alarming cries of a "jobless recovery" in 1992 seemed like a clarion call from another century. The U.S. was experiencing the tightest labor markets in history as the pool of available workers plummeted to a record low percentage of the adult population (Figure 5.3). Chairman Greenspan regularly expressed his concern that labor shortages would ultimately lead to rising wage inflation, which would depress corporate profit margins and potentially trigger a bout of price inflation in sectors where business had sufficient pricing power to pass along the higher costs to the consumer.

The jobless rate fell to a low of 3.9 percent in September 2000. This is not the lowest level in the postwar period. It was lower briefly during the

Vietnam War era in the '60s and during the early '50s. However, back then, the labor force participation rate of women was as low as 33 percent. By the late '90s, it had risen to nearly double that level. Never before in U.S. history had such a large proportion of the adult population been gainfully employed. Retirees were reentering the labor market as businesses, desperate for workers, were offering flextime and attractive compensation. The jobless rate for college graduates fell to a low 1.5 percent; and, lest you think that only the knowledge workers or the wealthy benefited from these gains, the jobless rate for high-school dropouts—the lowest rung of the knowledge ladder—fell to a record low 6 percent in December 1999. Businesses were willing to train these new workers on the job. Many companies located in places they would never have considered before—the inner cities—and trained welfare recipients and the long-time unemployed on the job.

There is evidence to suggest that a significant proportion of the "hard-core" unemployed who found jobs during the late-1990s boom will remain employed long enough to become a permanent part of the American working mainstream. Economists call this phenomenon "hysteresis," after the Greek word meaning "to be behind." In physics, it is used to describe the lagged effect of changing the forces on a physical

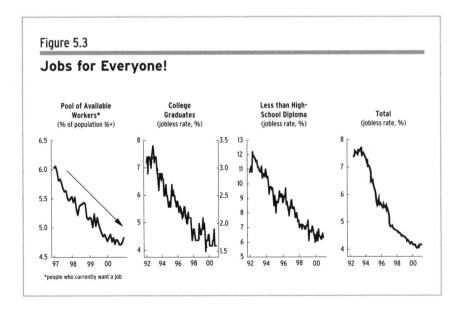

Figure 5.3

Jobs for Everyone!

mass. In economics, it describes the kind of behavioral change that may be happening to these newly employed people. It hasn't shown up definitively yet in the job statistics, but the idea has a strong proponent in former Treasury Secretary Larry Summers, who studied hysteresis as an economics professor at Harvard.

The boom in the economy was a remarkably effective social program because of the special efforts that business made to recruit, train, and retain workers. People's attitudes change when they don't have the excuse for not working—an excuse like a weak economy.[9] This will increase labor-force participation rates and therefore reduce the base level of the unemployment rate. Even as the economy slows, the no-longer-marginalized workers have an easier time of finding work because of the skills, experience, and habits they have attained.

The opposite effect has occurred in many European countries, with their secularly high levels of joblessness and generous social programs. A similar phenomenon is evident in Canada for the same reason. The U.S. has much less regulation, much greater labor mobility, unions are less powerful, and there is less government interference. The flexibility of the U.S. labor markets and the hands-off position of government foster an environment of creative destruction—the constant churning in the workforce. Layoffs continue high but, ironically, the jobless rate plunges as economic growth accelerates. The U.S. has a markedly lower jobless rate than Canada or many continental European countries such as Germany, France, and Italy, where labor market restrictions are more onerous and flexibility is more limited. Britain, on the other hand, adopted a more American-like system during the Thatcher years and Britain today has the lowest unemployment rate in the Group of Seven (G-7) countries, even lower than in the U.S.[10]

The strong U.S. labor market has truly been a boon for social policy. Recent studies suggest that it accounted for a big share of the fall in the crime rate. Jared Bernstein and Ellen Houston of the Economic Policy Institute, a Washington think tank, argue that as America's record-breaking economic expansion barreled on in the late 1990s, the decline in crime became ever more pronounced.[11] They conclude that it was really only after 1995 until the late 2000 slowdown that the economy was strong enough to substantially advance the opportunities for those most likely to commit crimes. The authors add that the enhanced job prospects were particularly beneficial to young African Americans, a group over-represented in both prison and the low-wage workforce.

Additional research has confirmed the Bernstein-Houston conclusions: youth violence fell sharply. It is the youth cohort that contributed most to the decline in crime in the late 1990s. An analysis of FBI data by Jeffrey A. Butts of the Urban Institute in Washington, D.C., found that from 1985 to 1995, arrests for murder, rape, assault, and robbery rose by more than 298,000 in the U.S., with youths under twenty-five accounting for over a third of the rise.[12] In the four years following 1995, these arrests declined by more than 150,000, with that same age group accounting for half of the drop. The declines were especially sharp for youths under the age of eighteen.

Much of the fall in youth crime can be attributed to the enhanced job availability for young people and rising real wages. This, in turn, increased standards of living, reducing child poverty and family stress. It showed many from multiple generations of underprivilege that hope was out there, things could change. Increased legal and police enforcement may have played a role as well, but demographics did not. The youth population in the U.S. actually grew over the past decade.

Wage Demands Remain Muted

Even in this period of remarkably tight labor markets, wage inflation remained surprisingly moderate. On the factory floor, average hourly earnings gains were relatively stable at an annual pace of roughly 4 percent. The broader measures of labor compensation also increased but still far less than many had expected.

Ironically, despite the strength in employment, labor insecurity continued to swell. In an early-2000 study by International Survey Research of employed Americans, one-third of respondents admitted that they were "frequently concerned about layoffs." Many felt the threat of skill obsolescence in this rapidly changing techno world. Others pointed to downsizing and mergers, which were a constant feature of the global landscape in the 1990s. Restructuring and mergers inevitably meant layoffs, and although the average duration of unemployment fell to decade lows, widespread unease continued. This kept excessive wage demands in check.

Also contributing to the softness in wage inflation was the continued decline in union power and the advent of nontraditional compensation methods, most notably, stock options. An increasing proportion of the workforce was compensated through stock-incentive plans, allowing these employees to share in profit gains while limiting the need for outsized salary increases. Inflation expectations of the workforce also cooled over the decade, reducing dramatically the psychology of cost-of-living demands.

Internet Drives Down Inflation

In contrast to other long postwar expansions, inflation actually declined over the 1990s (Figure 5.4). It became quite evident that most businesses had little pricing power and for many in the fastest growing sectors, prices were falling. Raise your price and you lose market share. Even the surge in energy prices at the end of the decade did little to increase the headline inflation numbers. Core inflation—which excludes food and energy prices—though up, ended the '90s at barely over a 2 percent annual rate.

The Internet was a major contributor to the disinflation. Consumers rule on the Net. Comparison shopping is easy; consumer information is readily available. When Amazon.com slashed the price of best selling books by 50 percent, traditional booksellers were forced to follow. E*Trade and Ameritrade sliced stock brokerage commission rates and Merrill Lynch was forced to follow. Consumers now go into automobile showrooms armed with information on dealer costs, thanks to sites like Autobytel.com, AutoNation, and CarMax. Moreover, the Net has reduced the costs of communication to near zero. And B2B exchanges have reduced the costs of production.

The Net has also gone a long way toward reducing the need for order-taking intermediaries. No longer do you need a travel agent to book airline tickets, or an insurance agent to obtain car or homeowners insurance. Whole industries are at risk of being wiped out unless they can

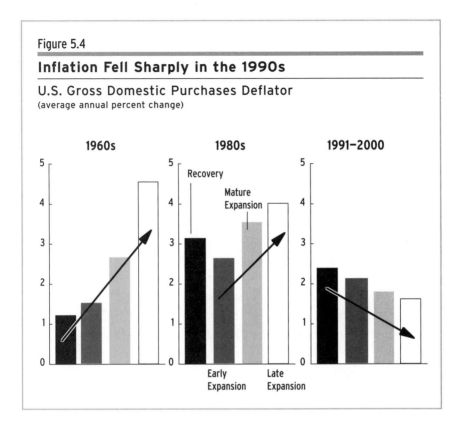

Figure 5.4

Inflation Fell Sharply in the 1990s

U.S. Gross Domestic Purchases Deflator
(average annual percent change)

figure out how to add value in the age of the Internet. Simply executing orders is no longer sufficient. Customers need advice, knowledge, and guidance. People still want to deal with people. Travel agents must become travel-experience consultants; stockbrokers become financial planners. The same will be true of real estate agents, automobile dealers, booksellers, music retailers, mortgage brokers, and other intermediaries. Without this added value, consumers quickly discover that they can do the job faster and cheaper online.

The Net itself has contributed to the surge in efficiency and streamlining, driving down costs. Deflationary pressures mount as consumers become more adept at bargaining online and researching buying options. Never before have markets been so transparent or information so easy to get.

Business Responds

In this environment, businesses had to keep their costs down or go out of business. Virtually every corporate leader is driven today by shareholder value, and the markets take no prisoners. The rate of turnover in the executive suites has never been higher as the number of big-cap company CEO firings hit a record level in 2000–2001. Often CEOs are given little time to prove themselves in this "what-have-you-done-for-me-lately" world.

Boards of directors have become ever more relentless in the pursuit of sustained competitive advantage, and market forces encouraged business to do whatever it took to enhance productivity. The only way to maintain earnings growth in the face of higher wage bills or rising energy costs was to improve the rate of return on labor and capital, to enhance productivity. And the tried and true way to do that was to invest in technology and streamline labor demand. Permanent layoffs continued to surge through early 1994. They dipped during the next four years, then they rose again in 1998 and accelerated dramatically when the economy slowed in 2000–2001. The initial responses to economic slowdown were dramatic production cuts, workforce downsizing, and the slashing of capital spending plans.

Oil Prices Surge—Inflation Still Modest

There is evidence of a real disconnect between energy prices and core inflation (Figure 5.5). Even the surge in oil prices in the late 1990s did not meaningfully raise the underlying level of inflation. After all, in the Information Age, oil just isn't as important as it once was. Gone is the heavy-metal-bashing industrial world of the past where oil was all powerful. Thanks to conservation efforts, energy consumption is way down, even in the Old Economy. Oil usage as a percentage of economic output has halved in the past thirty years. Energy costs represent a much smaller proportion of household spending than in the past and even at their peak in 2000, real oil prices—the price level after inflation is taken into account—remained slightly below the average level of the past three decades. Real oil prices this cycle were substantially below the levels

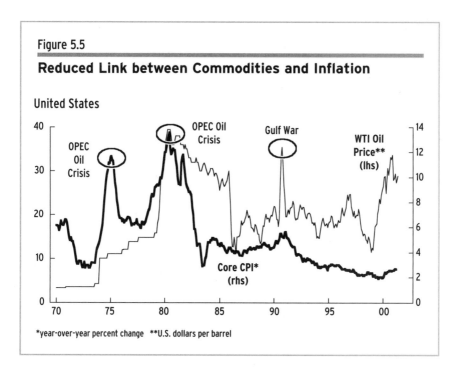

Figure 5.5

Reduced Link between Commodities and Inflation

United States

*year-over-year percent change **U.S. dollars per barrel

posted during the OPEC oil crises in 1973 and 1979 and during the Gulf War in 1991.

The rise in oil prices led to a commensurate increase in the prices of gasoline, electricity, and heating oil. Natural gas prices skyrocketed to record-high levels as past production cutbacks became painfully evident. Even so, headline inflation in the U.S., though up, remained below 4 percent year-over-year and core inflation maxed out at 2.6 percent in 2000. This is above the cyclical low of 1.9 percent posted in August 1999, but it is nothing compared to the inflation rates of old. Core inflation in the 1960s topped out at over 6 percent and in the 1980s it hit a whopping 14 percent.

Import Prices Fall

Falling import prices also kept inflation at bay, which only increased competitive pressure in the U.S. The strong U.S. dollar ensured that imported products were very attractive to value-conscious consumers. In no way could domestic companies raise prices and hope to compete either at home or on the world stage.

During the Asian crisis, the U.S. became the "importer of last resort," providing a strong domestic market for foreign products. Without this factor, the global economic rebound in 1999 would never have been so pronounced. As positive as this was for global financial stability, it led to an ever-widening trade and current account deficit in the U.S.[13] Many see this as the ultimate Achilles heel of the American expansion, as we will see in Chapter 9.

CAPITAL WAS CRUCIAL—THE 1990S

Cheap and readily available capital was the lifeblood of the New Economy boom and the driving force of economic expansion. As long as the stock market was booming, the capital continued to gush in. Aging (but not aged) Baby Boomers were busily adding to their retirement savings accounts and stocks were their favorite investment vehicle. Even so, savings rates headed downward as household borrowing and spending increased even more rapidly than investments in financial assets. It may be that there is a split in the population between savers and borrowers, and to some extent, this is no doubt true. But it is also apparent that people were leveraging their portfolios, buying stock on margin. Many were leaving capital gains intact—particularly in their retirement accounts—but borrowing to finance spending. A recent Federal Reserve study shows that high-net-worth households did just that—financed expenditures with yet-to-be-realized capital gains on their stock portfolios.[14] It was the top-quintile income earners that accounted for all of the decline in the U.S. savings rate. Low- and middle-income earners actually raised their rate of saving.

For the five years ending in 1999, the S&P 500 and the tech-heavy Nasdaq posted stellar returns. With the Nasdaq up a mind-boggling 86 percent in 1999 alone, no wonder Boomers were ready and willing to pour as much money as possible into equity mutual funds and the latest IPOs. The markets were red hot. Companies with barely a concept, let alone any earnings, were coming to market with astronomical single-day gains on their IPOs. Some proved to be real companies, such as Yahoo!,

Amazon.com, and Netscape, but many others were not and have since disappeared.

Much of the money funding American enterprise came from outside the United States, as foreigners sought a safe haven and higher rates of return on their capital. Despite all of the foreboding about huge current account deficits, the U.S. dollar continued strong, even after stock market performance waned in 2000–2001. Throughout the 1990s, the U.S. was the strongest economy in the world with the highest rate of return on capital. At its peak in March 2000, the U.S. stock market capitalization represented 52 percent of global market value, up dramatically from the 30 percent level posted in the late 1980s. Second biggest was Japan, with only 11 percent of total stock market cap (Table 5.1). The valuation of the S&P 500 as a percent of the economy surged in March 2000 to a record of over 150 percent. While it has subsequently retraced some of that gain, it remains historically high.

Table 5.1

G-7 COUNTRIES' SHARE OF GLOBAL EQUITY MARKET

MARKET CAPITALIZATION (PERCENTAGE)

	S&P PEAK (MARCH 24, 2000)	1989
United States	52	30
Japan	11	38
United Kingdom	9	7
Germany	5	3
France	4	3
Canada	2	3
Italy	2	1

STOCKS AS CURRENCY

As the stock market surged, businesses bought other businesses using their inflated stock as the means of payment. Merger and acquisition activity rocketed all over the world as businesses felt impelled to maintain or attain a leading edge as quickly as possible. Speed was crucial in the New Economy and talent was scarce. Companies with very high price–earnings multiples were able to buy other companies, capturing their talent and intellectual capital at a much faster pace than if they had tried to start the business on their own. It became an "eat-or-be-eaten" world, as virtually every company was subject to being either predator or prey, depending on their stock market value. New Economy giants like Cisco, Nortel, and Microsoft followed a deliberate policy of constant acquisition. This, in turn, fueled the IPO and venture capital frenzy, as the rate of return on start-up companies could be enormous with the giants sporting an open wallet. The virtuous cycle of more money creating more investment and, therefore, more money carried on until March 2000, when the dot-com and telecom stocks began to crash and burn.

THE WEALTH EFFECT

Household wealth more than doubled in the 1990s, accelerating in the second half of the decade. Stocks held directly or in the form of mutual funds, managed funds, and retirement accounts became the largest single component of family net worth, rising to one-third of total wealth. Residential real estate remained an important component as well, although equity in the family home as a percent of household real estate fell to record lows as households tapped home equity with second mortgages. Even so, the rise in house prices over the decade augmented the stock gain to improve household balance sheets.

The American household enjoyed an improving financial position. While debt-to-income ratios surged, the household net-worth-to-income ratio rose even faster. As a result, debt-to-net-worth plunged in the second half of the decade, thanks to the booming stock market and the voracious appetite for stocks from a large segment of the population (Figure 5.6). The surge in wealth was felt by the majority of families, with the middle-wealth cohorts experiencing the most significant percentage gains (Figure 5.7).

Implications for Spending

The ever-frothy stock market enticed American consumers to spend well beyond their means. Consumer confidence surged to record highs.

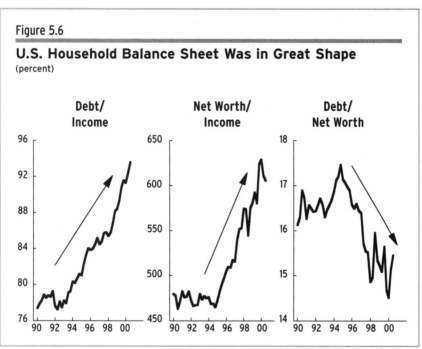

Figure 5.6

U.S. Household Balance Sheet Was in Great Shape
(percent)

Debt/Income

Net Worth/Income

Debt/Net Worth

Figure 5.7

Most Wealth Classes Benefited from Capital Gains

United States (percent rise in assets: 1995–1998)
Wealth Percentile

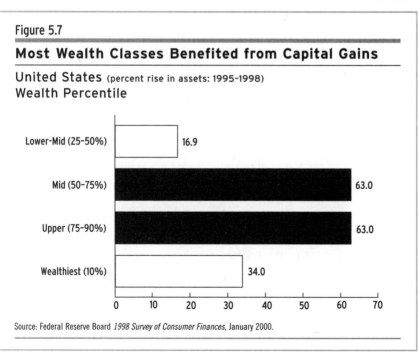

Wealth Percentile	Value
Lower-Mid (25–50%)	16.9
Mid (50–75%)	63.0
Upper (75–90%)	63.0
Wealthiest (10%)	34.0

Source: Federal Reserve Board *1998 Survey of Consumer Finances*, January 2000.

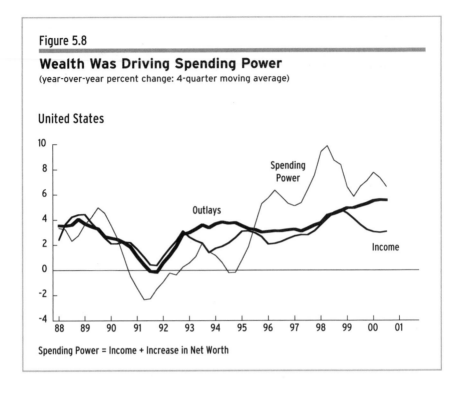

Figure 5.8

Wealth Was Driving Spending Power

(year-over-year percent change: 4-quarter moving average)

United States

Spending Power = Income + Increase in Net Worth

Personal net new savings flows were all but vaporized in response, as the wealth effect became an increasingly powerful source of support to consumer demand. Spending power—defined as income plus realized and unrealized capital gains—increased far more rapidly than income alone. The booming stock market allowed consumers to maintain their spending growth, despite the slowdown in income expansion in 1999 and 2000 (Figure 5.8). Many have suggested that this was the sign of a profligate consumer, unwilling to face the reality of slower income expansion and more volatility in asset values.

Was the Consumer Overextended?

A glance at the personal savings rate would suggest that yes, the consumer was overextended. As traditionally measured, savings—defined as personal income less consumption spending—fell into negative territory. This official measure of savings, however, is distorted.

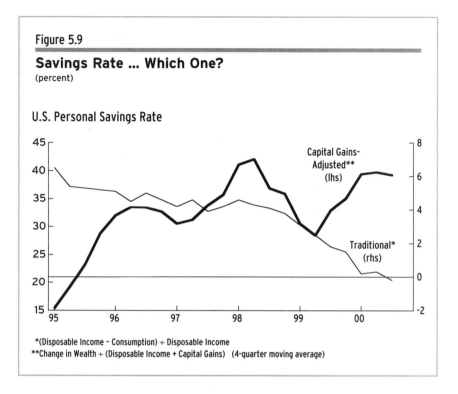

Figure 5.9

Savings Rate ... Which One?
(percent)

U.S. Personal Savings Rate

*(Disposable Income − Consumption) ÷ Disposable Income
**Change in Wealth ÷ (Disposable Income + Capital Gains) (4-quarter moving average)

Most importantly, it ignores the positive effects of capital gains on income but includes capital gains tax payments in consumption, thus depressing the measured rate. The general surge in personal tax payments as a percentage of income since the mid-1990s also contributed to the decline in the traditional savings measure.

Things weren't as dismal as they seemed, however. When realized and unrealized capital gains are included in a wealth-based measure of savings, the rate rose to nearly 40 percent of income and capital gains in the third quarter of 2000 (Figure 5.9). The problem is that unrealized capital gains can disappear, as we saw in 2000–2001. Even so, the market downdraft far from fully reversed the wealth gains of earlier years. Household net worth relative to income remained well above historical averages in mid-2001. But the dramatic slide in stocks in late 2000 and early 2001, significantly dampened consumer confidence, as we shall see. This slowed the growth in household spending from the breakneck pace of the late '90s, although the consumer sector still provided reasonable support to the slowing economy. As we shall see, it was the plummeting business spending and production that really precipitated the rout.

THE GREAT DEBATE

Economists and market watchers lined up in two camps:

- The *New Paradigmers* believed that the digital revolution had transformed the economy, rendering obsolete most of the old econometric relationships between growth, inflation, and employment. They estimated the long-run growth potential of the economy at about 4 percent, well above earlier conventional estimates of 2.5 percent. The extremists in this group breathlessly forecasted the end of the business cycle—tech expansion and rising productivity growth would go on indefinitely without the nasty cyclical worries of inflation or recession. Some not only justified the outrageous overvaluation of many dot-coms, but predicted a generation of essentially never-ending growth and prosperity—a "long boom." The dot-com and tech stock crashes of 2000, followed by the precipitous economic slowdown, flew in the face of their enthusiasm.

- The *Traditionalists* believed that the New Economy was a myth, mostly hype, and that the biggest impact of the technology revolution was a bubble in the stock market. For them, the "old fundamentals" remained in place. They saw inflation as the next big threat, and counseled for a reduction in economic growth to a level well below potential (which for traditionalists was 3 percent or less) to raise the unemployment rate to roughly 5 percent. They took the stock slide as proof that the New Economy was dead.

The first group pointed out that the unprecedented investment in IT since early 1993 led to a structural rise in productivity growth by making accurate information available to decision makers in real time, thereby reducing risk, mistakes, and waste. This caused a dramatic rise in the efficiency of business, boosting earnings growth, job creation, and overall economic output in the 1990s without causing inflation. They saw the stock market selloff and slowdown in 2000–2001 as the direct result of inappropriately tight monetary policy. The Fed raised interest rates six times from June 1999 until May 2000, thereby drying up capital and unnecessarily damaging the economy and financial markets. For them, inflation was never a threat.

Traditional economists were flummoxed by the developments of the 1990s. As growth continued to surprise on the high side, the shrill call for tighter monetary policy intensified. How could growth continue to drive the unemployment rate down without causing a marked rise in wage rates and overall inflation? Yet inflation was surprisingly on the low side. Even the Fed was perplexed. Over the latter half of the '90s, the Fed had the poorest forecasting record in its history.

What troubled traditional economists the most was the so-called Solow Paradox, named for Massachusetts Institute of Technology economist Robert Solow: "You can see the computer age everywhere but in the productivity statistics."[15] Productivity is notoriously difficult to measure. Often improvements show up in better quality and variety of products or services, factors that are rarely captured in the data. If forecasters couldn't understand the impact of computers, they were incapable of saying whether the productivity gains and inflation-free growth could continue. Errant estimates of productivity gains were in large part responsible for widespread overestimation of inflation and underestimation of growth in the '90s.

All but the most recalcitrant of the Traditionalists finally accepted that productivity growth accelerated. However, except for the gains in the computer industry, they saw it as a cyclical rather than a structural phenomenon. They concede that output can be stretched beyond capacity for some time, temporarily raising measured output per hour worked; but they are quick to point out that the next cyclical slowdown in demand will trigger a marked deceleration in productivity growth as business adjusts employment with a lag.

For this group, booms always lead to busts—no soft landings for them. They are convinced that strong economic growth, full employment, and prosperity rest on a knife's edge and could easily tip over into an inflationary outcome. The secular downtrend in the inflation rate over the past two decades is largely seen as resulting from a series of fortuitous supply shocks, all of which had only short-term implications.

NEITHER EXTREME CORRECT

Both sides in this polarized debate were wrong. As we saw in 2000, the New Economy is not immune to massive stock market losses and precipitous economic decline. Corporate earnings do matter and the old valuation metrics still prevail. Productivity growth will not move straight up because business investment in technology will decline when capital is hard to come by and earnings growth is falling. The New Paradigmers were irrationally optimistic and the excesses in their exuberance had to be wrung out of the system. By predicting stable, rapid growth and ever rising stock prices, they forgot that revolutions—digital or otherwise—are marked by surprises, reversals, and wild swings. During the Industrial Revolution, thousands of start-up companies failed because their business models were flawed and their efforts were misdirected. No one knew how to manage the emerging post-agrarian environment. The entire economy was re-invented. The upheaval during the period of development was immense and many people lost their shirts in stock market debacles, like today.

But the Traditionalists were also wrong. It is true that business is still around to pursue profits, and in that way nothing has changed. But how that profit will be made *is* changing. The move from the agrarian to the industrial world transformed just about everything—business structure, finance, distribution, urban development, and societal order. Today, on an even larger, accelerated scale, a new economic and social system is taking form. It too will transform everything.

The New Economy is far from dead. It is getting ready to launch its next phase. Information technology will fully converge with and, in turn, be remade by the biological revolution. Biology is the science of the Information Age. Faster, better digital capability is helping to unlock the secrets of the life sciences, while an improved understanding of biological systems will help researchers create the next stage of information and communications technology. Scientists at MIT today are building computers based on molecular systems. Biologists and other life scientists will be working hand-in-hand with computer scientists and engineers. Together, they will revolutionize business, economics, politics, and society. Generations from now will look back to see the next decade as a major turning point in human history. This truly is a Digital Revolution.

6

The Nasdaq
Bubble

W e all know now that the Nasdaq ultimately levitated in early
2000 to a height that was impossible to sustain, even under
the most optimistic of economic circumstances. Before we
examine the dot-com crash and the ensuing economic slowdown, it is
worth examining the underlying causes of the Internet bubble. In many
ways, the confluence of events since the early-1980s recession created just
the right tsunami for the bubble to grow beyond all reasonable
proportions—beyond most of our wildest expectations. Even the most
rabid bulls among the Internet analysts were, in the early years, too
conservative in their stock price forecasts. It was the "perfect storm." Just
the right set of parameters to create the biggest bull market in history, and
with it came the inevitable bust.

WHAT CAUSED THE BUBBLE?

Like most bubbles, this one was based on positive fundamentals that
became overinflated by mass expectations, euphoria, and hype. The
Internet truly is a revolutionary force for many aspects of business,

research, entertainment, communications, and household spending; it opened up a wide range of possibilities regarding its ultimate impact on the economy and profits. But before the appropriate business models could be developed to assure profitable transactions on the Net, the world began to believe dot-coms would virtually replace traditional bricks-and-mortar businesses, capturing their revenue streams while sporting a much lower cost base. This fantasy produced a seemingly reasonable expectation of very high profits. It disconnected the future profit story from the current substantial losses. Industry reports suggest that only three well-known B2C dot-com companies have thus far achieved sustained profitability: AOL, Yahoo!, and eBay. Most Net companies could never have lived up to the hype that accompanied their arrival.

Unassailed Chutzpah

If the dot-coms had nothing else, they had *chutzpah*—nerve, guts—in the pursuit of consumer awareness and "piece of mind." Super Bowl 2000— the top-rated TV show of the year (with audiences of roughly 135 million people)—was the dot-com Super Bowl. Ad time for the event ran as high as $3 million for a thirty-second spot. At those prices, you would think only the most blue chip of Fortune 500 companies with the biggest marketing budgets would even consider it. Yet, dot-com after dot-com, some of them start-ups with barely any revenues and certainly no profits, advertised during that game. For example, OurBeginning Inc., an Orlando-based online stationery e-tailer, which only launched its website in April 1999, was right in there with the others that included AutoTrader.com, Computer.com, E*Trade, HotJobs.com, Kforce.com, LifeMinders, Monster.com, WebMD, and Pets.com. Of these big spenders, two no longer exist—Pets.com and Computer.com.

OurBeginning seemed unfussed that it had only twelve full-time employees and had racked up revenues of just a little over $1 million. They paid an amazing $4 million to produce and air three pre-game ads and a fourth spot to run during the game. It cost them another $1 million for technology upgrades to handle the expected surge in traffic on their site.

OurBeginning's CEO, Michael E. Budowski, had chutzpah alright; but he was only following in the footsteps of other dot-coms that had used the Super Bowl the year before to enhance customer awareness. These included job-search sites HotJobs.com and Monster.com, which successfully created a lot of hype with clever ads during the 1999 game. Monster.com reported that their job searches per minute surged nearly 400 percent after the game.[1] These unabashed excesses in advertising were encouraged by consultants such as Forrester Research, quoted as saying that there aren't many other places that could compare to the Super Bowl in creating a mass market quickly. Maybe; but that didn't stop the dot-com stocks from crashing barely two months later. Clearly the excesses mirrored the jubilance of the markets at the time. Super Bowl advertising might have been a cool tactic, but it had little strategic significance. You can't build a business on cute tactics, regardless of how expensive and "in your face" they are.

What a difference a year made. Dot-com start-ups were conspicuous in their absence from the roster of advertisers for Super Bowl 2001. Instead, the list was full of heavy hitters such as Anheuser-Busch, FedEx, Johnson & Johnson, IBM, Dentyne, Frito-Lay, Hershey's, Pepsi-Cola, Visa, and Pizza Hut. E*Trade was back, one of only three dot-com advertisers. One newcomer, Cingular Wireless, marked its brand debut with several spots, including one with NFL players. Cingular is not your average start-up, however—it is a wireless venture of SBC Communications and Bell South.

Timing Was Everything

But the Nasdaq boom was not made purely from thin air and hype. The timing couldn't have been better. The emergence of the Net coincided with a number of underlying developments that were very positive for stocks. The mid-1990s followed a very long period of relative prosperity and stock market success. The recession in 1990–91 was mild and brief. Stocks had been doing well since 1982, the beginning of the long bull market in stocks. The substantial decline in long-term interest rates—generated by the secular downtrend in inflation—made stocks the only game in town and drove up underlying price-earnings ratios. People believed that the natural direction of stocks was up. Fifteen years earlier, that belief was rare. This optimistic view was nurtured by a growing spate of very positive books that pointed out the tremendous prospects for stocks in the future. Gurus such as Harry Dent were in increasing demand to explain the wonders of the coming *Roaring 2000s*.[2]

The underlying fundamentals were superb. U.S. businesses were forced to restructure in the early 1980s, thanks to the dramatic increase in global competitive pressure. Profit margins widened sharply a few years after the recession in 1982, reflecting the enormous streamlining, updating, and rationalizing that had occurred in Corporate America. Profits surged, outpacing the growth in GDP. This in combination with the rise in price-earnings multiples produced a very heady gain in the broad stock indexes.

Stocks Were Sexy

By the mid-1990s, public awareness of things financial had burgeoned. The proliferation of twenty-four-hour news coverage—spearheaded by CNN—started the process. It was accelerated by the onslaught of financial news networks. Suddenly everyone was following the latest in stock market developments as though they were plays in the Super Bowl. Breathless commentators from the floor of the New York Stock Exchange or the Chicago Board of Trade helped raise the temperature and the hype. Running for hours and hours each day, these networks had to "feed the beast"—fill the airtime with so-called news even when nothing much was happening. A constant series of talking heads were anointed expert status, filling the airwaves with "dramatic" developments and ten-second, "in-depth" analysis.

CNBC, Bloomberg News, and CNNfn were watched not only on the trading floors on Wall Street, Bay Street, and similar financial centers around the world, but they quickly became the property of Main Street as well. *Wall Street Week* with Lou Rukeyser on PBS on Friday nights became a national icon. Portfolio managers such as Peter Lynch in the U.S. and Frank Mersch in Canada were granted celebrity status. Brand-name equity analysts and investment strategists were in high demand. Everyone was optimistic.

The Internet itself contributed to Main Street's love affair with stocks. Investment information was readily available. Countless sites such as the

Motley Fool, Raging Bull, and James Cramer's TheStreet.com fueled the insatiable appetite for market chatter. The Net also dramatically reduced trading costs. Trading online was possible at a fraction of the former commission rates. Indeed, as we saw earlier, the online trading dot-coms drove down commissions in the industry. The acquisition of real-time market information and the availability of cheap real-time trading were democratized for the first time—anyone could have it.

Mutual Fund Bull Market

The boom in the stock market coincided with the proliferation of mutual funds. The mutual fund industry was given new impetus by the Employee Retirement Income Security Act of 1974, which created Individual Retirement Accounts (IRAs). But the industry didn't really take off until the beginning of the great bull market in stocks in 1982. That year, there were only 340 equity mutual funds in the U.S. That number had risen to over 4,200 by 2000. There are more mutual funds than stocks listed on the New York Stock exchange and they advertise heavily in the print, Net, and broadcast media. People are constantly reminded to save for college or for retirement. Many of the ads very effectively raise the guilt and anxiety level for those spendthrifts too short-sighted or undisciplined to regularly invest in the funds of Fidelity, Alliance Capital, Janus, or Vanguard. Others show the wonders of the worry-free retirement years, thanks to the advice of Paine Webber or Salomon Smith Barney. The mutual fund industry effectively raised the public consciousness about equity investments.

No More Big Brother Protecting You in Retirement

Investment clubs popped up everywhere. Psychology couldn't have been better and the Baby Boomers had hit investment age. Leading-edge Boomers were turning fifty and whole hosts behind them were in their forties. For many, accumulating wealth was essential because their employers were no longer going to take care of their retirement needs.

Augmenting the fury was the decline of the defined-benefit pension plan—the kind that pays you a guaranteed income after you stop working; with more and more people having to save for their own retirement, interest in every wiggle in the market was shooting upward. Everyone was ripe for the next hot tip.

All of the wealth that was created prior to the take-off in tech stocks in 1995 was in the hands of very optimistic investors who were willing to take a flyer on a hot tech stock. It was a great time to finance an important new innovation. In a bull market, everyone thinks they know what they are doing and nothing is so disturbing as watching your neighbor get rich. Everyone wanted in. This fertile soil encouraged risk taking of all types, with the most aggressive equity sectors seeing the biggest returns.

The New Metrics

Soaring price-earnings multiples did not seem to matter. Wall Street rode the euphoria for all it was worth. While investment dealers were raking it in on the IPO side, Internet analysts were creating a new system of metrics to value the intangibles so highly regarded in the New Economy. This was not all hype. Respected accounting guru and New York University professor Baruch Lev agreed that the New Economy had rendered traditional accounting conventions obsolete.[3]

The fact is that current accounting methods are geared to Old Economy companies, where the physical assets of the businesses are predominantly what create the value. In the Industrial Age, investing in physical assets such as factories and machinery reaped big returns. According to standard accounting practice, the cost of those items would immediately be posted on the balance sheet as an asset and could be amortized over a number of years.

In the New Economy, however, the intangible assets such as talent, intellectual capital, brands, and speed were key to success and value creation. New Economy companies invested in recruitment and training, research and development, and advertising; but none of these items could be amortized. They had to be fully expensed in the year they were incurred. Moreover, the intangibles themselves were rarely considered assets on the balance sheet. This immediately put the Internet companies at a disadvantage from a traditional valuation perspective.

So instead of looking at price-earnings ratios, analysts began looking at price-to-sales or price-to-revenues ratios. (In some cases, it even seemed to be price-to-concept ratios.) These ratios were compared to the forecasted growth rates of earnings (or revenues, or sales) in the so-called PEG ratios. In 1995, growth forecasts for the whole technology spectrum were staggering; in most cases they panned out, at least until 2000.

Lending credence to the new metrics, Baruch Lev himself has estimated the value of what he calls a company's "knowledge capital" and added it to the existing book value to give what he considered to be a truly "comprehensive" net asset value. *Barron's* reported these numbers in November 2000. According to Lev, balance sheets of many New Economy corporations ignore 70 to 90 percent of their true asset value. This view helped justify the enormous valuations of tech stocks.

Jubilation Continues, Fed by "New Era" Thinking

Early positive returns in the dot-coms as well as the broader telecoms, media, and tech (TMT) stocks encouraged other investors to jump in. Many had little investment experience and most turned a blind eye to the risks they were taking. Economists joined the chorus of others claiming that "this time was different." The most extreme New Paradigmers suggested that a cyclical downturn was nearly unthinkable—that 4 to 6 percent growth without inflation was sustainable on an indefinite basis.

Boomers saving for retirement had a very long investment horizon. They were willing to wait for profits to emerge in the Internet space—or so they thought—as long as the concept seemed right. This helped to fuel the IPO boom, providing the capital needed to feed the frenzy.

The belief that "this time is different" spread widely, particularly in reference to the importance of profits for the dot-coms. The most extreme New Economy theorists were ready to throw out the old economics textbooks. While they were right on many counts—including the fact that rapid productivity growth could support a strong economy without inflation—they did get carried away. There are many examples of "new era" thinking in the past.

Some Historical Examples

The same thoughts were rampant at the turn of the last century, and for good reason. The commissioner of the United States Office of Patents in 1899 recommended that his office be abolished because everything that could be invented had been invented, so spectacular was the wave of innovation in the late nineteenth century. History is littered with such foolish predictions about the future. This was the age of optimism when it was believed the wonders of electricity would soon revolutionize the world. Stock prices surged and peaked in June 1901. It was touted that stocks were held in the "strong hands" of long-term investors.[4] Those strong hands, however, did not prevent the market crash in 1907 or the dramatic plunge in stock values that took place between 1907 and 1920, when the market shed 35 percent of its value.

Another period of marked optimism was the roaring 1920s, as the automobile came into common usage, radio matured, and electricity moved beyond the city centers. Robert Shiller, professor of economics at Yale University, chronicles the media at the time and the incredibly positive statements of the day.[5] They include Professor Irving Fisher's infamous late-1929 assertion that stocks had reached a "high plateau." Fisher was not alone in his views. Others, such as Charles Amos Dice in *New Levels in the Stock Market*, published in August 1929, referred to the period as a "New World" and extolled the virtues of stock market investment.[6]

"This-time-is-different" thinking emerged once again in the mid-1950s. The Industrial Age was in full blossom and large corporations were growing rapidly as the U.S. emerged from the war as a global super power. The baby boom sparked further growth and optimism. By 1953, the stock market took off. It was argued then, as now, that businesses were better able to plan for the future and thus big swings in the business cycle could be avoided.

Television became the mainstream vehicle for mass culture, following in the footsteps of radio. Like the Internet today, television in the 1950s captured the imagination of the public and provided concrete evidence of technological innovation. It came into everyone's homes, significantly impacting people's lifestyles and attitudes.

The optimism continued through the Kennedy years, as "Camelot" reflected the positive sentiment of the time. The handsome, young president with his beautiful, charming wife and children were a mirror image of the way middle-class America saw itself. Throughout the 1960s, as Shiller archives, the looming goal of Dow 1,000 impacted market sentiment.[7] The Dow did not close above 1,000 until 1972—although it touched it intra-day in 1966—and was only to crash in 1973. It would not touch 1,000 again until 1982. That meant sixteen years of essentially no capital gains in the Dow Jones Industrial Index. The S&P 500 fared a bit better.

Back to the Future: The Virtuous Circle of the 1990s

In the 1990s a very positive virtuous circle emerged, further augmenting the stock market boom. The financing of start-ups with seed capital quickly paid off with IPOs—many of which surged to the moon on their first day—in turn encouraging more venture capital to pour into the space and more investors to take the plunge. Cheap and plentiful capital was just the rain the dot-com garden needed. The easing in monetary policy following the Asian crisis in 1998, along with the Fed-brokered bailout of LTCM, confirmed to investors that the Fed would always bail out the stock market. This was the so-called "Greenspan put"—the Fed could be counted on to be there to provide a bid. Figure 6.1 shows the correlation between the provision of liquidity and subsequent stock market movement.

The Fed nurtured the garden once again in late 1999. Fueled by fears of a Y2K debacle, the central bank aggressively pumped monetary reserves into the system. This was the final bit of fertilizer the already fertile soil needed. Dot-com and TMT stocks exploded. The Nasdaq rose over 20 percent in December 1999, taking the annual gain to a mind-boggling 86 percent. Stocks continued to surge in the first quarter of 2000. When the Nasdaq peaked on March 10, it was up another 24 percent year to date. The breadth of the stock market gain, however, was extremely narrow—a relatively small number of stocks shared in the rally.

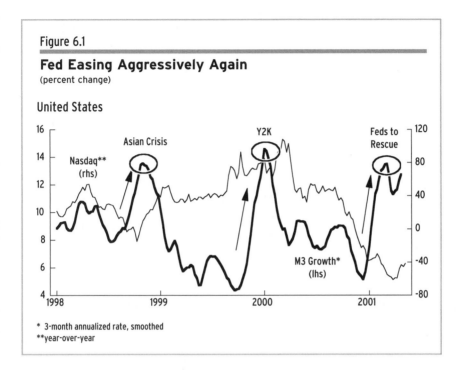

Figure 6.1

Fed Easing Aggressively Again
(percent change)

United States

* 3-month annualized rate, smoothed
**year-over-year

Forces Come Together

Supporting the euphoria as well was the growing notion that stocks were no more risky in the long run than bonds. Books such as Jeremy Siegel's *Stocks for the Long Run*, first published in 1994, and *Dow 36,000*, by James Glassman and Kevin Hassett, added to the positive view of stocks relative to other asset classes.[8] Glassman and Hassett were diehard bulls, asserting in March 1999, a year before the Nasdaq peaked, that perceptions of risk were declining, and rightfully so.[9] According to them, a small drop in the equity "risk premium" in valuation models would lead to a huge rise in predicted price-earnings ratios, so multiple expansion would fuel the further stock market rise to ultimately take the Dow to 36,000.

All of these forces came together in a giant crescendo. The public was willing and anxious to take the leap. The sky was the limit. Risk-aversion seemed to have fallen sharply. Wall Street profitably ran with the story for all it was worth. The media were willing accomplices. The Internet itself augmented the hype, as the plethora of investor websites and chat rooms fed the garden. The replacement of historical precedent with the dream of a dramatically different future is a common element of most bubbles. This process of story creation is a naturally occurring Ponzi or pyramid scheme.[10] The momentum players—buyers of stocks because they are rising—added the fatal positive feedback loop that carried the market to its dizzying top.

GAME OVER—MARCH 2000

Just as momentum was so positive on the upside, it had brutal effects on the downside. By March 2000, the Nasdaq was vulnerable to concerns about overvaluation. It had rocketed upward in 1999 only to be followed by the continued surge into the new year, but fewer and fewer stocks were sharing in the gain. At the Nasdaq's peak on March 10, the average stock was already 30 percent below its fifty-two-week high. Many were beginning to wonder if the depressed Old Economy stocks wouldn't provide better value and more stable portfolio returns. You have to give credit to Jeremy Siegel, who published a prescient op-ed piece in the *Wall Street Journal* on March 14, 2000, four days after the Nasdaq peaked, warning that the big-cap tech stocks were significantly overvalued.[11] I gave a speech with Siegel in late 1999, when he asserted his long-held views of the outperformance of stocks. But by early 2000, he realized it had gone way too far. Many others did not, but influential among the bears at the time was Robert Shiller, who published his book, *Irrational Exuberance*, with great fanfare.[12]

THE BUBBLE BURSTS

It was only a matter of time before the excesses of the Nasdaq boom would reverse—the bust was inevitable. In 2000, the Nasdaq plunged a gut-wrenching 39 percent, down 51 percent from its peak. The S&P 500 fared better, down only 9 percent, while the Dow Jones Industrial Average slipped a relatively modest 5 percent. The broadest measure of U.S. stock market performance, the Wilshire 5000, fell roughly 20 percent from its top, ending 2000 down 12 percent. The rout didn't end there. It continued into 2001 as the economy slid, with the Nasdaq down another 25 percent in the first quarter and the broader markets falling 12 percent further. Many well-known tech companies—the champions of the bull market such as Cisco, Intel, JDS Uniphase, Nortel, and Oracle—were down 70 percent or more from their peaks as their revenues and profits plunged.

Searching for the reasons for the dramatic and prolonged slide in stocks, particularly the dot-coms, brings us back to the Fed. Even though the Fed was hiking interest rates—they raised the benchmark fed funds rate in June, August, and November 1999 by 25 basis points each time—they nevertheless flooded the markets with liquidity in late 1999 to fight the Y2K phantom. Money supply growth surged around the turn of the year. This further ignited an already overheated economy and stock market. GDP growth in the fourth quarter of 1999 and the first quarter of 2000 zoomed to an annual average of 6.5 percent. Headline inflation was rising, owing largely to the rise in energy prices, and the hawks on the FOMC were clamoring for additional rate hikes. It was obvious that the Fed had overdone it in easing following the Asian crisis in 1998, and then again in gunning the money supply in late 1999. The Fed raised rates another 100 basis points culminating in May 2000. Inflation fear had continued to mount and the red-hot economy seemed to be unstoppable.

Many had argued that the tech sector would be impervious to the rising interest rates, but they were woefully wrong. While there were any number of other factors that helped grease the slide in stocks, the most fundamental was the tightening of credit. Cheap and readily available capital had been the lifeblood of Internet frenzy. Take it away and the frenzy died. The tightening actions hit the weakest borrowers first. The dot-coms were rapidly burning through cash. Pointing this out was a widely read cover story in *Barron's* in late March regarding the enormous cash-burn rates of the Internet companies.[13]

The telecom companies were also hit badly early in the process. The Internet "plumbing providers," such as AT&T, WorldCom, and other telecom carriers, were trashed almost as much as the dot-com stocks, even though these companies were at ground zero in the transformation being wrought by technology. For them, the problem wasn't only the availability of capital and the shift in investor sentiment, but also an antiquated regulatory environment coupled with their obsolete revenue models that depended too much on the unprofitable long-distance market.

A sudden scaling back of enthusiasm by some Wall Street strategists also heightened market fears. Abby Joseph Cohen, celebrated strategist at Goldman Sachs, pulled in her horns in March. The Blair-Clinton genome statement undercut biotech stocks at a crucial time when other tech stocks had already begun to tremble. Finally, Microsoft's legal battles threw more cold water on the market. Settlement talks collapsed in early April 2000 and the ruling against Microsoft came shortly thereafter, causing the Nasdaq to dip further.

The decline accelerated in mid-April with a distinct ramping up of the hawkish talk from the Fed and a brutal CPI report for March, which cast serious doubt on the New Paradigm view that we could sustain strong growth without mounting inflation. This prompted fears that the Fed would have to boost short-term rates further to curb inflation pressures and to cool the economy. The market's fears were justified. The Fed did indeed hike rates 50 basis points at the next FOMC meeting in mid-May, and the Nasdaq tumbled another 15 percent in the five days following the rate hike. Margin calls exacerbated the sell-off. Margin debt had soared in late 1999 and early 2000, hitting a record $278 billion in March, a jump of over 50 percent since the previous October.

The May rate hike would be the last, but no one knew that then. The U.S. economy was incredibly strong throughout the first half of 2000, which stoked investor concern that rates would have to move meaningfully higher still. Initial claims for unemployment insurance, a leading indicator of the labor market, hit a twenty-six-year low in the first quarter, and oil prices moved relentlessly higher.

More bad news drove the markets down. The already-listing dot-com sector was clobbered in June, when Ravi Suria, a credit analyst at Lehman Brothers, released a scathing report on the financial weakness of Amazon.com.[14] And then the parade of earnings warnings from tech heavyweights began in September—kicked off by Intel—and a broader tech sell-off commenced. Earnings were crushed on all fronts as it became increasingly clear in the fall of 2000 that the U.S. economy was slowing aggressively and that the slowdown was spreading fast around the world. Dow giants in the tech sector such as AT&T, Microsoft, Intel, and Hewlett-Packard plunged more than 50 percent from their fifty-two-week highs. And the pain didn't end there. Sector after sector in the non-tech world also took a beating as the U.S. and global economy slowed. Hardest hit among the Dow stocks were Home Depot, Procter & Gamble, Walt Disney, and Wal-Mart. It was not all bleak, however. The majority of listed companies actually finished 2000 up on the year, even as the dot-com fever broke and the TMT—telecom, media, and technology—stocks dived, taking the major indexes and market averages down with them.

THE CREDIT SQUEEZE

With the Nasdaq plunge, the IPO market collapsed, making it hard for companies to raise cash by issuing equities. Having seen that brand-name, large-cap tech companies could fall 50 percent or more in value, who was going to take a flyer on an upstart? Investors suddenly became more risk-averse, tasting the pain of a bear market. Net inflows of capital to equity mutual funds fell sharply. This ultimately caused the VC—venture capital—market to weaken. VCs were fearful that, with the demise of the IPO market, they wouldn't have an exit strategy and they wouldn't have enough capital to sustain the companies already in their portfolios. Many spent the money they had on propping up the top-tier companies they already owned and pulling the plug on the rest.

In the meantime, the junk bond market took a hit as corporate earnings prospects waned and the default rate rose to over 5 percent. In December 2000, Moody's Investors Service's twelve-month forecast of global speculative-grade defaults was just over 8 percent, the highest level since the 1990 recession. Rising defaults and bankruptcies, combined with volatility in the Nasdaq, helped erode investor confidence in a market that was already bleeding from cash outflows. Many investors avoided junk bonds issued by tech and telecom outfits—once investment darlings. As a result, investment banks shied away from bringing many deals to market. Interest-rate spreads over comparable-maturity Treasuries shot up, reaching more than 860 basis points (on an option-adjusted basis) at year-end 2000. This compared to a 450-basis-point spread one year earlier. The collapse in junk bond prices left little wonder that there was a record outflow of money from high-yield mutual funds.

The investment-grade corporate bond market deteriorated as well. Earnings disappointments and rising event risk battered the sector, as companies unveiled extensive restructurings to cope with industry changes or battled devastating lawsuits. Corporate bonds deteriorated relative to Treasuries across the credit spectrum. Even the interest rate spread on AAA-rated corporate bonds—the highest quality possible—hit a record level in early 2001, as fears of a hard landing in the economy increased and worries intensified that the debt problems in the junk sector would be contagious.

Credit risk increased fast. Moody's ratings downgrades exceeded upgrades at an accelerating pace. Companies that suffered downgrades included those that were already vulnerable, but also the telecom and auto giants considered to be bellwethers in the market. The casualties included Xerox, which descended into junk status, as well as Armstrong World Industries and Owens Corning, both sliding to the default level from triple-B owing to costly asbestos-related litigation. A number of traditional blue chips were also hacked by the rating agencies. For example, AT&T's plan to realign its businesses finally provoked a widely expected downgrade. For Ford Motor—arguably the most actively traded name in the investment-grade market—a large share-buyback program damaged the company's credit rating.

Wall Street was falling all over itself to keep up with the news. Having missed the Nasdaq plunge to a large degree, equity analysts were aggressively revising down their earnings forecasts—but not aggressively enough. The number and size of downward revisions were close to unprecedented. In mid-2000, I/B/E/S International posted S&P earnings forecasts for 2001 at a strong 14 percent. By year-end 2000, the 2001 outlook was a much bleaker 7 percent and the downgrades had not yet stopped. In 2001, analysts continued the downward revisions as company after company warned of earnings disappointments. Investors, riled at the after-the-fact downgrades, increasingly lost confidence in analyst forecasts. By the end of the first quarter of 2001, the earnings forecast for the year had been revised down again to a decline of 2.2 percent.

Then the banks cut back on syndicated lending—big loans that are parceled into chunks and sold off to other banks and investors such as insurance companies. An increasing number of banks tightened their credit standards to a point not normally seen except in recession. Even short-term commercial and industrial loans to fund inventories declined sharply. Worries about problem loans were at the heart of the concern; they had doubled since 1998. Nonfinancial commercial paper issuance plunged as well, making it difficult for businesses to use this alternative source of funding for their mounting inventories (those unsold goods on the shelves). The crackdown forced some businesses that couldn't get new loans to rely on previously arranged lines of credit. This is the corporate equivalent of living hand-to-mouth on credit card debt. Many banks began to rue that they had issued these lines so lavishly in the hopes of garnering other, more lucrative business. They became a ticking time bomb for bank credit quality and loan loss reserves, and the stock market began to reflect this in some troubled bank stocks. By the first quarter of 2001, financial stocks—banks and investment dealers—generally were sliding as credit concerns mounted.

These developments represented a sharp squeeze on corporations and happened much quicker than people expected. Troubled companies hit a wall and corporate bankruptcies surged well beyond the dot-com sector. Many worthy investment projects went unfunded.

Projects Flounder as Credit Tightens

The impact on the Internet revolution was undeniable. For example, the growing demand for broadband in the U.S. has gone largely unsatisfied. Both interactive cable and "digital subscriber lines" (DSL) require vast infrastructure overhauls that the financial markets became increasingly unwilling to fund. Stephen Wildstrom, a columnist for *Business Week*, put it this way:

> Stung by a sinking stock price and plunging profits from long distance, AT&T has abandoned its grand dream of reinventing itself as a provider of voice and data services over the cable network it purchased. Instead, it will spin off AT&T

Broadband, leaving open the question of who will finance the overhaul of the nation's largest cable network.[15]

The DSL situation was even worse. Verizon estimated that because of distance and other problems, only just over half of their subscribers will ever qualify for DSL service. Satellite access to the Internet, though available to some, requires substantial additional investment, and that means capital. Innovation and technological progress require abundant sources of risk capital; any drying up of that capital is devastating to the New Economy.

ANTIQUATED REGULATORY ENVIRONMENT DOESN'T HELP

What's more, the regulatory environment was a major deterrent in the swift development of broadband. This hurt the dot-coms. It can be argued that among the most potentially profitable dot-com models is the provision of services to the consumer. For sellers of goods, the issues surrounding who pays for all the customization and delivery is still a problem. But, clearly, a huge market exists for such services as movies-on-demand, music, 3-D games, e-books, and other intellectual properties of all sorts. This requires fast, reliable Internet connections in the home. Unfortunately, the provision of high-speed connections for most households seems to have hit enormous roadblocks. As of the end of 2000, only slightly more than 7 million of the 100 million American households had broadband access to the Internet. There were just 2.4 million DSL subscribers among the 120 million or so copper-connected U.S. homes and businesses, and there were roughly 4.9 million cable modem subscribers.[16] This has no doubt limited the growth of all B2C dot-com activity, although many people do shop online at work using the high-speed Net connections there.

The process of bringing DSL service to Baby Bell customers became a regulatory morass. Another pathway to fast, reliable connections was through cable modem, but that was held up as AT&T and Time Warner fought "open access" battles in Washington and in the courts. Wireless is another possible avenue, but it depends on the FCC doling out licenses to use the airwaves. The situation was not helped when the U.S. Justice Department shot down an attempt to merge WorldCom, a big provider of Internet backbone, with Sprint, a leading wireless provider. As telecom stock prices plunged, their willingness and ability to raise billions of dollars to build a national broadband system waned. Small businesses that depend on broadband connections are at their wit's end and some are falling into bankruptcy because they have to wait weeks or months for a line that works with questionable reliability. This problem provided another threat to the economy and slowed the progress of dot-com innovation.

Paradoxically, at the same time, there are those who argue there has been a glut of fiber-optic cable development, as evidenced by the dramatic decline in bandwidth prices in 2000 and low utilization rates for the vast network of cable that has been laid. For example, wholesale bandwidth prices between New York and London fell 45 percent in 2000, falling further in 2001. It appears, however, that some of the price decline resulted from the desperate attempt of the telecommunications carriers to grab market share at any price. Many are selling their networks' bandwidth at a loss. Newly founded communication companies have enormous debt obligations with interest carrying costs estimated at around $7 billion per year. In order to meet their debt obligations, many had no choice but to enter an all-out price war in the hopes of generating enough cash to stay alive.[17]

Meanwhile, companies such as Corning and JDS Uniphase that manufacture optical fiber slashed revenue projections as demand slowed. Equipment makers and suppliers were all hurt, including Nortel, Cisco, Motorola, and Lucent. The contract manufacturers—companies such as Solectron—that make the equipment for Cisco and others suffered as well. Stock prices plummeted—some as much as 90 percent. Also joining the debacle were the firms that lay the fiber—for example, Level 3, Qwest Communications, and Williams Communications Group. Their stock prices tumbled sharply, adding to earlier losses. Content companies and lenders also felt the pain as consolidation in the industry will no doubt be the ultimate result of the shakeout.

Over the past decade, there has been a surge in the laying of optical fiber, the tiny strands of glass that carry voice and data in pulses of light. According to the Telecommunications Industry Association, the annual deployment of fiber doubled from 1993 to 1997 and tripled by 2000. So the annual growth rate of new fiber deployed went from 20 to 30 percent in the mid-1990s to a peak of 68.7 percent in 2000. It is expected to grow by a much slower 24 percent in 2001, decelerating further in 2002.

Meanwhile, the reduced price of transporting data across fiber cable has sparked increasing demand, and new applications are growing rapidly. The problem still remains, however, that in the U.S. (less so in Canada and Scandinavia), the last-mile hook up of broadband access to the Net for households has faltered, even as the overall supply of fiber has surged. It will take some time to work off the overinvestment in cable, although that is likely to be relatively swift given the potential growth in demand. But the household demand for fast access must be addressed, and has thus far gone largely unmet. This inevitably slows the pace of Internet B2C activity and helps to explain why the growth in B2C space in the U.S. will pale in comparison to B2B commerce.

7

The Slowdown Comes

The economic slowdown that began in the second half of 2000 and accelerated in 2001 was the inexorable result of Federal Reserve policy. First came the inordinate provision of liquidity in late 1998 and again in late 1999 that fueled excessive spending and stock market speculation, and then followed the inevitable dramatic reversal, the draining of liquidity. The ensuing stock market plunge and credit squeeze dampened business and consumer confidence and turned the economy on a dime. The slowdown was abrupt and dramatic. Following five years of extraordinary growth and stock market jubilation, many believed a cooling off period for the economy was long overdue. But the obliteration of an estimated $4 to $6 trillion of wealth by the end of the first quarter of 2001 was more than most people bargained for.

The economic slowdown was rapid and forceful and risked getting out of hand. But just as the immediate cause of the precipitous slide in growth was the Fed, the ultimate rebound would, in the end, be Fed-based as well. This was not 1929 in the U.S. or 1989 in Japan—the beginning of a decade-long depression in stocks and the economy—but after the crash in the Nasdaq, many feared it might be. The media hype machine continued to pump out charts and stories showing the similarities, but in contrast to those periods, the central bank from the start aggressively cut interest rates and dramatically accelerated the growth in the money supply. In addition, Congress passed a meaningful tax cut. At this pace, I would worry that growth in 2002 might just accelerate too rapidly.

THE TIDES TURN—ECONOMIC SLOWDOWN

The gearing-down process started, not surprisingly, with a slowdown in the interest-sensitive sectors in response to the first bout of interest-rate hikes in the second half of 1999. Housing and auto sales slowed from staggering heights. Industrial production in the non-tech world weakened as well, exacerbated by the strengthening U.S. dollar and the resulting damaged competitive position of most non-tech manufacturing companies. As long as tech was strong, however, and consumer confidence held in, all was well. A modest slowdown was welcome, the deliberate result of the Fed's actions.

Then the Nasdaq plunged—first it was just the dot-coms and telecoms that collapsed, but after Labor Day 2000 the rout spread to all the techs and many non-tech companies as well. By October 2000, consumer confidence began to erode from near-record levels, and it eroded fast. Never before had equities loomed so large in the psyche of American consumers. Stocks were the largest component of household assets, having surpassed the value of residential real estate in the 1990s. Stocks as a percentage of U.S. gross domestic product (GDP) had risen to a record of over 150 percent in early 2000, up from 60 percent at the beginning of the '90s. The number of U.S. households owning equities, directly or through mutual funds, rose to 84 million from 52.3 million between 1989 and 1998, according to the New York Stock Exchange. With the fall in the stock market, most Americans felt poorer—the dot-com millionaires, pensioners, and middle-class families. In many ways, the stock market was the new and most powerful transmission mechanism of monetary policy. Fed tightening slowed interest-sensitive spending, but the resultant decline in stock prices did even more to dampen the pace of overall economic activity. The impact was both financial and psychological.

CONSUMERS SLOW SPENDING

For years, many warned that the consumer reliance on unrealized capital gains to fund their current expenditures was ultimately very risky. Traditional measures of the savings rate had fallen below zero, as I discussed in Chapter 5. But with the plunge in the Nasdaq in 2000, households finally saw how ephemeral their unrealized capital gains really were.

They finally reacted, triggered ultimately by the dramatic decline in stocks. It is difficult to ignore the loss of trillions of dollars in wealth. The Christmas 2000 shopping season was weaker than expected. Sales of personal computers actually fell below year-earlier levels; Gateway reported that its revenue over the Thanksgiving holiday was almost one-third lower than during the same weekend in 1999. The year's supposedly hot items—leather pants and jackets—piled up on the shelves of Gap stores everywhere. Auto sales plunged, provoking the industry to slash production. Auto factories from Detroit to Brampton, Ontario, sat idle as the industry wrestled with inflated inventories; thousands of layoffs were subsequently announced.

The auto industry was not alone in the slowdown. Basic industry manufacturing went into deep recession as industrial production plunged, except in the energy-related sectors. Even high-tech manufacturing growth, though still positive at first, slowed considerably. The rout there accelerated into 2001 as orders for high-tech equipment plummeted and layoffs surged. Purchasing managers reported a dramatic downturn in activity and price pressures dissipated.

Consumers reined in their most extravagant expenditures. Luxury retail chains, which reaped some of the biggest benefits of the decade-long boom in wealth, experienced a marked slowing of growth. Nieman Marcus, one of the last holdouts, saw sales decline significantly following more than a year of double-digit expansion. These were the last to feel the pinch. Companies like Home Depot and the Gap had suffered from weaker sales since mid-2000.

Pent-up demand had largely been satisfied by the huge buying binge of the long expansion. The demand for durable goods (those that last three years or more, such as refrigerators and cars), as well as capital equipment had been growing at a double-digit rate for years. Consumers seemed to reach a satiation point and businesses decided it was time to digest their acquisitions. With private borrowing totaling a record 130 percent of GDP, many began to think about paying off debt.

Oversupply of consumer goods was not all bad news. It certainly helped to dampen inflation. Businesses, in an effort to empty shelves, introduced deep discounts. Consumers enjoyed these discounts even during the Christmas season in 2000 and certainly in the subsequent months of weakened demand. But the discounts only wreaked further havoc on retailers' earnings.

ENERGY COSTS HIT HARD

The rise in energy prices also crimped discretionary income flows. For much of 1999 and 2000, however, the rise in energy prices had failed to curtail shopping, as consumers took out more debt and dipped into their savings in an effort to maintain their standard of living. But consumers were finally becoming overextended. In the third quarter of 2000, the average minimum monthly payment that Americans owed on their debt reached it highest level since 1987. They also spent more money than they earned during the quarter, something that never occurred in the '80s or '90s.

In many ways, households had been on a binge. Despite the booming economy, skyrocketing stock market, and tight job market, homeowners had opted to defer paying down their mortgage debt in the late '90s. Indeed, they consistently added to it. As a result, American homeowners' equity positions increased only moderately from the rise in home prices in the late 1990s, as consumers mortgaged a good deal of the gain. One in every four homeowners had a second mortgage, generally carrying interest rates in the 8- to 13-percent range. Many banks and finance companies allowed homeowners to borrow 95 percent, 100 percent, or even 125 percent of their home's appraised value. It is not surprising, therefore, that the plunge in the stock market and the ensuing layoff announcements would begin to cause many consumers to tighten their belts. More of a surprise was the degree to which consumption held up through the early part of 2001.

Threatened disruptions in energy service, particularly in California, were especially troublesome. Natural gas prices, in particular, spiked temporarily to a record $10 per million BTUs, rising fourfold from levels posted one year earlier. This led businesses that are heavy users of natural gas—such as fertilizer producers, chemical companies, textile dyers, and steel manufacturers—to shut down a large proportion of their capacity. All business inevitably felt the pain. Energy costs in the corporate sector rose more than 20 percent in 2000, according to the Bureau of Labor Statistics. That slowed production and business investment in 2001. The rise in energy costs also depressed corporate earnings outside of the energy sector.

The problems were the most acute in California and other western states that were affected by California's power grid. Disruptions and rapidly rising costs caused many businesses to cut production or to shut down altogether. Once the stalwart of the Californian economy, tech companies such as Intel threatened not to grow their business in the state, preferring to move new and, in some cases, existing operations elsewhere. California itself represents 13 percent of the U.S. economy. It is the sixth largest economy in the world. As its major utilities began to default on their commercial paper, it was clear that the Fed, the state government, and even the federal government would have to do something.

Vaguely reminiscent of the Orange County debacle of 1994 and Long-Term Capital Management in 1998, the Fed aggressively eased monetary policy in response to financial strains. In a surprise, inter-meeting move, the Fed cut rates 50 basis points in early January 2001 and then again at the end of the month. Chairman Greenspan tried to calm shaky consumers by suggesting that the economy—at near-zero growth in early 2001—would rebound in the second half of the year. But the "R" word—recession—was a daily headline in the news and the Bush Administration, anxious to quickly push through their tax cut proposal, fed the fires of economic concern. Declining stock prices and rising heating bills further rattled nerves.

Heating bills surged an estimated 50 percent over year-earlier levels in the winter of 2001. For homes using natural gas, which accounted for over 50 percent of the total, bills rose as much as 70 percent. This increase inevitably slowed demand for other products, which hurt business in general. The impact on inflation, however, was remarkably muted. As discussed in Chapter 5, most businesses were unable to pass off the higher energy cost onto the consumer. With demand softening, doing so became even more difficult. Besides, many manufacturers couldn't hike prices because they had to compete with European and Asian rivals, where less-stringent environmental regulations allowed natural gas prices to remain somewhat lower. Even the companies that did raise prices—such as United Parcel Service Inc., FedEx Corp., the airlines, railroads, and truckers—continued to experience weaker earnings as price hikes were limited by market forces for them as well.

The winter heating bills were followed by the summer driving season. Gasoline prices surged in the spring of 2001, further exacerbating the mounting burden of consumer spending constraints. Gas price increases also further dampened the profitability of companies in the transport industry.

OVEREXPANSION AND INVENTORY BUILDUP

Capital dried up, as we saw in Chapter 6, and the overextension of credit during the economic boom came home to roost. In many ways, the downturn was rooted in overcapacity brought on by a reckless capital-spending boom in 1999, accelerating in the first half of 2000, accompanied by a vastly overleveraged economy. While consumer borrowing during the boom was at record levels relative to personal income, the growth in business borrowing had been even greater—far surpassing the pace of economic expansion or consumer credit extension. Businesses had been drunk on cheap credit.

There were real concerns also that Y2K disruptions might make it impossible to conduct business as usual. In the fall of 1999, companies, afraid of being caught without critical parts, double and triple ordered from suppliers. The excesses were enormous, so the ensuing slowdown in capital spending was all the more dramatic. Technology companies such as Nortel, Corning, JDS Uniphase, Cisco, Oracle, and Sun Microsystems were unprepared for the dramatic plunge in new orders. Indeed, inventories at Cisco, Nortel, and Lucent ballooned 52 percent in the fourth quarter of 2000 as sales slowed to a crawl. Repeated earnings warnings ensued—not once, but quarter after quarter from late 2000 through 2001. And with each earnings warning, stock prices tanked.

Rising labor costs also dampened earnings. Wage rates had increased in lagged response to the tight labor markets. Productivity gains—though still strong in the fourth quarter of 2000 at 2 percent—were below levels recorded earlier and they fell sharply in early 2001. More importantly, they no longer fully offset the rise in wage bills. Unit labor costs increased dramatically in 2001. Most businesses, unable to pass these higher costs along to the consumer in the form of higher prices, slashed their payrolls instead. The labor markets began to slacken, evidenced by an increase in initial claims for unemployment insurance, a dip in help-wanted advertising, and a reduction in average hours worked. Finally, the jobless rate began to drift higher. There was no longer excess demand for labor in many sectors. Laid-off workers were having more difficulty finding jobs quickly and the once-fast-growing tech companies were slashing payrolls, the same companies that had clamored about labor shortages just a few months earlier. By mid-2001, the drop in job availability was a meaningful deterrent to consumer confidence. Barely a week went by without a major announcement of job cuts, and help-wanted ads all but dried up. Corporate recruiters reported a dramatic decline in employment openings and initial claims for unemployment insurance surged to their highest level since March 1992.

BUSINESSES CAUGHT OFF GUARD

Many businesses had been planning for the indefinite continuation of exceptionally strong growth. The disappointment was gut wrenching. Since 1995, industrial capacity had increased by roughly 5 percent per year—more than double the pace from 1980 through 1994. This helped to keep the lid on inflation in the robust years, as the economy did not bump up against meaningful capacity constraints (except in the energy sector) when the economy was strong. But when growth turned down, the industrial excesses were glaring. Production cutbacks were extreme and abrupt.

Retailers had been even more exuberant than manufacturers, embarking on a specialty store–building spree. The new stores—geared to a particular market segment, such as sportswear or lingerie—were expected to increase the industry's nationwide floor space by about 30 percent by the end of 2001. From 1995 through 2000, San Francisco-based Gap Inc. more than doubled its number of Gap, Old Navy, and Banana Republic stores to 3,500. It planned to increase that number by almost 20 percent more in 2001.

It wasn't just giddiness that led many retailers and manufacturers to overinvest. The warp-speed world of global competition meant that any profitable new business sector quickly attracted a flood of hopeful new entrants. An example is the market for sport utility vehicles (SUVs), which, because of rash overproduction, have become increasingly less profitable. In 1995, North American factories produced 1.7 million SUVs in thirty different models. In the next five years, the production capacity doubled and the number of models rose to fifty-two, according to Autodata Corp., a Woodcliff Lake, New Jersey, auto-industry research firm. This was one area where the unintended inventory buildup early in the slowdown was the greatest. American carmakers claimed they had actually tried to exercise restraint. It was Japanese and German manufacturers that flooded the market pioneered by the Big Three.

Overcapacity in the auto industry was one thing, but the more jarring development was a glut in high-tech sectors, where demand was supposed to keep up with whatever supply came onstream. Companies selling into new market segments had no historical markers to guide them in predicting sales patterns. Rapidly increasing demand and the potential for sky-high rates of return encouraged tech firms to bet on the high side when building plants or laying cables.

This sounded frighteningly like Japan in the 1980s, where corporate giants expanded confidently, proclaiming a new era of sustained higher growth. When financial and property markets collapsed and consumer demand plunged in the early 1990s, companies were left with far more capacity than they needed, deepening the economic morass from which Japan has yet to emerge.

Nowhere was the recent U.S. exuberance more evident than in the telecommunications sector. The 1996 U.S. telecom deregulation, combined with growing awareness of the new business frontiers opened by the blending of computers with phones, unleashed a barrage of new telecom companies. Hundreds were launched, raising money through IPOs and borrowings in the bond market. According to Lehman Brothers, telecom start-ups carried $74 billion in debt at the end of 2000.

But making inroads into the domain of the traditional suppliers was difficult. Old phone companies controlled 94 percent of the local business phone market by the end of 2000, and none of the new entrants had yet made a profit. Saddled with unfinished or underutilized fiber-optic lines, these companies reported they would slash capital spending in 2001 by more than 20 percent. This led to a dramatic decline in the revenue prospects of the telecom and fiber optic equipment providers. The stock price of these companies fell dramatically further, as we have seen.

The PC manufacturers had already felt the pinch. From Gateway to Dell, Hewlett-Packard, Intel, and more, stock prices plummeted. There were no safe havens on the tech side. Internet stocks fell further and even the biotechs were decimated as valuation adjustments abounded.

To be sure, overcapacity was not evident everywhere—capacity was tight in many important sectors of the economy. Airlines were flying with their planes near their fullest loads in more than twenty years. Oil companies had been careful in expanding drilling and refining capacity, one factor that had kept oil prices high. Yet new pockets of excess capacity kept arising, so that when consumer spending slowed, excess inventories became a widespread problem.

The New Economy information transformation was supposed to dampen the inventory cycle. But better market information alone can't always prevent excessive buildups, especially in the case of potentially profit-rich new technologies. There, the lure of outsized returns seems to justify the risk of overinvesting.

The after-effects of overinvestment in technology are likely to be less serious than the bricks-and-mortar overinvestment of the past. In the 1980s, for example, an overabundance of real estate investment burdened the U.S. with an excess supply of commercial office space that took years to work off. The difference today is that tech products, such as software and computers, depreciate relatively quickly; but with computers, the technology has matured, the rate of obsolescence has slowed from an earlier period, and businesses might wait somewhat longer to replace them, so spending might be delayed.

CAPITAL SPENDING BUDGETS SLASHED

Perhaps the biggest risk to the economy in 2001 was the bleak outlook for capital spending. Soaring business investment was a hallmark of the New Economy. Capital spending rose from an average of about 10 percent of gross domestic product in the 1980s to a stunning 15 percent in 2000. Even if they had wanted to—and they did not—businesses just could not afford to continue spending at that pace. They were overleveraged. By late 2000, the gap between corporations' capital outlays and their cash flow had never been wider. That meant that internally generated funds were increasingly insufficient to finance expenditures, just at a time when financing from external sources, such as banks and the credit markets, had become more and more scarce. In early 2001, banks reported a record tightening in credit standards for corporate borrowers.

In the face of slower growth, corporations were just as quick to cut their capital spending budgets as their payrolls and supply orders. Corporate outlays on equipment and software—the mainstay of the long expansion and productivity surge—fell at an annual rate of 3 percent in the fourth quarter of 2000 and dropped even more in the first half of 2001. CEOs at companies such as Nortel and Cisco reported that they expected capital spending plans to remain weak through most of 2001, adding a strong depressant to economic growth even when inventories were brought under control. Some of the reduced demand for capital goods inevitably would reduce imports, mitigating the dampening effect on U.S. GDP growth but damaging the economic prospects in the rest of the world, especially in Asia, the global leader in IT exports.

SLOWDOWN IN FAST FORWARD

Thanks to substantial business investment in inventory-monitoring systems during the long expansion, the response to the slowdown in sales was immediate and abrupt. Manufacturers in all sectors quickly called their suppliers and turned off the spigots. Production plunged and layoffs increased sharply. This was the just-in-time downturn. Armed with the latest in IT and under unrelenting pressure from Wall Street to protect profits, many businesses reacted with lightning speed to the relatively sudden slowdown in sales.

Reminders of the downturn barraged consumers daily, further dampening sentiment and exacerbating the slowdown. Ford, DaimlerChrysler, Amazon.com, Gillette, Dell, Nortel, and a multitude of others rapidly and forcefully cut the size of their workforces. Better information allowed business to quickly trim job rolls, close excess plant capacity, and cut spending on computers and other equipment. The response to the slowdown in orders was rapid and dramatic.

Not surprisingly, consumer confidence fell further. The growing tsunami of layoff announcements, further swelling with each passing week, spooked consumers. The drop in the University of Michigan survey of consumer sentiment from November 2000 to February 2001 was the second biggest in history. The Conference Board survey confirmed the result, but also indicated, ironically, that consumers were more worried about the future than the present. This was corroborated by the continued strong activity in the housing market, as new applications for mortgages increased and home sales edged upward. Lower interest rates were doing their job on that score at least. Even auto sales began to recover in early 2001, and consumer spending on services held in fairly well. By March 2001, it was evident, however, that further Fed easing would be needed. The Fed continued to slash interest rates as the labor market continued to weaken, and the surprisingly resilient first quarter GDP figures—first reported showing 2 percent growth—were quickly revised downward followed by mounting evidence of a further slowdown.

THE FIRST INTERNET DEPRESSION?

Technology, though only 10 percent of U.S. GDP, had accounted for one-third of the growth in the economy for the five years ending in 2000. More importantly, tech spending generated the gains in productivity growth that were so crucial to the noninflationary growth spurt over those years.

Take away technology spending and we risked the first Internet Age recession.

Michael Mandel raised just these points in his thought-provoking book, *The Coming Internet Depression*, released in October 2000. His prescient discussion warned about the three early danger signals of a coming Internet depression:[1]

- Simultaneous fall in tech stocks and a slowdown in business investment in technology.
- Slowdown in the rate of price declines for tech goods.
- Decline in the flow of venture capital and IPOs.

Ominously, all three warning signs were flashing boldly in late 2000, although the decline in tech prices reaccelerated sharply in 2001 with the weakness in demand. The New Economy virtuous circle had turned sour. In the virtuous circle, strong business investment in technology lifted productivity growth and helped to hold the line on inflation. This boosted profits and equity prices, which, in turn, reduced the cost of capital and so encouraged further investment and productivity gains. Meanwhile, faster growth in the U.S. resulted in a stronger dollar, which also helped to hold down inflation and interest rates and so supported growth.

Mandel warned of the virtuous circle turning vicious: A falling stock market, by raising the cost of capital and denting confidence, could reduce investment as well as productivity growth and profits—pushing stock prices down even more. Slower productivity growth would also push up unit labor costs and hence inflation, making it harder for the Fed to ease policy. Also, the dearth of capital and reduced profitability would discourage new entrants into business. This would diminish competition, which could increase pricing power and ultimately inflation. In addition, slower U.S. growth would push the dollar down, making it harder for the Fed to cut interest rates.

Mandel ignored one mitigating factor on the inflation front. When inventories rise, reflecting excess supply, prices come under downward pressure. We saw this in retailing as businesses slashed prices to move goods off the shelves. Tech manufacturers were also forced to cut prices to move product, which works its way through the technology supply chain, squeezing profit margins for tech companies even further.

The value of inventory also declines as it gathers dust in storage, particularly for technology products. The inventory-holding cost for a personal computer—the cost of capital plus the loss of value for the computer—could equal as much as 86 percent of the price over 18 months.[2] Once growth resumes and inventories are depleted, the robust long-term growth prospects for technology will be back in place.

Key to the prevention of an Internet Depression, according to Mandel, is an aggressive easing in monetary policy by the Federal Reserve, even in the face of what he believes could be mounting inflation pressure. Alan Greenspan apparently concurred, as he aggressively slashed interest rates and rapidly increased the provision of liquidity into the system. The Fed surprised many with the forcefulness and rapidity of its moves. Technology and the speedier flow of real-time information quickened the adjustment to slower growth. As Greenspan put it in Congressional testimony in February 2001, "Economic policymaking could not, and should not, remain unaltered in the face of major changes in the speed of economic processes."[3] By mid-2001, the Fed had slashed interest rates over a six-month period proportionately more aggressively than any time in the past.

REMINISCENT OF 1929 IN THE U.S. OR 1989 IN JAPAN?

We have seen central banks in the past wait too long to ease policy in the wake of a market meltdown, with disastrous results—the U.S. in the 1930s and Japan in the early 1990s. The U.S. in the late 1990s bore a strong resemblance to the lead-up to the stock market collapse in both earlier periods: the economy boomed, credit surged, and stock prices vaulted higher. Speculation and leverage increased dramatically as stocks rose, and there was no shortage of "new era" rationalizations suggesting that the good times would never end. The higher stock prices rose, the greater the euphoria. When the bubble finally burst, most were taken completely by surprise.

Figure 7.1 shows the similarities between the stock market in the three periods. However, a dramatic stock market decline does not necessarily cause a prolonged period of economic decline and stagnation.

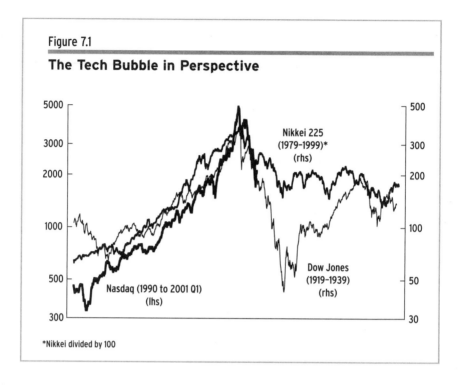

Figure 7.1

The Tech Bubble in Perspective

Nikkei 225
(1979–1999)*
(rhs)

Nasdaq (1990 to 2001 Q1)
(lhs)

Dow Jones
(1919–1939)
(rhs)

*Nikkei divided by 100

Both earlier episodes were, in large measure, the result of major policy errors rather than the inevitable fallout from a burst speculative bubble.

It is generally accepted that the Great Depression was not caused by the October 1929 stock market crash but by excessively tight monetary and fiscal policies, failure to respond correctly to the wave of bank failures, and by the 1930 passage of trade barriers under the Smoot-Hawley tariff. Between 1930 and 1933, the money supply fell by about one-third as the American banking system collapsed. That is unthinkable today.

Japan's protracted stagnation was also triggered by monetary and fiscal policy mistakes. In April 1989, Japan implemented a value-added tax of 3 percent. In January 1990, they hiked the capital gains tax rate from zero to 20 percent. The increase in taxes on consumption and investment quickly ended the Japanese miracle. In addition, the Bank of Japan boosted short-term interest rates from around 4.5 percent to 6.5 percent between March and December 1989, even though inflation was just 1 percent before the increase in the value-added tax. Then, just as the economy appeared to be getting back on its feet, the value-added tax was hiked again to 5 percent in early 1997. The tighter fiscal and monetary policy led to a deflationary downward spiral in economic activity. Moreover, the government failed to deal with the troubled financial sector. The Japanese government's efforts to spend its way out of the malaise through astonishingly expensive public works projects did not address the underlying problems.

In comparison to Japan, the U.S. has a healthy banking system; a more flexible market system, especially insofar as labor markets are concerned; and a much richer shareholder value culture. Japan still suffers from the perils of an elaborate system of cross shareholdings (*keiretsu*) that dragged down banks and corporations in the aftermath of the equity bubble. The U.S. does not suffer from this house-of-cards syndrome. Moreover, Japan's one-party political structure crimps its policy-making flexibility far more than America's two-party system. And Japan's asset bubble was far more encompassing and pervasive than the U.S. Nasdaq bubble. In Japan, not only did the stock market rise to enormous heights, but the property market displayed the same kind of excessive valuation.

In contrast to the policy mistakes of the past, the Greenspan Fed showed that it would not stand idly by and allow the self-reinforcing effects of the stock market's collapse to spiral into depression. Nor did the federal government stand in the wings. Aggressive easing in monetary and fiscal policy in 2001 guarded against the worst fears of the doom-and-gloom crowd.

STOCKS LEAD THE ECONOMY

The stock market anticipates movements in corporate earnings and economic activity. The market turns up long before the economy rebounds from a cyclical slowdown. The lead time has consistently been about four to six months, as shown in Table 7.1. The first-year returns after an economic slowdown have been sizable—averaging 37.5 percent since 1970, measured from when stocks began to rise (five months before the economic upturn). The sectors that declined the most generally led in the rebound.

Table 7.1

Stocks Rebound First (S&P 500)

Stocks Turn Up Early	Economic Rebound Starts Later	Stocks Lead Time (months)
June 1970	November 1970	5
September 1974	March 1975	6
July 1982	November 1982	4
October 1990	March 1991	6

Average Stock Rebound: 37.5% in First Year

A similar pattern is evident in the high-yield bond market: credit spreads improve well before the economic upturn. Indeed, the junk bond market generally leads the stock market. That is why many saw the decline in junk bond interest-rate spreads relative to Treasuries beginning in February 2001 as a harbinger of the stock market rebound to come.

This pattern materializes in a soft landing or a mild recession. A severe recession, however, prolongs the economic downturn and leads to a further drop in stocks. With Greenspan, Bush, and low inflation all on the side of investors, a rebound in stocks in 2002—or sooner—is a pretty good bet. Many, however, will not return to the heights of the pre-collapse era. While technology spending undoubtedly will, in time, resume its strong ascent, most stock prices in that sector will likely take years to exceed previous peaks.

8

Maybe the New Economy Isn't So New

Even with the dramatic slowdown in economic activity in late 2000–2001, you can't help but be excited about the future and amazed about the past. The decade of the 1990s was one of extraordinary expansion and growth, particularly over the last five years. And much, much more is yet to come. As we discussed earlier, the IT revolution, for all its glory, is still in its infancy. The world of infinite bandwidth—communication power—is now imaginable. This will mean ubiquitous, always-on computing and Internet access. The day will come soon when computers will be imbedded in virtually everything. And IT is not the only thing to look forward to.

We are on the precipice of major breakthroughs in medical science that will dramatically alter all of our lives. I would argue that the breakthroughs we will see in the next decade will dwarf all developments in medicine to date. These have tremendous implications, not just for the quality and quantity of our years on Earth, but also for our retirement planning, investment horizon, career planning, and general economic behavior.

Some have suggested that the development and broad use of the fuel cell to replace the internal combustion engine should also be seen as one of the seminal and important developments of the next ten or twenty years. And major discoveries in nanotechnology will, as we saw in Chapter 4, revolutionize manufacturing and so much more. Increasing returns to knowledge assure that the speed of change will be rapid in this, the Acceleration Age, and that the developments will be profound.

This is not new. Although the speed of acceptance of new technologies has certainly accelerated, an innovation cycle has been evident for more than two hundred years. Ever since the beginning of the first Industrial Revolution in the late 1700s, we have seen wave after wave of innovation roughly every fifty to sixty years. Once or twice a century, as Alan Greenspan has pointed out in many of his speeches, a new technological advance meaningfully alters the way the economy works, boosting growth, enhancing productivity, and often literally changing society. We saw it in the mid-1800s with the introduction of the railway and at the turn of the last century with the automobile, electricity, and the radio. The economic impact of these technologies is well known, but their social impact is equally as important. The electric lightbulb extended the working day and allowed for a new scope of evening activities—night baseball, for one. Prior to electricity, most of the population went to bed a lot earlier than they do today, not too long after sundown. The railroad allowed for the transport of people, not just goods, across great expanses. Remote towns could prosper as long as they had a railway station and regular train stops. Heaven help the town if the railroad decided to discontinue service. The car was the impetus for the development of the suburbs after World War II—the relative isolation of the housewife, the commuting dad, strip malls, fast food, drive-in movies, and the trucking industry.

These were not easy or instantaneous transitions. Often the pace of progress was halting at first, then overly euphoric, and then overly pessimistic, as the pendulum of human behavior and market psychology swung from one extreme to the other. The fact remained, however, that these technological breakthroughs had a profound effect on many aspects of life: the costs of production, transportation, and communication; productivity growth; the location of the population; the mass culture; and the political scene.

I believe that today we are in the early days of another upwave in the innovation cycle. This time, the breakthrough technologies are the Internet and the application of digital technology to the life sciences. We might also include fuel-cell technology and nanotechnology as secondary, but still significant, scientific developments. This period, as before, is fraught with risk and disappointment. Change is always difficult as many leaders in business and politics attempt to protect the status quo, fearful of change and innovation. Imagine how the stagecoach operators felt when the railroad came or how the kerosene and coal manufacturers reacted to the advent of electricity.

The dot-com crash should not be seen as the end of the upwave. Quite the contrary. While it was wrong to expect too much of the dot-coms, it is equally wrong to expect too little. We are in the early days of an upwave in the "Long Cycle." This is a once-in-a-lifetime cycle. It occurs every fifty or sixty years. In upwaves, expansions are long and strong and recessions are short and mild. Gyrations can be great, but the trend is up. This upwave, I believe, will last at least another ten to fifteen years, and maybe longer.

THE LONG CYCLE

Living in a world of tremendous volatility and change, we inevitably get caught up in the day-to-day orbit of our lives, our businesses, our careers, and our investments. But I believe it is important to look at the economy from a longer-term perspective, as well. Too much of my time is spent focusing on the very short-term movements in financial markets and economic indicators. And while monitoring the business cycle is what I get paid to do, it is useful and appropriate to put this cycle in an historical framework. I find it quite enlightening to think of the world in the context of the long wave—a decades-long cycle around which the shorter-term business expansions and contractions revolve.

The long wave was first spotted by Russian economist Nikolai Kondratieff in the 1920s and is sometimes called the Kondratieff wave.[1] It is a controversial concept; many quibble endlessly about how it should be measured. It is very difficult (virtually impossible) to pinpoint the exact dates of peaks and troughs in the long-term economic cycle. I don't think this really matters. The fundamental usefulness of the construct—the model—remains. The concept of a long wave has moved more into mainstream thinking in recent years with the endorsement of Alan Greenspan.

Greenspan and I have both accepted the concept of the long wave without necessarily attempting to map the precise dates of the cycle. There are significant statistical problems in doing so. Data are needed back to the end of the eighteenth century, well before government statistics agencies were set up to collect it. But nevertheless, those who have attempted to do the analysis conclude that a discernible long cycle in economic activity can be mapped out (Figure 8.1).

Kondratieff caused such an uproar with his cycle research in post-Revolution Russia that he was arrested and sent to Siberia. His work angered the Bolsheviks because it showed that downturns in capitalist economies were self-correcting. Kondratieff's work fell on a far more receptive audience in the United States. Joseph Schumpeter, with his now-famous theories of creative destruction, followed in the Russian's footsteps. Schumpeter is seen as the first New Economy thinker because of his interest in technological advance and its implications for economic growth. Continuing the research today is, among others, Stanford economist Paul Romer. As I discussed in Chapter 1, Romer analyzes the

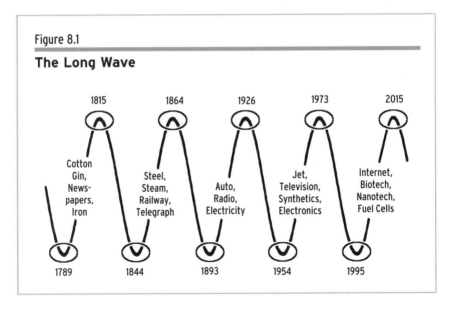

Figure 8.1

The Long Wave

importance of knowledge and ideas in the growth process, seeing these as intrinsic to growth, rather than as exogenous forces.[2]

Breakthrough Technology

It was not the computer, per se, that triggered the current upwave. We have had computers on our desks for twenty years. It was the networking of computers in a global information highway that spurred the forces of change, reducing the costs of communication to nearly zero and triggering a flurry of productivity-enhancing activities. The biotech revolution has barely begun. As I discussed in Chapter 4, we are on the precipice of major breakthroughs in medical science, and this combined with the developments in the nanotech world and fuel-cell research will continue to contribute to head-spinning change for the next decade or more.

In all upwaves, the new inventions or discoveries trigger an enormous disinflationary process (Figure 8.2). Businesses reorganize, costs decline, efficiency rises. The quality and variety of products increase. These factors combine to raise real wages and the standard of living. Family living standards rise even more than the economic numbers can capture, because the improved quality, service, and selection often cannot be readily measured. Prices fall, particularly for the new products and services that are introduced. The economic pie gets bigger, and though there continue to be disparities, for the most part, everyone is better off. Today there is the so-called digital divide— determined more by "know and know-nots" rather than "have and have-nots"—but the jobless rate fell throughout the 1990s across the knowledge spectrum. As we have seen, the biggest improvements were for the unskilled and untrained—the hard-core unemployed—who were finally lured into the job market by the booming economy and the desperate need for workers.

Upwaves are periods of considerable dislocation, often accompanied by intermittent periods of excessive optimism and pessimism. While jubilation may run hot and cold, the constant churning that innovation causes can be very painful. New must replace old, and new-new replaces new. The product life cycle can be very short. Many of the winning tech companies in the early 1980s are long gone—Commodore, Wang, Control

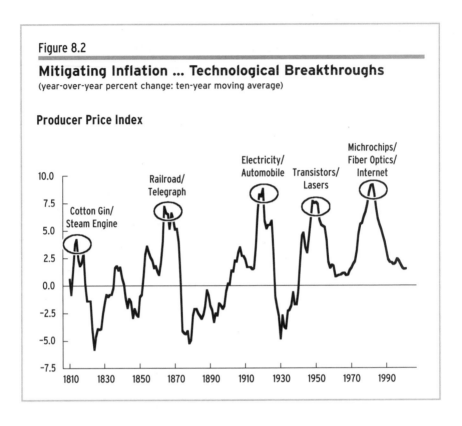

Figure 8.2

Mitigating Inflation ... Technological Breakthroughs
(year-over-year percent change: ten-year moving average)

Producer Price Index

Data. IBM was quick enough to move from the mainframe to PC and then on to network and Internet servicing. A less-nimble company would have long ago joined the ranks of Wang. Those people or regions that cannot or choose not to adapt are left embittered and often disadvantaged. It is not easy to ride an upwave, but it can be very rewarding.

Wars Also Play a Role in the Long Cycle

Military engagements have been instrumental in the timing of the long wave cycles. Defense establishments—in the U.S., Europe, Israel, and elsewhere—have led much of the advanced tech research in the world. Wars themselves are distracting, expensive, destructive, and inflationary. However, they also trigger substantial innovation. There is nothing like an armed conflict or a rabid enemy to get the scientific juices flowing, even if for the purpose of mass destruction. What we find is that once the war ends, the military innovations often can be put to lucrative and beneficial peacetime use. We saw this with the computer, radar, the airplane, anesthesia, the Internet—just to name a few. Even atomic research has found its civilian uses.

Turning points in the long cycle have often been associated with major military encounters. Some long-wave theorists attach importance to the popularity of the military engagement: the end of a popular war triggers an upwave, while the end of an unpopular war marks the beginning of a downwave. While this is highly controversial and may be putting too fine a point on the theory, for the United States, something like it can be seen in the long-cycle pattern (Figure 8.3).

Consider the coincidence of cycles with wars in American history. The end of the Revolutionary War—certainly a popular war in the Colonies—ushered in the era of the cotton gin, the threshing machine, and iron working. Transportation routes such as canals and roadways were the big infrastructure projects. The upwave ended with the relatively unpopular War of 1812.

The next upwave began around the time of the Mexican War and lasted for roughly twenty years, eclipsed by the devastation of the Civil

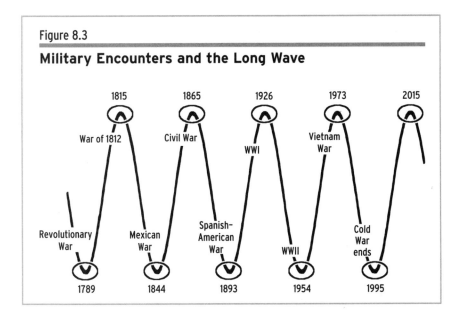

Figure 8.3

Military Encounters and the Long Wave

War. This was the period of the railroad, the steam engine, the telegraph, and the first telephones. The building of the American railroad infrastructure led to booming labor markets. Transportation costs plunged as the railway and steam ships allowed for the transport of goods across former regional boundaries. Cities and towns flourished along the routes. The prices of goods, most notably food, fell sharply as agricultural products were whisked from the Midwest farms to the East Coast cities. The prices of all household goods declined as wage rates rose. Real family purchasing power increased sharply. Productivity growth surged and communication capability rose dramatically with the telegraph.

This communication breakthrough, invented in the 1830s, increased the flow of information through the economy. Tom Standage, a journalist with the *Economist* magazine, has called the telegraph "the Victorian Internet."[3] However, the telegraph remained too expensive for the average consumer, so the transformation of communication on a broadly based scale awaited the telephone and later the Internet. The steam age moved production from the household to the factory; the railroad allowed for the development of mass markets and all of the economies of scale that they entailed.

The next major upwave followed the end of the Spanish-American War in 1898 and lasted until well after World War I. This was the age of electricity, the radio, and the automobile—a spectacular period of economic transformation. With electricity, the assembly line became possible. It took years for the full effect of the productivity gains to be measured, as businesses needed to literally rebuild their operations to take full advantage of the new technology, a phenomenon that has been well documented in the computer age as well. New technologies often initially create more problems and inefficiencies than they solve. This is what economist Robert Solow (cited earlier) was referring to when he said that the computer boom was evident everywhere but the productivity statistics.

Electricity markedly enhanced living standards in countless ways, reducing communication costs, transforming the production process, and removing the constraints of the rising and setting of the sun. Automobiles, radio, the first aircraft, the first office machines, photography, and the development of plastics all contributed to the improvement in living standards during this period. Automobile sales doubled in the 1920s, bringing with them similar gains in the demand for steel, glass, rubber, and highways.

But the population's move to the suburbs awaited the next upwave at the end of World War II. A swell of soldiers returned home to marry and start families. The Baby Boom began. The pent-up appetite for consumer products was ravenous. The technologies of the earlier upwave were adopted on a mass-market scale. Electricity touched off a spectacular wave of innovation in the home, from washing machines to vacuum cleaners. The liberation from the tedium of repetitive household chores had a lasting effect on the role of women and society at large. Adding to these innovations were the first computers, transistors, jets, rockets, lasers, and television. The leading industries were consumer durable good manufacturers, such as the automakers and electronics companies, as well as the producers of synthetic materials and petrochemicals. This was the Industrial Age—the age of chemistry. There was an enormous build-up of infrastructure: highways, airports, schools, libraries, television networks, and airlines.

The era ended with the end of the very unpopular Vietnam War in 1975, not long after the first OPEC energy crisis and the resultant recession. What followed was a period of stock market decline, economic stagnation, and inflation—the downwave. While the stock market finally began to recover in 1982, with the end of the period of dramatic monetary tightening, I do not date the next upwave—the current one—until well after the end of the Cold War in 1989. The Gulf War in 1990-91 touched off a moderate recession. The rebound was initially halting, as we have seen. I date the beginning of the current upwave at 1995. By then, the Internet was a force on the American scene; within two years a critical mass of households—roughly one-third—had adopted the new technology for home use.

WILD GYRATIONS

There are those who fear that the very acceleration in the speed of change will short-circuit the current upwave. Never before has a new technology been adopted as rapidly as the Internet. Does that mean that the Internet upwave may only have lasted five years, culminating in the

Nasdaq crash of 2000? I believe not. While we have seen a major meltdown in the value of TMT stocks, the underlying forces of expansion remain extremely positive. The complementary development of the mobile Net and limitless bandwidth will have a profound further effect on IT development, as I discussed in Chapter 3. The applications in the future will be enormously exciting, thanks to the development of voice-recognition technology and video streaming. As yet, less than 10 percent of the world's population is online; even in the rich world, the figure is only just over 35 percent. While the U.S., Canada, Australia, and the Scandinavian countries are ahead of the pack, the opportunities for global growth of TMT businesses in these countries are immense.

But the news won't be all positive, as we have so painfully seen. In every upwave there are excesses—speculative bubbles—that often burst with surprising ferocity. We lived through that in 2000–2001. History has shown us that technology-driven downturns can be traumatic, particularly when the new technology has captured the imagination of the population.

Take, for example, the railroads, which dominated the economy in the second half of the 1800s, just as IT does today. During this period, whenever railroad expansion took a breather, the economy and the markets were pummeled. A slowdown in railroad construction helped trigger the panic of 1873, an economic contraction that lasted until 1879. The failure of railroads, such as Philadelphia & Reading Railroad Co. in 1896, and the resulting financial panic helped cause the near-depression and widespread layoffs of the 1890s. We marked this tumultuous period as one of a downwave, but I do not believe that the dot-com sell-off marked the beginning of a downwave this cycle. Too much is yet to happen with the Net and other burgeoning technologies. An information technology revolution remains in place, with bullish implications for long-run productivity and growth. The U.S. is in a long wave upturn that began in the mid-1990s and still has many years to run. Nevertheless, technology is a cyclical sector and there was substantial overinvestment in IT during the boom years—especially in 1999 and the first half of 2000. It is likely, therefore, that IT investment growth will contract in 2001 for the first time since 1991, as the excess capacity is worked off.

In a similar vein to the railroads in the nineteenth century, the expansion of the auto industry was a major thrust for the boom in the early twentieth century. Between 1893 and 1914, there were 1.7 million automobiles registered in the United States, but by 1920 there were more than 8 million and by 1929, there were in excess of 23 million cars. Auto demand peaked in 1929 because the Fed raised interest rates and because the car-buying needs of Americans were temporarily sated after a decade-long splurge. At first, the rest of the economy seemed to hang in. But without the impetus from the car industry, the boom could not continue. The result was the October 1929 crash and ensuing downturn, which hit the automakers and their suppliers first and hardest. It wasn't until the Fed started easing monetary policy years later that the auto industry began to recover.

Fortunately, the Fed is a lot more savvy today and understands the importance of the technology sector for the future well-being of the economy. When the tech stocks plunged in 2000 and the economy weakened sharply, the Fed responded quickly.

The past offers some good news for the present. Despite the viciousness of the railroad and auto-led downturns during earlier downwaves, the industries came back stronger than ever. The 1890s slump was followed by a resumption of railroad expansion. From 1895 to 1915, the number of passenger miles traveled by rail nearly tripled as Americans took advantage of fast, cheap transport. In addition, cheap shipping costs contributed to the rapid productivity growth of the early twentieth century.

Moreover, like today, the railroad and automobile booms led to the entrance of too many competitors, many of which went under when the economy slowed. Between 1900 and 1910, a whopping 485 automobile companies entered the industry only to ultimately disappear, just as today hundreds of dot-com companies have shut down or been swallowed up by the giants in the sector. These shakeouts are healthy. They did not damage the long-term soundness of the auto industry. The collapse of auto sales in the early 1930s brought substantial consolidation, as well-known carmakers such as Pierce-Arrow, Auburn, and Franklin went under or were greatly weakened. But overall, the auto industry emerged from the Great Depression with its position at the core of the economy more solid than ever. Sales rebounded in 1936 and 1937, and big automakers became the major powerhouses of the economy, a role they maintained well into the postwar era. While we will not see the same concentration in the B2C world as in autos, consolidation is likely in the optical network manufacturers and the telecoms.

The implication for today is clear. No matter how long the tech slowdown lasts and how weak tech stocks become, we will have an information-led economy. This does not mean, however, that the 2000–2001 tech slowdown did not do damage. It did, in terms of the overall economic expansion and certainly in terms of the trillions of dollars of wealth that were obliterated. But there is more to this upwave than just the Internet, and the Net itself will continue to expand. With biotech, nanotech, and fuel-cell technology, this could be a much more powerful upwave than some of its predecessors. Moreover, as history has shown, the tech sector will once again emerge as a leading propellant of growth.

THE NEW ECONOMY: DOWN BUT NOT OUT

The Old Economy is morphing into the New in every sphere. Using the Internet for B2B activities, as we have seen, Old Economy companies are streamlining and dramatically enhancing productivity. In today's world, information from global positioning satellites is used to navigate trucks on the road and robotic arms swing auto parts into place on the assembly line. New breakthroughs in digital technology and the life sciences are finding their way to traditional resource industries. Seismic soundings have dramatically increased the success of wildcat oil drilling.[4]

The Fed understands how important it is that advances in technology and productivity gains continue unabated. The same message was voiced in the Clinton Administration's last Economic Report of the President. It showed that productivity gains had spread far beyond the IT sector into all areas of the economy. The gains in productivity growth since 1995— the true hallmark of the New Economy—are structural, not just the short-term result of an upturn in the business cycle. The President's Council of Economic Advisors estimated that "a structural acceleration of productivity of greater than 1 percentage point has taken place."[5] A combination of investment in information technologies, improving education and skills of the workforce, and enhancements in the way capital and labor are used throughout the economy are central to the augmented performance.

Better business practices across sectors have been evident. The report shows that, for example, improvements in distribution and supply chain management led to an acceleration in productivity in wholesale and retail trade. Gains emanating from heavy IT investments buoyed performance in the financial and business services sector. Productivity gains were also evident in sectors as diverse as trucking and health care.

DOT-COMS: FROM DEIFIED TO DEMONIZED

Too much euphoria on the upside has now given way to too much pessimism on the downside. It was wrong to hold the dot-coms in such esteem in 1999, but it is equally wrong to find them at such fault in 2001. These Internet companies disrupted tradition and spurred established companies to create new business strategies and models. Now traditional companies of all sizes are understanding and exploiting business on the Net. Many of these firms lost significant market share to the dot-coms, at least initially. But smart ones watched them attentively and adopted some of their innovative entrepreneurial practices.

Indeed, at the 2001 annual meetings of the American Economic Association, Stanford economics professor Robert E. Hall argued that the dot-com stock market boom was not an irrational bubble, but a rational assessment of the prospects for their future earnings, given the knowledge at the time.[6] Contesting the work of Robert Shiller (and others), cited earlier, Hall believes that stock prices move rationally with the expectation of future returns. In other words, the stock market operates on the principle of registering the properly discounted value of the future cash that shareholders expect to receive. Cash-flow growth is the key to understanding the movement in the market. Hall states that it is "illogical to condemn astronomical price-earnings ratios as plainly irrational without investigating the prospects for growth in future earnings."[7]

Hall joined the ranks of those who have highlighted the enormous value of intangibles for many of today's companies, especially for the technology users such as insurance companies, banks, and business-service firms. There is a strong association between the use of computers and software and the value of these intangibles imbedded in stock valuations. Companies that have a significant "body of technical and organizational know-how"—types of property Hall calls "e-capital"[8]—have the highest imbedded intangible-capital valuations. Industries with low levels of intangibles—and, therefore, rationally low price-earnings multiples—include utilities, oil and gas extraction, primary metals, and airlines.

Unlike Shiller, Hall sees the stock-market boom of the 1990s as eminently consistent with the rational evaluation by investors of future returns; indeed, often investors were too cautious in their forecasts. He used Microsoft as an example of a firm that had immense and rational value owing to knowledge and proprietary technological savvy. The growth rate of cash earned by such tech leaders and innovators has been phenomenal. According to Hall, "A dollar invested in Microsoft stock in 1990 resulted in a claim on \$1.38 in after-tax earnings in 2000 alone. Obviously the market in 1990 guessed absurdly low about Microsoft's cash-flow growth."[9]

Hall argues that the main reason why stocks of new Internet companies soared to wild valuations in the first instance was because investors initially believed that only the start-ups would be able to adjust nimbly enough to harness the productivity-enhancing powers of the Internet. Most investors and analysts thought that old-line companies would lack the creativity and imagination, not to mention adaptability, to take the lead online. When Old Economy companies surprised everyone by showing they could effectively compete with the dot-coms, investors realized their mistake, painfully. It became obvious, finally, that the benefits of IT breakthroughs were accruing to the big shots as well, not just to the brash new dot-com start-ups with untried and unorthodox—and most importantly, unprofitable—business models. Valuations suddenly appeared ridiculously high for the start-ups and their stocks plunged—helped along, to be sure, by their extraordinary cash-burn rates and the Fed-induced drying up of cheap capital. This along with the meltdown in the telecom stocks triggered a cyclical slowdown in the economy, which, as we have seen, spiraled throughout the tech sector and the stock market in general.

Smart traditional companies embraced the Net and digitized their business models and processes to leverage the Net in every aspect of their businesses faster than originally expected. They began to garner the benefits in terms of rising revenues relatively quickly. Their contribution to the revenue and job growth in the New Economy far exceeds that of the dot-coms.

The dot-com bubble may have burst, but the New Economy is far from dead. The New Economy was always about productivity gains and innovation, and it still is. Old Economy companies have embraced the Internet and enhanced their economic performance. Dot-coms are a relatively small part of the New Economy, never representing more than 9.6 percent of revenues, according to a recent study co-authored by Andrew Whinston, a professor at the University of Texas.[10] But the dot-coms have played an important role and will continue to do so.

In the foreword to this book, business strategist Don Tapscott makes a compelling argument that the dot-com fireworks distracted the attention of financial media and business schools from a much larger economic transformation that was precipitated by the Internet: the demise of the vertically integrated corporation. Vertically integrated companies perform a host of functions beyond their core competencies. Functions such as sales, marketing, service, design, and human resources have traditionally been performed in-house because the time, expense, hassle, and risk of partnering with other companies that specialized in such services outweighed the benefits.

With the Internet's arrival, this is no longer the case. Companies can focus on what they do best and partner with other companies to do the rest, using the Internet as the means to coordinate and collaborate their energies. Business webs that allow partners to provide different goods and services are developing throughout the economy. These include sites such as CharlesSchwab.com, LendingTree.com, Travelocity.com, and Siebel.com. Many projects are starting to be executed in much the same manner as a Hollywood movie is produced. The producer, director, screenwriters, actors, cinematographer, and stage hands come together, work intensely, produce a film, and then disband to collaborate with different people on the next film. The ability to identify, bring together, and orchestrate the energies of many disparate entities will distinguish the winners in tomorrow's economy.

DOT-COMS PROVIDED MANY LESSONS

Established businesses wouldn't have acted so quickly were it not for the competitive threat from the online firms. Consider Amazon.com—a truly revolutionary business model. It introduced consumers to a whole new way of enjoying convenience, selection, and price. It not only changed the book business—forcing, for example, Barnes & Noble, the largest bookseller in the U.S., to reexamine its own business model and set up its own dot-com—but it has also impacted retailing in general.

The Net has revamped B2B relationships, resulting in greater value, efficiency, cost reduction, and service. For example, General Electric's former CEO, Jack Welch, mandated an Internet strategy for each of the firm's many business units. The speed of response was accelerated by the threat of competition from dot-coms, at least in some sectors.

The pure-play Web companies accelerated decision-making, taking the concept of "quick and nimble" to new heights. Dell Computer, for example, took the lead with its customized, on-demand production of individual PCs. This approach enhanced consumer expectations about service in all sectors. In addition, the dot-coms altered the standards for boards of directors. Passive boards may have dominated the Old Economy, but in the dot-com world, boards are active and involved. Traditional businesses took notice.

Maybe most notably, the dot-coms changed the talent side of the equation. In the late 1990s, a whole host of successful business managers, MBA grads, and just plain folks left the Old world for the New. Many were burned and many returned, but one thing is certain—they will always remember the excitement of the New Economy entrepreneurial spirit and rapid innovation. The early success of the dot-coms caused a brain drain and labor shortage in the Old Economy, at least initially. Businesses suddenly became very aware of the issues surrounding how to attract, retain, and motivate talent. Established businesses reevaluated their personnel, incentive, and compensation policies. Flex-time, job sharing, training programs, and interesting, innovative incentive plans were introduced. Perks such as daycare, family care, concierge service, health clubs, massages, family counseling, and on-location medical services were offered by many large businesses to keep the talent they so desperately needed.

Investment banks, consulting firms, and professional-services firms were forced to adjust their compensation and profit-sharing systems as many of their ranks headed for the dot-coms and many of the top graduates of the leading professional schools opted for the entrepreneurial world. While the dot-com meltdown of 2000 and the subsequent economic slowdown dampened a good deal of the enthusiasm in 2001, the appeal of consulting and investment banking to the future crop of MBA graduates may well be diminished. Historically, these had been the hot areas, but increasingly, many ambitious young people have something else in mind. The Internet has captured their imagination. Start-ups are not uncommon today in dorm rooms and garages.

Many of the changes the Net companies created in the work environment were healthy and lasting. More casual dress codes and less hierarchical structures have tempered the often stilted and formal cultures of traditional big business. Key professionals today work in teams and on projects, rather than in the traditional pyramidal structures with fixed job specs. People make job choices based on their interest in the nature of the work and the opportunity for learning and growth on the job. Title and rank are no longer as important.

New Economy businesses realized the key to future success is in attracting and keeping the right people. Talented individuals invest their human capital for a piece of the action and for the knowledge it provides. Job-hopping is common. Gone are the days when people joined a firm upon graduation with the intention of staying for forty years.

Surviving dot-coms and new entrants to the Net will learn from the failures. The freedom to fail is a key ingredient in the success of the U.S. as the global technology leader. Older firms have been forced to be more adaptable as well. While the many early B2C dot-com models did not work, new ones will take their place. Internet commerce will blossom and ultimately flourish.

INTERNET GROWTH

Despite the slowdown in the economy and the crash in dot-com stocks, the Internet Economy continued to grow rapidly. The fourth semi-annual survey by the University of Texas Center for Research in Electronic Commerce, funded by Cisco Systems, showed continued strong growth in 2000.[11] They found that the Internet Economy generated an estimated $830 billion in revenue that year—representing a 58 percent increase over 1999 and a 156 percent gain over 1998. They divide the Net Economy companies into four groups: infrastructure, applications, intermediaries, and commerce. All posted enormous revenue growth in the first half of the year.

The infrastructure companies include the telecoms, Internet service providers, backbone carriers, network hardware and software firms, PC and server manufacturers, security vendors, and fiber-optics makers. This group—which includes names like Epoch, WorldCom, Corning, Juniper, and Hewlett-Packard—enjoyed just over 63 percent growth in revenues in the first half of 2000.

Growing at a 57 percent pace over the same period were the providers of Internet applications such as Web consulting, commerce and multimedia applications, development software, search-engine software, online training, and databases. Some of the companies in this sector are Microsoft, Adobe, Accenture, Oracle, SAP, and Organic. Topping even this stunning growth pace were Internet intermediaries such as online travel agents, brokerages, portal/content providers, ad brokers, advertisers, and content aggregators, with a 103 percent surge over the period. These are companies like Yahoo!, Charles Schwab, Commerce One, ZDNet, and DoubleClick.

Finally, we have the Internet commerce firms, which enjoyed 62 percent growth in the first half of 2000, despite the crash in their stock values. These are the e-tailers, manufacturers selling online, fee/ subscription-based companies, airlines selling tickets online, and Net entertainment. Among the names in this group are Target, Amazon.com, Southwest Airlines, Dell, and Road Runner Sports.

The stock market shakeout was even more pronounced in the second half of 2000, as the Internet Economy slowed along with the rest of the economy. Even so, the more subdued growth rate in the Internet Economy was still far from shabby. In addition, according to the report, the Internet Economy directly supported more than three million workers.[12]

EARLY DAYS YET IN THE INTERNET REVOLUTION

The Internet opportunity is largely ahead of us. In the next phase of the Net, literally billions of digital devices will be connected to an increasingly powerful, high-speed, broadband, multiformatted Web. A wide array of new applications and services will help companies leverage the Net to communicate and manage their relationships with customers and suppliers more effectively and efficiently. By 2003, virtually all but the smallest businesses will have a Web presence, and many of these will as well.

Mobile e-commerce is also growing rapidly. The proliferation of mobile Internet devices will be spectacular. The "voice Web" will contribute to this as telephone functions and voice services will become available online. Voice, data, and video are converging rapidly into a single Internet-based capability.

Bandwidth will continue to grow. George Gilder notes that the bandwidth on a single cable is already a thousand times greater than the average traffic on the entire Net three years ago. More information can be sent over a single cable in one second today than all the information that was sent over the entire Internet in one month in 1995.[13] This continued explosion in communication capacity will facilitate the development of B2C e-commerce as well as entertainment on the Web, where full-motion video, an e-juke box, and interactive games are already starting to become available. Other portals, such as interactive TVs, media-rich PCs, MP3 players, and game consoles, will leverage the entertainment content. Critical mass is a necessary condition for profitable growth of entertainment on the Web. Many suggest it will take roughly 18 million households with high-speed connections to create the mass needed for lift-off in this area. We aren't there yet. As of the end of 2000 in the U.S., only about 7.3 million households had high-speed connection, but that number is growing rapidly and is forecast to rise to over 20 million by 2003.[14]

B2C SITES—NOT ALL FAILURES

The great Net shakeout does not imply that all dot-coms will fail. Many survivors have strong revenue streams and good prospects. The leading online retailers are, by any measure, big, successful companies. The three bellwether stocks that carry the standard for the B2C world—Amazon.com (a book, music, and more retailer), Yahoo! (a portal), and eBay (an auction site)—have become remarkable businesses. Despite the depressed advertising market in 2000–2001, Yahoo! still had revenues of more than $1 billion annually and operating margins of over 30 percent. The other dot-com bellwether, eBay, is also profitable and growing by more than 90 percent per year. Amazon.com restructured its business in early 2001, slashing payrolls and closing a warehouse and a call center in an effort to assure operating profits in the following year. All three e-businesses have expanded outside the U.S., dominating nearly every market they invaded. For example, with eBay's acquisition of iBazar—the French auction site—eBay became the undisputed online-auction victor in Europe. Yahoo! has local sites throughout Europe, Asia, and South America. Moreover, all three are already among the world's best-known brands.

Amazon.com has proved that an e-tailer can, in at least certain categories, beat the bricks-and-mortar competition. Shoppers love the virtually unlimited selection of books, music, and videos—complete with ratings and reviews—and its fast-growing electronics business turns around its inventory two to three times faster than offline competitors. Yahoo! invented the portal and used the Net to create a media behemoth that originates practically no content of its own. It has evolved from a simple directory to a media and commerce giant that has become a Web leader in everything from financial information to personal ads. eBay has proven that the Web is a terrific means to create an efficient market where none previously existed.

Consider how eBay compares to, for example, Sotheby's. eBay is solely an intermediary—it has no inventories and does not direct transactions. It simply provides the unattended software on a Web server that allows a seller to conduct an auction, receive payment, and ship the merchandise. No one at eBay is directly involved in the process. For what is essentially a mating service, bearing zero marginal cost to the company, eBay receives between 7 and 18 percent of the sale price. Its capacity to conduct auctions is nearly unlimited.

The model for Sotheby's is very different and far less efficient. Trained auctioneers and other personnel must assess, store, and handle the merchandise. Showroom space is limited, as is the number of auctions that can be conducted at any one time. Inventories are expensive to insure and the number of people who participate in the auction is limited. For all but the most expensive goods—and possibly even for them—the eBay site, which attracts a huge audience, is preferable for the seller; and it is the seller who chooses the locale and pays the fees. Network effects are strong. As eBay grew, more people wanted to use the site, encouraging further growth. This process allowed eBay to beat any fledgling competitors.

Without doubt, even the strongest of Internet players have had their problems and may find that they need a bricks-and-mortar connection to excel in the future. As the sector matures, its leadership may consist of fewer pure-play firms. For example, Yahoo! could well benefit from a traditional content producer, particularly as AOL has merged with Time Warner.

THE DOT-COM MODEL—PROFITS ARE ESSENTIAL

Other dot-coms are improving their financial performance, indicating they are learning as the Net evolves. However, many are still struggling. They are not just facing off against each other anymore, they are competing against established businesses and traditional business models. The struggle to turn thin gross margins—the raw profit before paying salaries, advertising, warehousing, handling, and other overhead costs—into bottom-line profits is daunting for many. But the true power of the Net will not be realized until it is profitable. Productivity growth must be translated into bottom-line earnings. The potency of the technology is unassailable, but profits—or the promise of them—is vital. There is no future in losing money and making it up in volume unless increased volume really does reduce costs.

The industry is in a period of dramatic soul-searching agitation. Yahoo!, for example, began charging companies that list products on its online auction site. Amazon.com and Bluefly—an online seller of designer clothing—have raised prices and shipping fees. Barnes & Noble is selling downloadable books on its website and offering big royalties to lure authors.

Bertelsmann AG, the German media powerhouse, broke with the rest of the music industry to cut a deal with Napster, instead of suing it like so many of the other giants in the music industry. The trick was for Napster—with Bertelsmann—to come up with a way to distribute music online without violating copyright laws. Napster announced in early 2001 that it would be charging a monthly subscription fee to reimburse royalties to recording companies—a significant shift from its free song-swapping beginnings. Napster lost an appeal to overturn a lower court ruling that it must stop offering music under copyright, so it stayed alive by screening the file names that passed through its computers, blocking the exchange of pirated tunes. However, its users have delayed this effort simply by using aliases for band names. Meanwhile, Napster and many other companies, including the record labels, have been scrambling to create a digital rights management system that would be convenient and allow payment. If the music industry pushes Napster too hard, its 50 million clients will go underground, using copycat programs, technology, and sites. Some alternatives are decentralized, unlike Napster, so they couldn't be shut down with a single power switch, making court orders harder to enforce. This fact may buy Napster time to "legitimize" itself in the eyes of Recording Industry Association of America.

Companies like Bertelsmann recognize that the old business model is no longer viable. It is working hard to develop an innovative new one. But this isn't so easy. As many unprofitable dot-coms have found, people underestimate how long it takes to come up with a new business model that works—for the consumer and for the shareholder.

Some Budding Attempts

Consider, for example, one of the Net's better-known brands, Priceline.com, which made news in late 2000 when one of its highly publicized lures from the Old Economy, Heidi Miller, former CFO of Citigroup, fled along with other key executives after only a brief stint. Priceline's "name-your-own-price" or "demand collection" system is one of the pioneering ideas in e-commerce. Yet the company has lost millions of dollars and its stock sank from a high of nearly $96.00 on March 13,

2000, to a low of $1.31 at year-end. Its core business has been selling airline tickets, but it moved beyond that with little success, as the name-your-own-price system seemed to put off consumers.

Most importantly, Priceline has trouble turning a profit even in the airline-ticket business, because its expenses are so high. Priceline buys tickets for unsold seats that the airlines heavily discount, then marks them up to earn a gross margin of 9 to 12 percent, compared to only 5 percent for offline travel agents. The rub is, the company has poured its gross margins from the airline tickets, as well as hundreds of millions of dollars raised in its stock offerings, into largely failed forays into other product lines. Also depleting cash were their expensive computer systems, high-priced software programmers, and glitzy ad campaigns featuring William Shatner.

Priceline could be profitable tomorrow if it cut costs and focused on the core airline-ticket business, but even there it is running into trouble. The airlines themselves want a piece of this action. Like so many other pure-play dot-coms, its success—at least in terms of revenues—has lured the traditional players into its markets. A number of the major airlines backed a competing start-up, Hotwire.com, that sells cheap airline seats. While Hotwire doesn't tell customers up front which flight they are taking or how many connections they will need to make to get to their destination, it does reveal the price of the ticket, rather than requiring the consumer to bid. Many consumers are put off by Priceline's complicated system that requires a user to guess what the ticket will go for, place a bid, and then check back later to see if the bid was accepted. Hotwire may well force Priceline to reduce its gross margins. Priceline is still struggling with its pricing model, assuming that the airlines will continue to give it first crack at cheap seats because it does not reveal the true price of the ticket, theoretically protecting them from having to match the price for other customers.

Priceline, like so many other dot-coms, is in a make-or-break period. Execs are reconsidering their pricing model and their nontravel businesses. Many analysts are skeptical, suggesting their best option may be to merge, be taken over, or go private. In the meantime, the cash is running out.

Other Examples—Bluefly and Webvan

Bluefly's blueprint was similar to so many other dot-coms: Undercut the prices of the traditional bricks-and-mortar businesses and make up the difference through the efficiencies and reduced-cost structure of a Web-only business. In Bluefly's case, the product is designer clothing; it calls itself "the outlet store in your home." For Bluefly, like so many other dot-coms, the efficiencies did not surface. Indeed, in many ways its costs are higher than for traditional retailers.

In this business, profit begins with markup, the amount retailers charge above what the goods cost them wholesale. Bluefly's strategy was to keep the markup low to attract shoppers and to assure they return. This certainly was good for the Bluefly customer, but hell for the Bluefly shareholder. Bluefly's gross margin was only 28 percent, well below the more typical 48 percent at Lands' End (which sells its own private-label merchandise at much bigger markups) and the 40 percent at Macy's parent, Federated Department Stores Inc. After expenses, Bluefly has been losing millions.

The thinking was that without the traditional costs of stores, clerks, and catalogs, the online outlets could thrive on very thin profit margins that would drive their unwired competitors out of business. But this business model did not work, not for eToys, Pets.com, Garden.com, Furniture.com—or for Bluefly. Taking orders directly from customers, whether by phone like the catalog companies or by the Net, requires expensive computer systems underpinned by customer-service representatives. It also means operating a warehouse or paying someone else to do it, keeping a ready supply of the most popular items, handling the items one by one, and shipping them at often great expense. The logistical problems can be enormous. And then there is the high rate of returned merchandise, much higher than that for store-based shopping where the items can be touched, seen, and tried on. This is why most catalog companies sell largely their own brands for which the markup can be much greater. Even traditional retailers such as the Gap or department stores like Sears, Saks, and Bloomingdale's intersperse their own brands throughout the product lines and pitch them heavily.

Bluefly and the similar dot-coms' only choices are to raise markups and to reduce costs. This means they have to get goods for less and/or charge more to the customer. Suppliers do discount larger volumes of goods, so scale is important. Fulfillment costs also fall as volumes rise. As well, return rates can be reduced with better information and descriptions on the site. But, even with all of this, analysts feel that Bluefly and the others must raise price to achieve the 38 percent gross profit margin some say is necessary for an online company to prosper. This is tough because shoppers do a lot of price comparisons online— more than in the stores—because it is so easy. This is one of the beauties of the Net, at least for customers. This enormous price pressure was the death knell for many dot-coms. But consumers also like the convenience, selection, and service of the Net, and they will be willing to pay for it. For example, when Bluefly raised its shipping charges in the summer of 2000, there was no customer backlash.

But, clearly, the challenges are real for the online retailers. Volumes are crucial, but growing sales require costly advertising and rock-bottom pricing. Repeat orders and big orders are the key. Online grocer Webvan has found it impossible, thus far, to turn a profit on the average order. The margins are just too thin and the costs of delivery and handling are too high for most items. That is why the traditional dairies and grocery stores gave up their home-delivery services years ago. Other than in high-income, densely populated areas like Manhattan, these services disappeared in the 1950s. (Remember the milkman?) Also, consumers have to plan ahead to order online. For items like groceries, many will want to continue to just pop into the store when the need arises.

There is demand, however, for the convenience and service of online (grocery) shopping. With the surge in busy two-income families with young children, it is a real lifesaver for many professional women. A frequent-buyer program might help to lock in customers. But the beneficiaries of this 1950s-style convenience are going to have to pay for it, and the Webvans of the Net are going to have to make sure their service, product quality, and selection are consistently up to snuff. These sites are in the process of widening their product offerings to include a growing array of high-margin products, such as cosmetics and nonprescription drugs. They could also act as the "last-mile delivery" operation for other Internet and traditional merchants—such as dry cleaning, photo finishing, and book and flower delivery.

For Webvan, time is running out. It was founded by Louis Borders, the reclusive mathematician who started the eponymous bookstore chain. He focused exclusively on building a complex inventory management and distribution system, which turned out not to be worth the money. With operations in ten cities, the company burned through $100 million in cash a quarter. It was also overzealous in its expansion plans, setting out to enter twenty-six cities long before it had proved that its model worked. Webvan abandoned these plans, but the jury is still out. The stock price fell 99 percent from its high. If Webvan fails, it will be by far the biggest financial disaster the Internet has yet seen.

Not the First Such Challenge: Radio Struggled Too

The Internet companies do not face this challenge without historical precedent. Radio in its early days provides an illuminating case study. It took years for a viable business model to develop in the radio industry, well after the public had fallen in love with the new medium. The model that finally emerged was not immediately obvious. Radio began as a way for one person to communicate with another. Radio Corporation of America (RCA), founded in 1919, charged a fee to sender or recipient and prospered by undercutting the price of telegrams.

This changed when radio broadcasting became popular in 1922. Radio was truly the first WWW, as the early RCA logos sported the buzzwords "World-Wide Wireless."[15] The transition to broadcasting shifted the viable business model in uncertain ways. Everyone knew the new medium was wildly popular, but no one knew how to make real money at it. At first, RCA made money selling radios. To encourage sales, RCA and other radio manufacturers, universities, and churches sponsored radio stations to provide content. But this was quickly seen to be unsuccessful.

Some suggested a tax on listeners. The British charged radio owners a fee to finance the BBC. One obvious solution was paid advertising, but in the early days these were tough to sell and quite controversial. Just as in many locales there still are no ads before the trailers at big-screen movie theaters, ads did not show up on radio until national networks were created. In the 1920s, ads were seen as an intrusion at best and unethical at worst.

While ads did work for radio and TV, it is unlikely that they will be the answer for Internet companies. Radio and TV are mass-market media, with pre-arranged, set programming. The Internet, instead, offers customized content. The business model must reflect that. Amazon.com is betting that if it gets big enough fast enough, it will be able to charge enough to make money. We will see.

Subscriptions and fees may be part of the answer. Satellite radio stations are charging low monthly fees. Many dot-coms are looking for new revenue streams. A natural one for some would be to offer their valuable software technology to other noncompeting companies for a price. Some are already moving in this direction. Yahoo! is building private-label corporate portals—intranets for a company's employees— for internal use and setting up conferences over the Net. The fees for this will not be chicken feed. Yahoo! is hoping to earn roughly $200 million for this service in 2001, accounting for a fifth of expected revenues that year. Yahoo! had little choice but to diversify given that online advertising fell sharply with the economic slowdown.

Others are following a similar strategy. eBay is hosting storefronts for small and medium-sized merchants, similar to Amazon.com's zShops. Amazon.com has taken this a step further, however, with its agreement with Toys "Я" Us, which pays to sell its products through Amazon.com's software and warehouses. Amazon.com is planning to do similar deals with other retailers whose products are too limited or seasonal to warrant their own stand-alone site. Quite a few smaller e-tailers—from Ask Jeeves to Respond.com—are also selling private-label versions of their sites to big companies in an effort to move away from excessive dependency on consumer shopping revenues.

The B2B space offers other possibilities similar to eBay's fee-for-service system. Commerce One, a leading B2B company, gets most of its revenue from selling and servicing its software. It plans, however, to charge for each transaction on its electronic marketplaces.

Certainly the enhanced service, selection, customization, and convenience of the Net is here to stay and worth paying for. Customers will become increasingly used to all that the Net has to offer and will refuse to go back to the long lines and low inventories of bricks-only shopping, even as the traditional retailing experience improves in response. But shoppers will have to be willing to pay for this in some way. The Net participants will figure it out, but it will take time, and the shakeout in 2000–2001 was very much to be expected. The 1922 radio euphoria was followed by a meltdown. Of the forty-eight stations that were first in their states, twenty-seven went out of business by 1924. It took this kind of churning for the new business model to emerge.

THE FUTURE IS BRIGHT

As the Internet economy heads into full throttle and a more mature stage of expansion commences, the bio-economy is heading into its growth phase, when hot new industries appear and mind-spinning developments occur. During the next twenty years, organic biotech will intersect with inorganic infotech, materials science, and nanotechnologies. The pace of change will accelerate and the gains will be breathtaking.

We are in the early days of this upwave in the long cycle—the innovation cycle that has boosted productivity growth and increased living standards in astonishing ways—and the best is truly yet to come. Although these technological breakthroughs are not without their problems and challenges, the U.S. and the rest of the world will benefit from them. Many people, however, are frightened by them. We turn now to a look at globalization, the spread of capitalism around the world, and the leadership of the U.S. in the technology revolution.

Four

Globalization

9

The Synchronized Global Economy

The weakness in the U.S. economy inevitably impacted the rest of the world. If proof were needed that the global economy was more synchronous than ever before, the economic slowdown of 2000–2001 was Exhibit A. Just as the U.S. expansion over the 1990s led the rest of the world upward, the slowdown beginning in late 2000 ultimately spread as well. Similarly, stock markets are increasingly synchronized. The dominant players in each country's equity markets are generally multinational corporations, listed on many of the major exchanges. Capital flows freely across borders and information is readily available worldwide. In essence, there is increasingly a global stock market. Companies in the same sectors move similarly around the world. Diversification can be better achieved through investments in different sectors, rather than different countries. During the stock market rout of 2000 and early 2001, TMT stocks, for example, plummeted not just in the U.S., but in bourses all over the world. Earnings warnings for Nokia, for example, negatively impacted Ericsson and Motorola as well.

STOCK MARKETS MOVE IN CONCERT

After surging in late 1999, European stock markets turned in March 2000, congruent with the Nasdaq slide. In the five months from mid-October 1999 to early March 2000, the Dow Jones Stoxx pan-European index jumped 37 percent. Technology and media stocks led the way with a 150 percent surge, while telecom shares more than doubled. The turning point in Europe could well have been the U.K. auction for the third-generation (3G) wireless spectrum, which began March 6. By the time it ended one month later, the British government had dislodged $34 billion from the European telecom industry for just five licenses in one country. The infrastructure was going to cost many billions more to build, and the German, French, and Italian auctions were still to come. Ultimately Germany's auction took a similar haul, while it was "more reasonable" in France and Italy.

In Europe, where cell phones are more common than PCs, the kind of seed money the yet-to-be-proven 3G wireless service would require could not be ignored. As it finally hit home, telecom stocks plunged, followed quickly by media and technology stocks. For U.S. investors, the declines were inflated by the falling euro. While the broader market indexes in Europe declined in line with the S&P 500—far less than the Nasdaq—the TMT stocks, the group that many still hold as the bellwether for Europe's future growth, fell 40 to 50 percent and more from their highs. Market psychology was badly damaged. The Internet's power to transform businesses is real, and the cell phone is the best way to reach most Europeans. But in the near future, businesses in those sectors will have considerably more difficulty getting the capital they need.

Asia's stock markets were pummeled as well. In Japan, for example, the Nikkei index declined 27 percent in local terms in 2000, and 35 percent in U.S. dollars. The hands-down worst market in Asia was the Kosdaq venture index—Korea's equivalent to the Nasdaq—which was down a gut-wrenching 82 percent in U.S. dollars. In Taiwan, the Taiex fell 47 percent; Singapore's STI was off 25 percent; Thailand's SET plunged 52 percent; and the list goes on.

Asia's bellwether Internet stocks—Softbank, Hikari Tsushin, and Pacific Century CyberWorks, which made history when it bought Hong

Kong Telecom from Cable & Wireless—all slumped. As worries mounted that slowing PC sales would result in inventory buildups, chip stocks slid, including Samsung, Taiwan Semiconductor Manufacturing, Fujitsu, and Hitachi. As the appetite for risk waned, multiples shriveled on Indian software stocks. The wireless darlings also fell, including China Mobile and Japan's NTT DoCoMo, which in late 2000 unveiled plans for a stock offering to help finance its acquisition of a stake in AT&T Wireless.

The strongest stock market in the G-7 in 2000 was the Canadian TSE, supported by the oil and gas stocks and a strong financial services performance. Yet it too was battered badly by the tech meltdown. At one point during the year it had been up more than 35 percent—boosted by technology, especially its bellwether, Nortel, as well as the energy sector. The index was crushed in the final third of the year. It posted its worse single-day loss in history in late October when Nortel reported disappointing revenue forecasts. The TSE ended the year up 6 percent in Canadian dollars and 2 percent in U.S. dollar terms, but it was pummeled once again by Nortel in the first quarter of 2001 as the company admitted that earnings prospects were worsening with the global capital-spending slowdown.

Just as the stock markets everywhere fell in concert, they also bounced together in the spring of 2001. Equity markets worldwide are connected at the hip, reflecting the interconnectedness of national economies. Sectors behave similarly around the world. Increasingly, equity analysts in each country must follow sectors on a global basis, mirroring the globalization of the economy. The relevant competitors in each sector are headquartered in different countries and what happens to one affects the others.

In addition, the home marketplace and economic backdrop is often not the only, or even the primary, determinant of earnings. For example, an investment in Nokia is not a play on the Finnish economy just as Nortel is not a play on the Canadian dollar. These businesses, and a whole host of others, are multinational companies with most of their activity outside the home market. As economies everywhere move increasingly in congruity, greater stability in a portfolio could be achieved by investing in different sectors across country lines (for example, oil and gas stocks along with technology) than by owning, for example, the Nikkei as an offset to the Nasdaq.

The inventory cycle is also global. Multinational corporations, operating around the world, dominate a rapidly increasing proportion of the U.S. economy and stock market. The average company in the Dow now derives about 40 percent of its revenue from outside the U.S., up from 35 percent in 1988. This makes U.S. business more dependent than ever before on economic conditions elsewhere. In 1999, companies such as Microsoft, Intel, and Procter & Gamble warned that their earnings were softening as a result of waning sales overseas and the depreciation of non-U.S. currencies. Europe looms largest for U.S. multinationals, as it represented just under half of all global affiliate income in 1999. That is why the decline in the euro was so negative for the earnings of companies such as Coca-Cola, Minnesota Mining & Manufacturing, Heinz, and Gillette, and why the euro's partial and temporary recovery in early 2001 was so positive. Conversely, foreign economies are impacted more than ever by developments in the U.S. and elsewhere. From an economic perspective, we are truly living in a global village.

SLOWDOWN SPREADS

The U.S. is at the center of the global economy, representing a record 30 percent of world output. U.S. companies now make up almost half of all global corporate profits, which represents a 15 percent increase from a decade ago.

Global interdependencies are widening. When U.S. auto sales slowed in 2000, automakers quickly reduced production in Detroit, Canada, Mexico, and much of the rest of the world. Auto giants in Europe had been far too optimistic in their forecast of global demand. In another sector, slowing American demand for IT weakened the nascent expansions in Asia, a region that accounts for nearly 50 percent of the world's total IT exports. Surging U.S. demand explained about half of Asia's total economic growth in the first three quarters of 2000. Asia, therefore, inevitably felt the brunt of the cyclical slowdown in IT in the U.S. Export growth slowed dramatically in Korea, Taiwan, Singapore, and even China. Europe, on the other hand, sustained less damage from the IT downturn. Apart from mobile telephones, Europe is far less involved in the global IT production cycle than other regions.

Rising energy costs also contributed to the decelerated growth in Europe and Asia, dampening consumer discretionary spending. These commodities are priced in U.S. dollars, which were becoming increasingly more expensive for foreign purchasers until late 2000. (Even in the first half of 2001, the yen and euro were relatively weak.) This combined with the negative wealth effect from the stock market meltdowns spelled real trouble. Falling asset values exacerbated the already dismal situation for weak Japanese financial institutions, which had offset rising credit costs by realizing gains on equity portfolios. The U.S. slowdown clearly spun around the world.

U.S. DOLLAR HOLDS IN WELL

The U.S. dollar strengthened significantly during the long economic boom of the 1990s. The firm dollar played an important role in prolonging the expansion, even though it made U.S. exports less competitive. It reduced the cost of capital for American companies and attracted foreign capital inflows. Foreigners' willingness to pour money into dollar assets enabled the U.S. to maintain strong growth in capital spending. Huge foreign purchases of U.S. stocks and bonds provided direct support for those markets, supplying the funding needed for the enormous U.S. capital-spending boom.

Many feared that a tech slowdown centered in the U.S. would trigger an exodus of foreign money, driving down the dollar and putting pressure on the Fed to raise interest rates. The slowing economy and the uncertain outlook for Wall Street did undermine the appeal of dollar assets. Foreign investors had grown accustomed to a double play on their investments in the U.S.—appreciating currency and appreciating assets. The risk was that these investors might go home and take their money with them. The U.S. needs to borrow more than $1 billion a day to finance its current account deficit—the broadest measure of its trade imbalance (including the investment income deficit)—and this leaves the dollar very vulnerable to the changing whims of overseas investors.

The downward drift in the dollar in early 2001 was surprisingly muted. Foreign investors became more risk-averse and the dismal performance of the tech stocks in the first part of the year did not help.

But the U.S. was not alone in the stock market correction. Nor was it alone in the economic correction. The Japanese economy, having languished for more than a decade, weakened further. The Bank of Japan eased monetary policy, at least symbolically, but with interest rates already so low their ability to use the monetary levers was limited. Japanese fiscal stimulus had already run its course as well. Japan's fiscal deficit was enormous. With a federal-debt-to-GDP ratio approaching 150 percent—the highest in the G-7 and a record for any major industrialized country—the room for further pump priming was limited. Japan was disadvantaged domestically by its rapidly aging population. And when IT exports to the U.S. slowed, any hope of economic expansion—meager as it was—all but disappeared. For this reason, the dollar-yen exchange rate remained relatively strong.

The U.S. dollar did weaken moderately with respect to the euro in early 2001, but that did not constrain the Fed's ability to lower interest rates in the face of weakening economic activity. From the perspective of the U.S. economy, a depreciating dollar was a good thing because it gave American exports a competitive edge in a world of slowing economic growth. Unlike other central banks, the Fed does not conduct monetary policy on the basis of currency considerations. Instead, inflation and domestic growth, as well as financial-market stability, dominate its policy objectives. Moreover, as the Fed aggressively eased in 2001, most of the world's other central banks eventually followed along. The European Central Bank was a laggard, but finally it too succumbed to the pressure to ease.

The U.S. plays a unique role in the global financial system. It is the only superpower and it has the only reserve currency. It will remain a safe haven for the foreseeable future.

THE U.S. TRADE GAP—WHY THE WORLD NEEDS IT

Many market watchers and academics have argued for years that the Achilles heel of the U.S. economy is its looming trade deficit and growing dependence on foreign capital inflow. With U.S. consumers and businesses continuing to soak up imported goods and capital, many have wondered at what point the trade deficit would get too wide, stalling the great U.S. economic engine. They argued that the U.S. was too reliant on foreign capital to fund its business- and consumer-spending binge. They predicted the dollar would finally plummet as foreign investors took their money home, causing the stock and bond markets to tailspin and the economy to tank.

The Case for Concern

In 2000, the current account deficit surpassed 4.5 percent of GDP, its highest level in history. The ratio continued to rise further in 2001. This is by far the largest current account deficit in the G-7 (Figure 9.1).

A trade deficit means that a country imports more than it exports and borrows from abroad to cover the difference. The problem is that at some point, foreigners may wonder whether the borrower is capable of paying

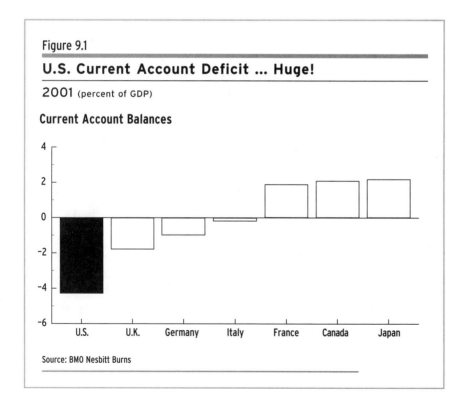

Figure 9.1

U.S. Current Account Deficit ... Huge!

2001 (percent of GDP)

Current Account Balances

Source: BMO Nesbitt Burns

them back. And when foreigners get worried enough, they may decide it is time to pull the plug. For countries other than the U.S., history tells us that, on average, foreigners generally reach their tolerance limit at a deficit ratio of just over 4 percent of GDP—which the U.S. surpassed in the fourth quarter of 1999. The fear is that confidence in the U.S. will suddenly collapse. At the very least, capital flows could dry up.

No Crisis in Sight

Instead, the dollar continued strong through most of 2000, outpacing all the world's major currencies, and U.S. long-term interest rates fell sharply. Through the end of 2000, there was no sign that America had exceeded its credit limit with other countries, even though the stock market had sold off. After all, stocks fell everywhere. But the risks are there. Foreign ownership of U.S. stocks is proportionately far smaller than its ownership of bonds, especially government bonds. But the government bond market is rapidly shrinking with the paydown of debt. It is highly unlikely, therefore, that foreigners would, en masse, dump U.S. Treasuries when there are so few—virtually no—substitutes. Quite the contrary—the global demand continues to grow faster than the supply. As of 2000, foreigners owned 11 percent of American stocks; but they held a whopping 44 percent of the outstanding volume of government bonds[1] and 22 percent of corporate bonds outstanding. Their direct investment in the U.S.—investment in businesses and real estate— was double their U.S. equity holdings.

It is always possible that something unexpected could put the currency in serious jeopardy. Once the process begins, the herd instinct could cause it to snowball. The Cassandras would tell us that as the dollar falls, import prices in the U.S. would rise, increasing inflation and causing the Fed to raise interest rates. As the economy slowed and earnings momentum turned down, stocks would sell off sharply, further escalating the dollar decline. This is the stuff of which nightmares are made, especially Federal Reserve nightmares.

Let's Look at the Facts

Things are not nearly as bleak as the doomsayers would suggest. The widening trade deficit in recent years was a reflection of strength, not weakness. The U.S. economy was the strongest in the world; not surprisingly, therefore, U.S. demand for foreign products outpaced foreign demand for American goods. The U.S., however, has a surplus in the service account that is expected to widen meaningfully over the next decade. Some predict it could ultimately surpass the deficit in goods. The U.S. dominates the trade in services. Worldwide, cross-border sales of services were around $1.3 trillion in late 2000, most of which was booked by U.S. providers. Services sold by the number-two exporter, Britain, totaled only $100 billion.

Moreover, service exports are probably woefully understated in the U.S. accounts. A proliferation of free-trade agreements around the world has blurred the boundaries between countries and made service exports that much more difficult to measure. Consider packaged software as an example. Its delivery can be via CD-ROM in a box, loaded onto a computer by the manufacturer, or downloaded via the Internet. While overseas sales of software by U.S. companies topped $13 billion as long ago as 1995, the most recent data in the U.S. balance of payments show software exports of a mere $3 billion. Clearly, accounting errors abound.

THE U.S. TRADE DEFICIT HAS SPURRED GLOBAL GROWTH

The deterioration in the U.S. trade position helped the Fed maintain a low level of inflation. Imports were a key safety valve that diverted some of the excessively strong growth in domestic demand to foreign producers. The 1998–99 global slowdown following the Asian crisis took some pressure off productive capacity constraints in the U.S. What's more, the States became a welcome market for the products of the crisis-threatened economies, allowing them to rebound more quickly. For most of the past quarter-century, in fact, the U.S. economy absorbed the world's surplus products and capital. Import prices fell as the U.S. dollar strengthened, increasing domestic competition and reducing the pricing power of

American companies. This meant that the ensuing Fed tightening would be more muted and generalized inflation pressures would remain at bay.

The massive inflow of foreign capital to the U.S. stock market reflected the higher rates of return that could be earned on these investments relative to most anywhere in the world. Particularly from 1995 to 1999, U.S. business investment in technology surged, owing to a sharp rise in its rate of return. Over the same period, household savings flows slowed. Foreign capital inflows (and a burgeoning U.S. government surplus) were necessary to finance the investment spending boom. It was this very boom that triggered the surge in domestic productivity growth, lengthening the expansion, enhancing corporate profitability, and reducing inflation. Living standards rose sharply as a result. The earnings generated in foreign coffers by the booming U.S. stock market and rising currency helped them as well. It was a win-win situation.

THE DEFICIT ISN'T AS BAD AS IT SEEMS

The trade deficit is not the problem that people make it out to be. For one thing, U.S. export shipments have been rising; they grew 13 percent in 2000. Exports help manufacturers offset a softening in domestic demand. Overseas demand for high-tech equipment increased throughout most of 2000 and should trend higher as the rest of the world adopts New Economy technologies. In 2000, these high-tech exports, though decelerating, still grew roughly 25 percent, accounting for one-third of the increase in total exports, before adjusting for inflation. Other foreign shipments were also strong, but grew at a smaller 10 percent pace.

Still, exports made up no ground on the surging imports, which rose nearly 20 percent in 2000, starting from a much higher level. Nearly $3 out of every $10 spent on goods in the U.S. went to buy an import.

TRADE DATA ARE MISLEADING—MEASURING THE WRONG THINGS

The preoccupation of politicians and economists with the trade deficit as a means of "keeping score" is, however, outdated and misleading. In some cases, it is downright dangerous as it spurs a growing degree of protectionism and antiglobalization fervor. Imports and exports as they are measured today are dated concepts, left over from the accounting systems and economic models of the nineteenth century. They not only measure the wrong factors, but they measure them erroneously.[2]

Accurately measuring the goods that are traded is difficult enough, but it becomes even more complex for services and the other intangibles in the economy. For example, imports used to be a simple concept: products from a foreign country. But today's imports from Taiwan, for instance, include items assembled from components that were originally *exported* to Taiwan from other countries.

In addition, at a time when many large corporations have operations all over the world, the use of imports and exports as a measurement of national economic health is desperately outdated. Roughly 25 percent of total imports to the U.S., for example, are from foreign affiliates of American companies.

So the official definition of U.S. exports and imports is misleading and broadly understates the relative American competitive position. The reason is that sales of American goods or services to foreigners only count as an export if the goods or services are produced in the United States. But so much of American foreign sales are produced outside the country by foreign subsidiaries of U.S. companies—substantially more so for the U.S. than for any other country. According to Joseph Quinlan, an economist at Morgan Stanley and an acknowledged expert in the field of foreign direct investment and trade, "The extraterritorial span of corporate America is unsurpassed on a worldwide basis."[3] More than 23,000 U.S. foreign affiliates are scattered around the world. The combined total output of these companies is greater than the GDP of most countries. They employ huge numbers of people and, collectively, they are the largest exporters in the world. If you add back in all of the sales of these U.S. affiliates abroad—from Microsoft Singapore to McDonald's Moscow—and subtract out the similar sales in the U.S. of foreign products produced in the States (for example, Honda Ohio), voila! The U.S. would have a trade surplus (Figure 9.2).

Also inflating the trade deficit is the difficulty in measuring the exports (and imports) of knowledge products. Customs officials often

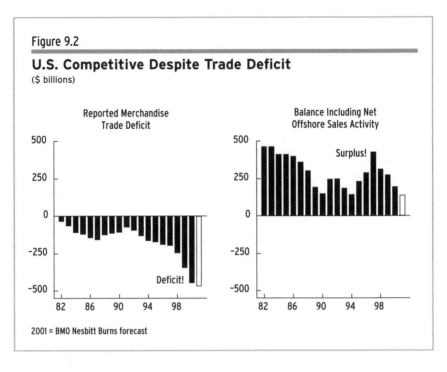

Figure 9.2

U.S. Competitive Despite Trade Deficit
($ billions)

Reported Merchandise Trade Deficit

Balance Including Net Offshore Sales Activity

2001 = BMO Nesbitt Burns forecast

value a computer file, for example, according to some arbitrary and irrelevant measurement system, even though the data may imbed thousands of hours of exported (or imported) labor. Often products of the highest value today are intangible or invisible. As service exports grow, they too may "disappear." The more successful service providers will set up shop in their customers' countries. We have seen this, for example, in the management consulting arena. Most large U.S. consulting firms now have offices all over the world. Their overseas sales are no longer counted as exports.

Quinlan reports that sales of U.S.-owned affiliates in foreign countries dwarf U.S. exports by a factor of two-and-a-half to one.[4] American firms compete more by setting up businesses in foreign countries—foreign direct investment—than by arm's-length trade. In short, the companies in the S&P 500 are the world's greatest export machine.

With today's globalization of production, sales by foreign affiliates of multinational companies have surpassed exports as the primary means of satisfying foreign demand. According to the United Nations, this changeover occurred in the early 1980s. Sales by all foreign affiliates reached roughly $11 trillion in 1998; world trade of goods and services ran only around $6.6 trillion that year. For the U.S. alone, in 1998, the value of exports stood at $0.9 trillion, while sales by majority-owned affiliates totaled $2.4 trillion.

This is ignored in the hand wringing over the current account deficit. The traditional measure of the trade balance misleads in assessing overall economic activity or competitiveness. U.S. companies have pursued a direct-investment strategy—building companies overseas to service home and foreign markets—more aggressively than their counterparts in most other countries, largely because of the relative strength of the U.S. dollar immediately after World War II. The dramatic appreciation of the yen until 1995 encouraged Japanese multinationals to follow the same strategy. In fact, as of 1997, there was roughly three times more Japanese direct investment in the U.S. than U.S. investment in Japan. Some of that disparity, however, was the result of Japanese barriers to entry and regulatory restrictions.

With one of the most open markets in the world and a large, prosperous middle class, the U.S. buys a vast amount of foreign goods (increasingly produced by U.S. companies with foreign workers). In addition, the U.S. absorbs the world's surplus savings that cannot be more profitably invested elsewhere. If the U.S. were not to do so, the return on capital to foreigners would be lower. This would be inefficient and improvident. Imagine the fate of Japanese or European pensioners if they were locked solely into low-interest domestic savings vehicles.

No Debt Trap

As productivity growth surged in the 1990s, augmenting the potential, noninflationary growth of the economy, the sustainable current account ratio also rose. This was reflective of an inevitably rising trade deficit, as we have seen. Plus, if intra-firm trade is exaggerating the real trade deficit, then foreign claims on the U.S. created by the same deficit are also exaggerated because many of these so-called foreign firms are American. Even more important, the U.S. is the world's key-currency country. It plays a central role in providing global liquidity and reserve assets. In today's world, the U.S. could not suffer the classic "debt trap" that so many traditional economists are concerned about.

The U.S. dollar will continue fluctuating to equilibrate global financial flows. Multinational companies adjust their intra-firm trade flows accordingly, helping to stabilize the system.

BOTTOM LINE ON THE CURRENT ACCOUNT DEFICIT

The U.S. current account deficit plays an important role in the stability of the global financial and economic system. The U.S. acts as a worldwide clearinghouse, helping to absorb the world's excess capital and goods. The dollar is used as a reserve currency for global central banks. They helped fund the deficit to the tune of more than $50 billion in 2000. The world needs dollars to conduct day-to-day business. The world's major commodity, crude oil, is bought and sold with dollars. Developing countries export and import with dollars.

Global dollar demand is also strong because of currency needs in countries like Russia, Turkey, and much of the developing world. There, the demand for U.S. dollars is strong, as domestic currencies are seen as less reliable. The dollar is the "unit of exchange" in the global underground economy. Try doing a multimillion-dollar drug deal in rubles or loonies (Canadian dollars). It is also the peg for currencies in Hong Kong and Argentina. Unless the euro or the yen begins to take over these key currency functions, which seems unlikely in the foreseeable future, the U.S. current account deficit will be the cushion and it will provide no imminent threat to the outlook.

10

Global
Capitalism
Problems and Promises

Never before have economies around the world been so closely synchronized. Never before has the inventory cycle been so multinational. The interconnectedness of the world's economies is stunning. It is tough to find a true safe haven when things begin to go wrong. The devaluation of the Thai baht in mid-1997, a seemingly innocuous event, sent shock waves through the global financial system that ultimately led to the Russian default and the threatened demise of Long-Term Capital Management and, potentially, many large banks in the U.S., Europe, and Asia. The economic slowdown in Asia in 1998 dramatically reduced the demand for oil, driving down prices to near-record lows in a matter of months. A slowdown in U.S. auto sales in late 2000 quickly spread to reduce auto production in Canada and around the world.

This is not entirely new. In the late nineteenth century, trade flows as a percentage of the economy were near current levels. Measures of total trade (exports plus imports) across industrial countries are not much above levels that were posted just over a century ago. We have seen a dramatic increase in trade in the past fifty years, but this mostly reverses the declines in the early twentieth century. Trade flows, however, capture only a small part of multinational economic and financial interaction today, as foreign direct and financial investment have surged. In Chapter 9, I detailed the importance of the activities of the foreign affiliates of American corporations—the multinationals—in widening the spread of global capitalism and the interdependencies of national economies.

A century ago, net capital flows across the industrial world (as a proportion of GDP) were often greater than they are today. This integration of global financial markets was made possible in part by technological advances, including the laying of the transatlantic cable in 1866. Like today, open markets allowed capital to flow to the most productive uses where the rates of return are deemed to be highest. This meant that national investment was not limited to the pool of national saving. Although the system produced inevitable dislocation, mispricing, and panic at some points, it reliably funded the opening of new economic opportunities, the development of the U.S. frontier and those around the world. A significant part of the most important infrastructure built over the century—including canal systems, thousands of miles of railroad track, and bridges in countries all over the world—were financed through international trade and finance.

In the nineteenth century, the movement of people was even more pronounced than today. Able-bodied people and their families were more likely to relocate. With the great waves of immigration, it was not uncommon in some countries that migration would change the population by 10 percent in one decade. Restrictions on immigration since then have slowed the tides of population movement, although in the past fifteen years immigration into the U.S. has picked up once again. But the reduced influx of largely unskilled labor in the U.S. provided the impetus for capital and managers to relocate to tap the pool of lower-cost workers available in other countries. Over time, this has driven up job growth in many parts of the world and increased real wages. International trade benefits all nations. This has been a basic economic precept for the past two centuries. Free trade promotes the underlying competitive forces of the division of labor and comparative advantage, fostering stronger growth and rising living standards around the world.

Businesses benefit from increased market size. In the New Economy, the return you can capture from an investment grows strictly in proportion to the size of the market where you can use it. If, for example, Bill Gates could have sold his Windows operating system only in Washington State, it would not have been very valuable and he would not be a multibillionaire today.

INCOME INEQUALITY WIDENS

However, what freer trade does not appear to do is to narrow the gap between rich and poor, at least not in the aggregate data. While increased global trade benefits all participants, raising living standards everywhere, inequality in the world economy has not diminished. It appears that technological progress benefits all, but the leaders in the tech revolution—both between countries and within countries—benefit disproportionately. We have seen this within the U.S., where knowledge workers have benefited disproportionately. This makes intuitive sense in the Information Age. If in the New Economy the most important creators of value are knowledge and creativity, then the most talented in the society stand to benefit the most from the growth and change generated by the technological advance.

The data support this notion. While the jobless rate for high school dropouts has plunged since 1992 thanks to the growing labor shortages through the 1990s, the aggregate data still confirm a widening income gap by educational level. Even though the supply of highly educated workers has risen significantly, demand has outpaced supply and the value of higher education has increased. The proportion of the working-age population over the age of twenty-five with at least a bachelor's degree has risen from 16 percent in 1979 to 26 percent in 2000.[1] The median worker with a college degree earned 80 percent more than the median worker with a high school degree in 1999, compared to a 37 percent differential in 1979.[2] It is not surprising that the rapid technological change over this period favored the highly educated— those who are best able to lead and create in the Information Age.[3]

Moreover, at least some of the value imputed to a college degree is likely to be a return to continuing investment in knowledge. It is much more likely for the highly educated to continue to invest in their own human capital through lifelong learning, an essential for success in the New Economy. Even the best computer science graduates at MIT will be obsolete in a few years (or months) if they don't keep up with advances in their field.

The advantages of educational achievement are no less evident for the income of countries than for the individuals within a country. With rare exception, the richer countries have a better-educated population than the poorer ones. The key to success in raising income levels has largely been the provision of good public education for all. But that is not so simple. It requires a certain degree of political stability—war-ravaged countrysides and social upheaval are not conducive to learning—and it also requires sound government financing, which presupposes a solid macroeconomic foundation.

Traditional economic theory—the paradigm of perfect competition and the traditional neoclassical growth model first formulated by Robert Solow—suggests that inequality between rich and poor countries should fall as barriers to trade fall. Opening up trade barriers permits countries to specialize in the products or services in which they have a comparative advantage—the ones they produce most efficiently. Trade encourages the transfer of leading-edge technology and know-how. Theoretically, the wages of workers and the return on capital in rich and poor countries should tend to become more similar. Workers in poor countries should benefit more than workers in rich ones as both types of economies become more efficient; relative wages in the developing world rise. In theory, poorer nations get far larger payoffs from investing in skills and capital than richer ones because of the law of diminishing returns—the less one already uses a factor, the more one gains from added increments.

Economists have preached that as global trade increases, average output per person should become less disparate around the world.[4] Unfortunately, this just has not happened, at least on a broad scale—not because trade has failed, but because of the continuing gap in the ability of many emerging economies to provide a well-educated and technically savvy workforce. The most notable success stories have been the Asian tigers, but for the world as a whole, income inequality has been roughly stable for more than a century.

INCOME INEQUALITY REMAINS

Output per worker among advanced countries has tended to converge, but the gap between the advanced and the developing world has not diminished. The good news is that output per worker has risen dramatically throughout the world. Even so, there remain large pockets of poverty. According to the World Bank's *World Development Indicators 2000*, the 3.5 billion inhabitants of the low-income countries had an average gross national product per person of a mere $2,170 in 1998.[5] The middle-income countries, with a populace of 1.5 billion, averaged $5,990 per person that year, while the high-income countries, with only 0.9 billion in population, averaged $23,420 per person. As a group, the richest countries generated eleven times more income per capita than the poorest countries.

We have seen the growth surge in East Asia—countries like Singapore, Taiwan, South Korea, and Hong Kong—leaping from third-world to first-world status with the freeing of trade. Yet there has been little overall progress in much of the rest of the developing world on a per capita basis. Income in Latin America increased by only 6 percent in the past twenty years. Average incomes in sub-Saharan Africa and the former Eastern bloc have actually contracted over that period. The World Bank reports that the number of people living on $1 a day has edged downward only slightly over the past decade to 1.2 billion people.

Looking back, it appears that the gap between rich and poor has not narrowed. If anything, it may have widened. Work by Lant Pritchett shows that in 1870, per capita income in rich countries was nine times that in poor countries, compared to eleven times in 1998.[6] While low-income countries have enjoyed a substantial increase in income, so have the rich countries. The net result is that worldwide inequality has not diminished over the past 130 years. This period included times when trade barriers were quite high. If, instead, we make the comparison between 1960 and the present, a period during which trade barriers have fallen markedly, the same result follows, little change in income inequality.

According to Robert Summers and Alan Heston, gross domestic product per person in 1960 in the rich countries was ten times higher than it was in the poor ones, compared to eleven times higher in 1998.[7] This certainly refutes the notion that income convergence would result from freer trade.

RELATIVE INCOME GAINS TODAY REQUIRE SKILLED LABOR

In a recent study, economist Eli Berman of Boston University and others investigated the paradox of why some nations remain so much poorer than others.[8] The answer seems to lie in the nature of technological change; it requires knowledge, which means a well-educated workforce. Many have highlighted poorer nations' lack of institutions that protect property rights and enforce the rule of law. While this is important, Berman's extensive study suggests that technological progress depends on a well-trained workforce equipped with state-of-the-art computers, software, and the like.

Poorer nations have trouble catching up, therefore, because they lack the skilled labor and IT to allow them to benefit disproportionately from innovation and technological change. We have seen this in the continued wide relative income gap between the U.S. and, for example, India, Bangladesh, and even Mexico and China. The good news is that poorer countries that take aggressive action to substantially raise education levels and boost capital investment—as Korea, Singapore, Ireland, and others have done—will reap enormous returns.

The East Asian economies are likely to benefit more from IT than Africa or Latin America because they have achieved a sufficiently educated population base to exploit the technology. Africa lacks many of the economic and legal institutions needed for a thriving information economy, and most of Latin America and Africa are well behind Asia in educational achievement.

Electronics already represent roughly one-third of East Asian exports. For example, South Korea has adopted the Internet more ardently than most. By the end of 2001, 20 million of its 48 million people are expected to have Internet access. The workforce is relatively well trained, as government expenditures on education as a percentage of the economy are higher than for many rich countries and the labor force is very hard working. Cultural predilections towards education and hard work are characteristic of the countries that excel, especially in the Information Age.

A more competitive Korean economy, however, is essential for the efficient use of knowledge. The government is using the Net to force increased competition. State-owned firms must make 50 percent of their purchases online by 2001. All government procurement will be on the Net by 2002. The government is finally addressing the inefficiencies created by the long-standing system of cozy, opaque, crony capitalism. The *chaebols*— huge conglomerates protected historically by government—and their suppliers have historically faced little competition. It is hoped that B2B supply chains will provide greater transparency and competitive pressure.

For the entire developing world, IT access alone is not enough. Opening up markets, breaking up telecom monopolies, and improving the quality and access to public education are also essential.

GLOBALIZATION VILIFIED

But the bulk of the emerging world remains relatively poor. This may help to explain why in the past decade globalization—meaning the spread of market capitalism around the world—has generated such negative sentiment in some circles. Its ability to narrow income gaps between rich and poor nations has been grossly oversold. There are some dazzling success stories, but they are relatively few in number and that is unlikely to change anytime soon.

We have witnessed the protests of the past few years in Seattle, Washington, D.C., Quebec City, and Prague—the turbulent and sometimes violent street theater of incensed young middle-class Westerners who defame multinational corporations for exploitation and environmental rape. Ironically, the emerging countries that are supposed to be the victims of global capitalism do not support these protests. The poor countries fear that labor or environmental restrictions will reduce their competitiveness and slow the inflow of foreign business to their nations. Nevertheless, the protesters have been heard. Many may be on the political fringe, but their concerns are real and need to be addressed.

We have seen a dramatic surge in globalization in the past twenty years as the end of the Cold War, the demise of socialism and communism, the Internet and other advances in IT, and East Asia's remarkable success contributed to a surge in international capital flows. Exports have swelled for two decades while foreign direct investment has risen sharply, but growth has been uneven and poverty in the developing world is still widespread. It is obvious now that trade liberalization on its own does not lift all ships equally. Inequalities and distortions remain, and some are exacerbated. Poor-country governments have long been remiss or ineffectual in preventing labor, human-rights, and environmental abuses. The evidence is clear: some multinationals have contributed to these abuses.

GLOBAL CAPITALISM SPURS GROWTH

Even with all of these problems, globalization undeniably contributed to the New Economy boom in the U.S. and elsewhere. It has created millions of jobs and enhanced training opportunities from Bangalore to Brazil. It has developed whole regions, bringing electricity, phone service, and sewage to some 300 million families in developing nations. It has transferred nearly $2 trillion from rich countries to poor through financial markets—bond and equity investments and commercial loans. It has had tremendous political effect as well, toppling dictators and causing enormous student unrest by making information freely available in once protected and sheltered societies. Today, the Internet has obliterated much of the power of censorship and dictatorial control of information. It has the power to narrow the commercial and cultural gulfs separating rich and poor nations.

The benefits of globalization are so potent, so obvious, that the threat of the protestors becomes all the more serious. It is essential that the progress continue. After all, the New Economy is undeniably global. There is no turning back this clock. It is also crucial, therefore, that the costs of globalization be addressed, mitigated, and, where possible, eliminated. There are many examples of reckless investment causing harm. But these hazards can be addressed by better corporate and government policy. Free markets are good, but they have produced disparate results in different countries and regions.

Too much of the foreign investment in these countries is subject to little if any environmental or human-rights restriction. While the industrial world has enacted a whole host of worker and environmental safeguards since the nineteenth century, the developing world has not and many there argue that such restrictions would only hurt the people they are meant to help. Child labor laws, for example, have huge support in the West, but developing nations argue that these children would rather work than starve, and many of their families support this notion. Political tensions, world war, and social dislocation undid the previous golden age of globalization in the late nineteenth century. If the gap between rich and poor countries continues to widen, the benefits of today's global capitalism could also be at risk from the political tensions they create. This is evident from the hailstorm of protest that accompanies every global trade summit.

Trade and inflows of private capital are essential to achieve strong, sustainable growth and to reduce poverty. Key also is the spread globally of mandatory education for everyone. The wonders of the economic surge in East Asia were largely the result of widespread, quality public education for the population at large. Almost everyone in Hong Kong, Taiwan, South Korea, and Singapore received a high school education when their countries' export drives began decades ago. In too many developing countries, quality education is available only for the wealthy or elite. Women are not adequately educated in much of the emerging world. In most of Central America, for example, much of the population never makes it to fifth grade. In consequence, poverty rates are horrific.

In a global economy where competitive advantage is increasingly dictated not by physical endowments like gold and oil, but by talent and knowledge, countries where only a small proportion of the population is educated at even a high school equivalency, let alone college or graduate levels, are at an extreme disadvantage. In too many developing nations the upper classes have a vested interest in keeping the rest of the population in subjugated conditions. As long as this is the case, little progress will be made.

Developing countries with stronger educational systems—such as Chile, China, and Malaysia—enjoy higher growth and lower poverty levels. In direct contrast, countries where fewer than 75 percent of the *male* population finishes fifth grade—such as Guatemala, India, Nigeria, and South Africa—have more poverty and lower overall growth rates. Not that there aren't very well-educated people in those countries, but the undereducation of the masses inevitably acts as a dead-weight drain on the rest of the population and the economy as a whole.

Governments in the emerging world must first deliver political stability, sound economic management, and an educated workforce before the gains from free trade and open capital markets can be fully realized. East Asia enjoyed the fruits of globalization because these basic criteria were satisfied. They are not in place in most of Africa, Latin America, the Moslem Middle East, and parts of the former Eastern bloc. A broad base of development is needed for the benefits of openness to show through. Reasonable legal and financial systems are also important criteria for economic development. China is addressing these issues now, but more needs to be done. Russia, for example, is only beginning to recover from the corruption, capital outflow, and economic collapse of the 1990s.

OPENNESS IS NOT A PANACEA

In order for countries to benefit from freer trade, governments must make the best use possible of inflows of foreign capital and expertise. Governments must have business-friendly policies that attract foreign firms and allow for the development and growth of domestic tycoons. These multinationals and homegrown successes train workers, invest in technology, and nurture the local infrastructure and local suppliers. Also important are the basic provision of political stability, solid macroeconomic management, good public education, a legal system that protects property rights, and a society in which prosperity is widely shared.

Weak government or ineffective law enforcement can hold back development. China, for example, has good labor laws, but they are often not enforced. Working conditions in much of the developing world are appalling. But most of these workers would never suggest that they would be better off had the multinationals never come to their country.

Thanks largely to the enormous inflow of foreign capital to China, for example, urban per capita incomes have grown more than tenfold since the markets were first opened in 1978. Chinese industry exported $250 billion of goods in 2000. Much of the income from the shoe, toy, electronics, and garment factories on China's wealthier East Coast has spread far into the poverty-stricken interior. China's economy has made great strides. Having moved from basic, assembly-line, low-tech manufacturing, it is now advancing in electronics and machinery. Millions of very well-educated engineers and computer and basic scientists have helped China become a major exporter of computer equipment, telecom gear, and auto parts.

Mexico is learning to imitate these developments. While exports have surged thanks to NAFTA, roughly half the population still lives in poverty. Education levels are low; only half of Mexicans have completed sixth grade and just 20 percent enter high school. Roughly half of exports come from assembly operations that have done little to promote the development of the local economies because most of the parts and materials are imported. Nevertheless, the productivity of Mexican workers is improving and so, therefore, are living standards.

Some multinationals are beginning to upgrade their operations in Mexico in light of the increasing supply of well-qualified technicians. As an example, Delphi Automotive Systems has opened an R&D center in Ciudad Juarez that employs 700 engineers developing products Delphi sells all over the world. IBM and Hewlett-Packard have manufactured personal computers in Guadalajara for many years, but since NAFTA there has been a major influx of new computer and telecom equipment plants, which have increased jobs and provided substantial training. These plants invest in modern technology and employ lots of engineers. Since 1995, the jobless rate has plummeted and most factory workers now earn at least twice the minimum wage.

The government of Guadalajara works hard to support the labor needs of the booming manufacturing sector. High schools are encouraged to produce the skills that are in high demand. Job training for new hires is subsidized and incentives are provided to woo multinationals to locate in the region.

There are great divergences in economic progress in the former Soviet bloc. Hungary and Poland are successfully attracting new businesses and driving their economy upward, while Romania and Bulgaria are underperforming. Different approaches to the demise of communism and the ensuing privatization help to explain some of the differences in economic performance since the end of the Soviet Empire in 1991. The Czech Republic and Russia essentially issued shares in local factories to its citizens. This put insiders and inexperienced people in charge of the enterprises. In Hungary, in contrast, the factories were sold to both local businesspeople and multinationals. This dramatically accelerated the process of redevelopment and growth.

It could take years, if not decades, for some regions to truly benefit from the fruits of economic openness. Even with the liberalization of trade in sub-Saharan Africa, as an example, growth has fallen from 3.5 percent in the 1970s, when global growth in demand for natural resources was strong, to only 2.2 percent in the 1990s, when the fastest growing sectors were information and communications technology. Stability, infrastructure, and skills are sorely lacking in this region.

MULTINATIONALS HAVE A SOCIAL RESPONSIBILITY

While it is important that emerging-country governments take the lead in implementing the policies that were so successful in places such as East Asia, multinationals—which account for the bulk of direct cross-border investment and one-third of all trade—have a social responsibility as well. This is especially true in countries where basic human and worker rights are not guaranteed.

Sweatshops are still all too common. The National Labor Committee, based in New York, issued a report in May 2000 listing abusive labor conditions in sixteen randomly chosen Chinese factories that produce for U.S. companies.[9] For example, Wal-Mart produced Kathie Lee handbags at a Qin Shi factory where exorbitant charges for room and board reduced the net average take-home pay to 3¢ per hour, or $3.10 for a typical ninety-eight-hour workweek. A shocking 46 percent of the labor force earned nothing at all and were in debt to the company. They were housed sixteen to a room, fed two inadequate meals a day, and subjected to physical and verbal abuse. Some were held as indentured servants; their identification papers were confiscated and they were permitted to leave the factory only one-and-one-half hours per day. The report also stated that the Wal-Mart audits were a "total farce."

In another horrifying example, Timberland produced shoes in a factory in Guangdong Province that required sixteen- and seventeen-year-old girls to work ninety-eight-hour weeks in factory temperatures reaching 100 degrees Fahrenheit. They handled toxic glues and other solvents without gloves and complained of high dust levels, excessive noise, and strong chemical fumes. Workers were threatened and coached to lie to U.S. company auditors. Any workers attempting to defend their rights or form an independent union were imprisoned—as was the common practice in China. These shocking examples of worker abuse are appalling and must be corrected. Self-policing by the multinationals apparently, from these examples, does not work. However, in some cases, the attempts to audit the factory conditions were thwarted by local managers. The issues are complex and difficult.

With these enlightening revelations, multinationals have come under increasing scrutiny, which has threatened a consumer backlash at home, dramatically damaging the brand. To assuage critics, companies such as Levi Strauss, Mattel, Nike, and Royal Dutch Shell Group have drawn up their own guidelines and invited outside inspection to ensure that they comply with them. Many developing countries adamantly resist the discussion of labor or environmental issues in the WTO because they fear that Western protectionists will safeguard jobs at home by dictating principles that drive up labor costs in the developing world.

Changing business practices in response to well-meaning lobbying efforts can create more problems than they solve. For example, soon after a bill was proposed in the U.S. Congress in 1993 to prohibit imports from countries that allow children to work in factories, garment makers in Bangladesh fired 36,000 workers under the age of eighteen; most of them were girls. The alternative for many of these children is starvation. Most of the girls did not go to school but instead took more dangerous jobs or became prostitutes.

In July 2000, the United Nations launched a program called Global Compact to get multinationals to endorse a set of basic human rights, labor, and environmental principles, which are monitored by outside groups. Many companies signed up. The extremists see these self-regulated programs as self-serving window dressing. But the globalization of the future must be tempered with rules and restrictions. Widespread gains in the workplace are unlikely until workers are able to unionize or systems develop to punish transgressors of international codes. But the changes that have been made voluntarily by multinationals prove that not every factory is or need be a sweatshop for the global economy to prosper.

While the problems remain and increased trade cannot be expected to eliminate global poverty on its own, that is no reason to deny the benefits of globalization. Developing countries, such as Mexico and China, have enjoyed rising standards of living thanks to the burgeoning influx of foreign business activity. The combination of farsighted domestic government policies and a business-friendly environment can reduce poverty and create a thriving middle class.

It may not be reasonable to expect, however, that we will see a significant reduction in income inequality between the richest and poorest nations of the world in the near future. Consider the advantages the United States has in the New Economy relative to an emerging nation. The U.S. has a well-educated, diverse, and disciplined workforce and is able to attract talent from all over the world. It has many innovative and highly profitable corporations that have access to the most recent research and technology. It has a well-functioning and innovative capital market and financial system, which provides funding not just for established businesses but for promising start-up activities as well. It is a deregulated economy, relatively unencumbered by bureaucratic or regulatory restrictions. Taxes are moderate. The country enjoys tremendous political stability—even during the thirty-six days in late 2000 when the presidential election result was uncertain, the demonstrations were orderly and the rule of law prevailed. The U.S. has a long history of democracy and a well-established justice system. Unlike many developing countries, the military is under firm civilian control. Maybe most important of all is attitude. The U.S. has a long history of rags-to-riches success. People believe in themselves and aren't afraid to take risks.

These absolute advantages are more important than ever in today's information-driven economy, where speed, flexibility, innovation, and knowledge are so crucial to commercial success. The direct economic benefits of successful creativity will tend to be concentrated in the most advanced countries to the extent that creative individuals and firms benefit from geographical proximity. The rich may well get richer, but the poor will get richer too. The global economic pie will continue to grow and everyone will enjoy a bigger piece.

11

The Global Leader in the Technology Revolution
Will the Lead Narrow?

T o this point, the New Economy has mainly been an American phenomenon, with scant signs of a gain in productivity growth in the major European countries or Japan. Canada has jumped on the American upwave and Britain has enjoyed a dramatic decline in unemployment, but the real driving force of the technology revolution to date has undeniably been the United States. Many expect it to remain that way because the tired "old" economies of Europe and Japan lack the necessary entrepreneurial verve and innovative spirit. Some have espoused the view that the biggest gains from a new technology come, not from its invention and production, but from its implementation and exploitation. If this proved to be true, then over the coming years, as the Internet and biotech revolutions spread around the world, the U.S. lead would diminish. But what is more likely is that global growth leadership will remain in the countries that most successfully foster an environment of creative destruction and disruption—a milieu in which constant innovation allows new to replace old on an ongoing basis. In this the U.S. excels, although other countries are increasingly attempting to copy the model.

Inordinate benefits flow to the innovators, the creators of knowledge. Increasingly in the New Economy, as we have seen, value creation arises from the contribution of the intangibles emanating from brainpower, intellectual capital, and talent. Speed is also crucial, as network effects enhance first-mover advantage. The ability to respond quickly to change and innovation—flexibility in labor and capital markets and the willingness to take risk—is key to success in the future. The United States has a strong competitive advantage in these areas. The rivals to U.S. hegemony in the future may be surprising. Rather than the large economies of Europe or Japan, the next great competitors may blossom from the more agile economies of Europe and Asia—those that nurture a climate conducive to innovation and growth.

THE U.S. IN THE LEAD

From 1995 through 2000, average annual growth in the U.S. was 4 percent, compared to 1.7 percent in Germany and only 1.4 percent in Japan. The differences in growth per capita were smaller because the U.S. population grew more rapidly, but rapid population growth relative to other countries in the G-7 is a strong competitive advantage for the United States. Only some of the disparity in growth over this period can be explained by differences in each country's relative position in the economic cycle. By any measure, the U.S. outperformed the others.

The U.S. lead in IT and the Internet will give it a big advantage for many years to come, presenting European and Japanese high-tech firms with formidable barriers to entry. Europe has only a handful of world-class technology producers that could rival the likes of Microsoft, Cisco, or Intel. Of the world's fifty biggest IT companies by market cap, forty-one were American, six were European, and only one was Japanese as of year-end 2000. The technology sector accounts for nearly 10 percent of the U.S. economy, compared to 7.5 percent in Japan and 6 percent in Europe. The U.S. also holds the lead in biotechnology and nanotechnology.

The real benefits from IT, however, go to those that adopt it, rather than to those producing it. This means that Europe and Japan could also enjoy a boost in productivity growth if they were to step up spending on IT hardware, software, and telecommunications. This has begun, but they still have a long way to go to reach the pace of tech investment in the U.S. In fact, U.S. businesses overinvested in technology in 1999 and the first half of 2000, leading to a sharp reduction in tech spending later that year and into 2001. This was one of the important factors in the ensuing economic slowdown.

Key to global growth leadership is productivity growth. Along with the U.S., the other countries that enjoyed a rise in productivity growth in the 1990s compared to the 1980s include Australia, Denmark, Finland, Canada, Sweden, New Zealand, Portugal, and Ireland. Declines were posted in Spain, France, the Netherlands, Belgium, Japan, Greece, Italy, Germany, and Austria.[1] There is a significant productivity gap, for example, between the U.S. on the one hand and Germany and Japan on the other.

Europe and Japan do not need to create cutting-edge technology to close the gap. They can make their economies more productive simply by adopting or imitating American technology and B2B commerce. The U.S. has the first-mover advantage, which is so important for corporate profitability and stock market returns. But it is often much cheaper to catch up than to be the trailblazer. The prices of IT products have fallen sharply since 1995 and product improvement continues to be spectacular. Sometimes countries can leapfrog into the newest technologies without having gone to the expense of building the old. The wireless telephone development in Europe and Asia is an example of this. They essentially skipped over analog and leapfrogged the U.S. with more advanced wireless cellular phone systems. It is well documented that the U.S. has fallen behind Europe and parts of Asia in the wireless revolution.

Second movers get to cherry-pick the developments that work. For example, as European companies begin rethinking their plans to develop the wireless Internet, American companies can observe, possibly allowing them to avert costly expenditures on network capabilities that customers may not want. And consumers, similarly, might avoid buying unnecessary devices and services that don't pan out. In other words, for once the U.S. consumers and communications companies will let someone else be the guinea pig.

For Europe and Japan, the same advantage holds true in IT and the Internet. They can miss the more painful developmental stages and adopt the tried and tested technology that makes the most sense today. Many of the original bugs have been worked out and the costs are far lower than they once were.

A LOT OF CATCHING UP TO DO

Corporate America has been streamlining and restructuring aggressively for decades, eliminating unnecessary management and revamping antiquated business practices. Japan and Europe, in contrast, can look forward to bigger cost savings simply because they are so much further behind. They have plenty of archaic business practices and economic waste yet to be purged. But the structural rigidities in both regions will slow the process, assuring that productivity will remain low and prices high relative to the U.S.

The Internet, inevitably, will help to level the playing field. The Net increases transparency and competition. E-commerce could also help to transform Japan's famously inefficient and expensive distribution system. Although productivity in many of Japan's manufacturing firms is higher than in the U.S., in retailing it is only half as high. If consumers can buy much more cheaply from abroad, as the Internet helps them do, then domestic producers and retailers will be forced to lower their prices. This will take some time to work out, however, as cross-border B2C activity is still relatively limited. Most U.S.-based e-tailers are reluctant to ship even to Canada, let alone to Japan. The shipping, handling, and customs issues seem to preclude it for now. Imagine the logistical and payment problems, not to mention expense, associated with shipping small packages to Japan. But as American dot-coms follow the lead of Amazon.com, eBay, and Yahoo! in opening operations overseas, the Net will begin to be a real alternative to the high-priced offline retailers in Japan and Europe.

Restrictions on discounting and store hours will also have to be eased. It may be hard to believe, but in Germany there has been a law prohibiting discounts of more than 3 percent off manufacturers list price. This caused companies such as Wal-Mart enormous problems when opening in that country. It was only in late 2000 that German economic minister Werner Mueller agreed to eliminate some of the constraints that deter the use of e-commerce. Similar restrictions on retail trade are prevalent throughout Europe. How silly the limits on store hours, price discounts, and promotions seem in the cyber world.

The Internet also offers Japanese firms a way to cut out the huge array of enormously inefficient intermediaries. The longer the supply chain, the bigger the potential gains from B2B e-commerce. Cyberspace supply chains are already popping up in Japan. The promise of 20 percent reductions in production costs is real. But the impediments are real too. The Japanese system of economic cross-ownership, *keiretsu*, makes any meaningful change very difficult. Many manufacturing companies have equity interests in their suppliers, retailers, and financial institutions. The process of breaking these "I'll-scratch-your-back, you-scratch-mine" relationships has been glacially slow. Crony capitalism is still rampant in many parts of Asia, making it very difficult to increase competition and raise productivity growth.

Deregulation in the telecommunications industry is also important. A recent study by the OECD showed a tight correlation between Internet usage and access charges.[2] These charges are generally much higher in Europe and Japan than in the U.S. Things are changing, however. Nippon Telegraph & Telephone introduced a flat-rate, high-usage Internet access service—aimed primarily at small offices and heavy individual users in Japan. Even so, Internet usage fees are roughly 30 percent higher in Japan and Europe than in the U.S.

The U.S. economy has slowed and the pace of productivity growth posted in 2000 was not sustained in 2001. So much progress on the corporate front has already been made in the U.S. that some have argued that growth per capita in Europe and Japan could exceed the U.S. pace over the next decade. This is debatable. If it were to happen, however, it would not jeopardize America's economic supremacy; it would only narrow the lead.

Technology Around the World

Technology usage is growing rapidly around the world, but meaningful disparities still exist. The U.S. and Scandinavian countries dominate in per capita Internet, computer, and cellular phone access. Finland is clearly the tech capital of the world in terms of the ubiquity of tech products.

The Internet

Internet use is highest in the U.S., Finland, Iceland, Norway, Canada, Hong Kong, and Sweden, in that order.[3] The language of the Net is predominantly English. This gives the Anglo-Saxon countries a huge competitive advantage. Japanese and Chinese, for example, do not lend themselves easily to keyboard application, explaining in part the comparatively low Net usage in these countries. Among the larger economies, Internet use is lowest in India, China, Portugal, Italy, Spain, France, Ireland, Japan, and Germany. The Netherlands, the U.K., Israel, and Singapore, for example, have more Internet connections, population adjusted, than Germany, France, or Japan. The gap is narrowing, however.

Computers

The U.S. dominates the PC world with fifty-four computers for every one hundred people in 1999, representing 32 percent of all computers in use worldwide.[4] Of course, there are many American households with more than one computer, but it is estimated that more than 60 percent of households now have a PC, or more than 70 percent of households with children. Following the U.S. in computer penetration are, not surprisingly, the same countries that rank high in Internet usage— Sweden, Finland, Iceland, Norway, Australia, Denmark, and Canada. The Netherlands, Singapore, and the U.K. are also high on the list. Japan stands at thirty-two computers per one hundred people, similar to the ratio in France, Germany, Luxembourg, and Israel. Lowest on this list would be India, with only one-half computer per one hundred people, and China with one.

Cellular Phones

While Europe and Japan are lower in PC ownership than the U.S., they are generally well ahead in cell phone ownership, and roughly half of all cellular phones in Japan are used to access the Web. At the top of the cell-phone league is Finland—home of wireless giant Nokia—where 68 percent of inhabitants had mobile phones in 1999. Finland has the most tech-savvy population in the world, ranking very high in cell phone and PC ownership, as well as Internet usage.

Next in cell phone penetration are Norway, Sweden, Hong Kong, Italy, Austria, Denmark, and Korea—all with 50 percent or more penetration. This is amazingly high given that it includes children and the elderly. Interestingly, 38 percent of the population have cell phones in Japan, compared to 31 percent in the U.S. and only 28 percent in Germany. For Canada, the penetration is even lower still, at 21 percent. For most Europeans and Japanese, the cell phone will be the vehicle of choice for the Net, even with all of its limitations in terms of screen and keyboard size and flexibility. China boasts the fastest-growing Internet and mobile phone markets, yet as of 1999, only 3 percent of the population had one. Beijing is worried about e-dissidents using the Net to push for greater freedom.

ECONOMIC FLEXIBILITY—EASY TO START A COMPANY

It helps an economy to excel if starting a new business is relatively easy. In the U.S., start-ups have surged over the past decade, and many of these upstarts, as we have seen, have threatened the competitive position of the giants in numerous sectors. This is an important part of the process of creative destruction that is so crucial to the health of an economy. Without it, growth will be limited and productivity will stagnate. Starting a new business is much more difficult in Japan or Europe than in the U.S. Capital is not as readily available for new enterprises.

Things are improving, however. The introduction of the euro has helped to fuse small and fragmented financial markets into a single, more dynamic whole, making it easier for companies to bypass cautious commercial bankers and go straight to investors. The euro's arrival also triggered a spate of merger and acquisition activity across the Continent. This economic restructuring will eventually help to raise productivity growth.

The U.S. has the largest, deepest, and most liquid capital markets in the world. U.S. venture capital spending more than doubled to nearly $60 billion in 1999 and surged once again in 2000 to $103 billion. And according to a study by Samuel S. Kortum of Boston University and Josh Lerner of Harvard Business School, a dollar of venture capital produces six times more patents than a dollar spent on R&D.[5]

American investment and commercial bankers are in a class of their own, dominating business financing worldwide. Financial innovation—the asset-backed securities market, junk bonds, IPOs, and the like—continues to augment liquidity, providing capital for new businesses. Bank lending dominates in Japan and in Europe relative to the U.S., and banks have historically been reluctant to loan money to new businesses. The regulatory environment, which involves an enormous amount of red tape that is very costly to deal with, also impedes new businesses in Europe and Japan.

MONETARY AND FISCAL POLICY

It is important that monetary policy adjust to the realities of the New Economy, accommodating relatively strong growth and understanding that it does not necessarily lead to inflation. The two biggest central banks in Europe, the European Central Bank and the Bank of England, are much more hawkish on inflation than the Fed, raising interest rates in the past decade at the slightest hint of inflation—real or otherwise—thus choking demand needed to justify hefty business investment spending. Faster growth would also ease the longer-term burdens of funding the retirement of aging populations in Europe and Japan.

Historically, tax rates have also been enormously burdensome in Continental Europe and Japan. High taxes discourage work; they are a disincentive to growth. The Thatcher-Reagan reduction in tax rates in Britain and the U.S. in 1979–80 spurred economic growth, encouraged capital formation and investment, and enhanced entrepreneurial spirit.

Top personal income tax rates, for example, are roughly 40 percent in the U.K. and the U.S. (and are slated to fall in the U.S. with the 2001 tax reduction), compared to 56 percent in Germany and 50 percent in Japan.

According to the *World Competitiveness Yearbook 2000*, real personal taxes (after deductions) were most conducive to enterprise and hard work in Hong Kong, Singapore, Malaysia, the U.S., and the U.K. in 1999.[6] In contrast, personal tax burdens most discouraged work in Belgium, Sweden, Denmark, Russia, Germany, France, Finland, and Canada. Corporate tax rates on profits were highest in Germany and Canada in 1999, although they are slated to come down in both countries. Indirect taxes—those that are dependent on spending rather than income or profits—are lowest in Hong Kong, the U.S., Singapore, and Japan, while they are highest in Europe, especially Scandinavia.

Countries around the world, including much of continental Europe, Japan, and Canada, are slashing tax burdens for corporations and individuals. But the U.S. is doing the same thing. Given the much smaller social welfare system in the U.S., and the predilection for "small government" compared to most other countries, it is unlikely that the U.S. advantage on the tax front will disappear or even narrow very much.

SKILLED LABOR—THE KEY COMPETITIVE ADVANTAGE

Another constraint on the spread of the New Economy around the world is the insufficient number of highly skilled, computer-literate workers. Europe and Japan, with a dearth of young people and a declining population base, will have trouble finding such workers quickly, particularly given their strict restrictions on immigration. Engineers comprise 40 percent of all college graduates in China, and India graduates huge numbers as well. Asia accounted for two-thirds of the worldwide increase in college and other post-high-school enrollments in the 1990s. Indian universities turned out 125,000 engineers each year, second only to the U.S. While they are welcome in the U.S. and other Anglo-Saxon countries, foreign engineers have not been as well received historically in much of Europe and Japan.

Although China and India have large numbers of highly skilled workers, they represent a very small proportion of their populations. Less than 3 percent of all people between the ages of seventeen and thirty-four were enrolled in any form of post-secondary education in those two countries in 1999, compared to 20 percent in Thailand, 17 percent in Canada, and 16.2 percent in the U.S. The ratio was 13 percent for Japan and only 9.4 percent for Germany. The illiteracy rates for adults over age fifteen are also shockingly high—17 percent in China and a horrifying 44 percent in India. That compares to well below 5 percent in the U.S., Canada, Europe, and Japan.

ISRAEL—TALENT IS NOT ENOUGH

Israel boasts the world's largest number of doctors, scientists, and engineers per capita—boosted by the large influx from Russia and South Africa. Israeli defense training has also augmented the high-tech talent. As a result, New Economy companies are booming, rendering Tel Aviv one of the top-ten tech cities in the world. Tiny Israel is the world's leading technology incubator after the U.S., highlighting the importance of a highly educated workforce. More than 4,000 tech firms have sprung up there, most founded by veterans of elite technology units in the Israeli armed forces or brainy Jewish émigrés who left jobs as scientists in the former Soviet Union. Seemingly overnight, technology has become one of the main drivers of the Israeli economy. However, there are conflicts with traditional Israeli kibbutz socialism, the legacy of which has been inordinately high tax rates.

Hundreds of Israeli technology start-ups have migrated to the U.S., in particular to Delaware—the most popular corporate domicile in the U.S. Israeli firms that shift their paper homes to Delaware are, in essence, exporting tax revenue, job opportunities, and expertise to the U.S. They often shift their headquarters and leave only R&D units in Israel.

The rush to the States began in 1998 after Israel liberalized its currency-control laws and made it easier for Israeli citizens to set up offshore companies. Since then, more than 1,000 companies have designated Delaware as their corporate headquarters. They benefit through better access to capital and customers. But arguably the biggest benefit is the escape from punitive Israeli tax rates. Entrepreneurs who start businesses in Israel face a capital gains tax rate of 50 percent, more than twice the rate in the U.S.

The clear lesson here is that the New Economy is global. As the Israeli case shows, intangible assets flow across country borders to the most preferential locale. In most cases, that means the United States. The response of other countries around the world may narrow the U.S. lead in the future, but it is very unlikely to erase it.

THE CHINESE OR INDIAN THREAT TO U.S. LEADERSHIP

In both China and India, an elite minority of the population is extremely well educated, entrepreneurial, and at the leading edge of technology; but the vast majority is still underprivileged and poorly educated. There are some meaningful successes in places such as Bangalore, India, and Shanghai, China.

Indian Software Expertise

Ever since the early 1980s, the software industry in Bangalore has been home to a growing number of tech companies where well-trained, English-speaking, Indian computer programmers toil for the likes of Texas Instruments, Microsoft, and Infosys. There are many thriving homegrown tech companies as well, as India's universities and technical schools churn out world-class technicians and programmers who are paid a fraction of the wages they would earn in America. Many of India's engineers telecommute for U.S.-based companies, and others emigrate.

Indian software exports have been growing by 50 percent per year, reaching $8 billion in 2000 and accounting for over 10 percent of total exports. More than 180 of the top 500 multinationals outsource their IT needs to Indian companies. R&D spending was up from an average of 2.5 percent of revenues in 1997–98 to 3.5 percent in 1999–2000. However, India lacks IT-savvy accountants, lawyers, and venture capitalists with management expertise. And a strong IT sector is not a panacea for underlying poverty in the rest of the economy. A few are getting very rich, but the gap between rich and poor in the country is widening.

Moreover, telecommunications systems, power, roads, and airports require major upgrades. Thanks to a highly regulated telecom industry and lack of competition, most Indians have no access to telephones or the Internet, and supply bottlenecks mean that phone lines are often jammed.

Dramatic Economic Reform in China

China has been more successful in providing IT to its people, with three times as many telephone lines and Internet users as India (population adjusted) and twenty times as many cellular phones. It is increasingly apparent that the second most popular language on the Internet by 2005 could well be Chinese. According to the state-affiliated China Internet Network Information Center, China's online population has mushroomed from fewer than one million users in 1997 to more than 22 million today. Some predict that number will rise to more than 120 million by 2004—particularly as the Web becomes available on cable TV and mobile phones, both of which already reach roughly 100 million Chinese households. Net usage is emblematic of an enormous economic transformation that is taking place in the country. China is in the midst of a far-reaching economic reform program. With it comes the risk of political, social, and economic instability, although the government today is in full support of Net usage.[7]

The reform process began in 1978, spearheaded by Deng Xiaoping, creating a two-tiered economy—the government controlled sector and the smaller, more innovative market economy. Over the following twenty-plus years, nearly half of the economy was liberalized to market forces, while half remained under strict government control. The privatized sector is arguably less restricted than the private sector in Japan or Korea during their enormous growth phase in the 1960s and 1970s. Since reforms began, there has been a foreign direct investment (FDI) boom in China that is rivaled only by the FDI in the U.S. and the U.K. This investment set the stage for a boom in Chinese exports and intensified competitive pressure in domestic markets, which has led to meaningful deflation. As evidence of the significant improvement in Chinese living standards, the World

Bank reclassified China in 2001 from a poor country to a middle-income country. Rising from the ranks of the poor is a huge boon to the 1.3 billion people in the world's most populous nation, and clearly much of the gain is directly attributable to the economic reforms.

Without doubt, China's ascension to the World Trade Organization (WTO) will encourage further integration with the global economy. As with Mexico's entry into the NAFTA in 1994, China's entry into the WTO will likely give an additional boost to FDI by improving financial transparency and strengthening the rule of law. In the case of Mexico, FDI increased from $3 billion annually before NAFTA to $13 billion in 2000. WTO membership, therefore, will further support China's role as the regional growth leader, as well as force domestic companies to become more efficient in an effort to compete.

The challenge of increased foreign competition also has huge implication for social reform. In recent years, state-owned enterprises have been laying off workers at a rate of five million per year. WTO membership will increase that figure considerably. The government is preparing to reform the banking system and capital markets as well, which will also be disruptive. These reforms are slated to be gradually introduced through 2010 or so, ultimately allowing much more foreign control of the financial services sector than in other Asian countries. It is hoped this will increase the availability of capital and help to address China's enormous retirement funding problems, which are similar to those in much of Europe.

There are still many unattractive aspects to this rapidly changing country. Many of the poor are getting poorer. Workers and peasants are often abused, with no recourse. Some would argue that health care is worsening and educational standards are declining.[8] The rule of law is still very weak and corruption is rampant, while environmental degradation is widespread.

Economic volatility and dislocation in China are likely to cause social unrest. Human rights violations will receive continuing international scrutiny, particularly as China enters the WTO. The Internet will notify the Chinese public of these violations, with the possibility of further inciting agitation or worse. Ultimately, a shift to democracy will be necessary to insure the genuine rule of law over the long term. It is doubtful, however, that this will occur soon. Economic liberalization is causing enormous increases in unemployment and other economic hardship. Political unrest will likely escalate. It is questionable whether a democratic regime could preside over the economic transformation that is now occurring. Chinese leadership simply would not risk it. This will make it very difficult for the West, feeling the pull between the encouragement of economic reform, on the one hand, and totalitarian rule, on the other.

At the same time, China has many things going for it. The Chinese diaspora, those Chinese living all over the world, provides an important and well-educated network of wealth and influence. Moreover, there is a growing entrepreneurial class in China. Returning overseas students and local academics-turned-businesspeople are starting and running a myriad of infotech and nanotech companies. These key players will only become more important given that, according to the World Bank, China's private sector is growing at 70 percent per year. And while human rights violations are still a serious problem, there is some evidence that personal freedoms have expanded.

China and India: Challenges Remain

While educated workers and the middle class are increasing in both India and China, the overwhelming proportion of the population in both countries is ill educated and submissive to the rule of the elite. Life for too many of them remains a struggle to survive. Much will have to be done before either India or China enters first-world status in the New Economy. Those who are threatened by their competitive potential underestimate the problems that remain.

For China, the weight of a totalitarian government, limited public education, unprofitable state-owned enterprises, human rights violations, inadequate legal and judicial safeguards, a rudimentary financial system, and corruption must be addressed and altered before it can truly threaten U.S. hegemony in the New Economy.

China once was the global technology leader. Six hundred years ago, China was the most technologically advanced country in the world. Centuries before the development of the West, it had invented the printing press, gunpowder, the compass, the water-powered spinning machine, and even spaghetti. By 1400, it had in place many of the innovations that triggered the Industrial Revolution in Britain nearly four hundred years later. But China's technological progress went into decline, because its rulers kept such dictatorial control on the new technology that it could not spread. And while there were many brilliant Chinese thinkers and innovators, the bulk of the population was uneducated and very poor. The same remains true today, and until it changes, China will remain a relatively low-income country. The potential is great, however. The sheer size of the country with its 1.3 billion people, and the Confucian principles of hard work, loyalty, discipline, saving, and education, bode well for the potential of a China with greater freedoms and equality of opportunity.

In India, as well, the education system for the elite is excellent, but the mass of the population is illiterate or close to it. Human development—which includes economic, social, and educational factors—is low. Women are subjugated. The general infrastructure is inadequate and inefficient and productivity is weak. Public finances are also inefficiently managed. This means that many of the brightest minds in India will continue to be lured away to the developed world, damaging the chances of substantial improvement over the short run.

THE DIMENSIONS OF COMPETITIVENESS

The U.S. has topped the ranks of the World Competitiveness Scoreboard—prepared by the prestigious International Institute for Management Development (IMD), an independent think-tank in Lausanne, Switzerland—for eight consecutive years (Table 11.1).[9] The U.S. lead, in fact, is widening.

The IMD suggests that there are four dimensions that help determine a country's competitiveness.[10] In each of these dimensions, the U.S. has a unique and strong position, but other countries, as well, are now making gains. The dimensions are:

- Aggressiveness versus attractiveness
- Proximity versus globality

- Assets versus processes
- Individual risk-taking versus social cohesiveness

Table 11.1

MOST COMPETITIVE ECONOMIES IN THE WORLD

1. United States	6. Hong Kong
2. Singapore	7. Ireland
3. Finland	8. Sweden
4. Luxembourg	9. Canada
5. Netherlands	10. Switzerland

Source: *The World Competitiveness Yearbook 2001* (Lausanne, Switzerland: International Institute for Management Development).

Aggressiveness versus Attractiveness

This dimension examines the degree to which a country attempts to aggressively export products and engage in FDI rather than, on the other hand, make itself attractive to foreign companies, thereby hosting the FDI. The traditional path to competitive success historically has been aggressiveness in trade—actively promoting exports and the development of foreign affiliates. Germany, Japan, Hong Kong, Taiwan, and South Korea have followed this strategy. Aggressiveness generates income and wealth for the home country, but not necessarily jobs. It increases domestic profits and stock market capitalization.

More recently, a number of countries have opted to follow a strategy of attracting foreign investment. While this does not impact the profits or wealth of domestic companies directly, it does enhance domestic growth. Recipients of FDI garner the benefits of job creation and training as well as leading-edge technology and business practices. To be attractive, host countries often provide monetary incentives for corporate relocation— such as low tax rates, rebates, and R&D credits—which can be costly; but they are often more than repaid in boosted domestic growth. To help the lure, it is also important to provide a well-educated labor force. Ireland and Singapore have followed this strategy with great success. Ireland has invested heavily in education, providing a young and qualified workforce that has strong IT skills. The education system in Singapore is excellent, particularly for science and technical training, as well as economic literacy. The U.K. used to be aggressive but has now become attractive. Switzerland did the opposite. Once attractive, it is now following the aggressive strategy.

According to the IMD, the United States is the only country that is both aggressive and attractive. U.S. multinationals build operations in countries all over the world, and exports from within the U.S. are also sizable. The total of exports and net sales of foreign affiliates far exceed American imports, as we have seen. But the U.S. is also a magnet for FDI, being the host country for a large number of foreign businesses. Having the wealthiest consumer market as well as low production costs, the country is an attractive venue for foreign manufacturing and service companies. The U.S. is also a lure for capital and talent. Record inflows of foreign capital in the 1990s helped to finance the capital-spending boom.

Moreover, the U.S. enjoys the largest net inflow of foreign students in the world, many of whom stay after graduation, particularly now that immigration restrictions have been relaxed (especially in the high-tech sector). Between 1985 and 1996, foreign students accounted for two-thirds of the growth in science and engineering doctorates in the U.S. According to the National Science Foundation, enrollment of science and engineering graduate students rose 2 percent in 1999—the most recent year for which statistics are available—after five consecutive years of decline. The biggest gain, 12 percent, was in computer science. Foreign students on temporary visas were the main factor in the 1999 rise. Many of them planned to stay and work in the country. In the 1999–2000 school year, international students studying in the U.S. reached 514,723, up 5 percent from the previous year.[11] The countries that sent the most students were China, Japan, India, South Korea, Taiwan, and Canada.

The universities and colleges in the States are second to none, although education at the primary and secondary levels leaves much to be desired. This means that for the bulk of the population, a better education is available in many parts of Europe and Asia. This is a serious problem and helps to skew the U.S. distribution of income toward the top. In today's knowledge-based economy it is essential for the U.S. to improve the educational standards for all of its population. This is a major political issue and is hotly debated by the Bush Administration and the Congress.

The U.S. is also the least likely of all countries to lose its most highly educated people to other locales. The brain drain seems to flow mostly in one direction—toward the Stars and Stripes. This has been a troublesome issue for many countries. Until just the past few years, Ireland suffered an exodus of many of its most talented people—an exodus that began with the potato famine in the mid-1800s. With a series of fiscal measures to improve its attractiveness—tax cuts, infrastructure and R&D spending, and a large investment in education—Ireland has now turned the tide and enjoys significant net in-migration, thanks to the strong tech sector and the development of so many large multinational businesses. Canada as well has always been subject to a brain drain to its closest neighbor, particularly in the past twenty years or so when growth significantly lagged the U.S. and the tax gap widened. NAFTA has eased immigration restrictions, making it easier for Canadians and Mexicans to get a green card. The U.S. has also been the beneficiary of the influx of highly educated people from Russia, South Africa, China, and India.

Proximity versus Globality

Proximity versus globality refers to the dichotomy between the local economy, which services domestic residents, and the export-oriented sector, the companies with international operations. It also represents the dichotomy between the protectionists and the globalists. Even a large domestic economy, such as the U.S., is becoming more global. Globalization is on the rise and countries with high domestic living standards and operating costs, such as Germany and Switzerland, are going through a period of acrimonious adaptation and transition.

The Netherlands plays this dichotomy in an interesting way. The local economy, or economy of proximity, is quite insular and highly regulated. Labor and commerce laws are strict and the social welfare system is very generous. But there is also a very powerful global sector that is fully privatized and mostly deregulated. The Netherlands is home to many very successful multinational corporations. The five biggest are Royal Dutch/Shell Group in energy; ING Group and ABN Amro, which are banking colossi; Unilever, a leading consumer products company; and Fortis in insurance.

Assets versus Processes

Wealth creation today is increasingly based on innovation and know-how, called "processes" by the IMD, rather than the physical assets of the economy. Countries may be rich in physical assets—land, people, and natural resources—but still be uncompetitive and therefore relatively poor. We see this in Russia, India, and Brazil.

Relying too heavily on a rich endowment of assets has made some countries complacent. For too long Canada, as an example, believed that its economic wealth would continue to be assured because of its rich bounty of physical assets. During the two decades from 1975 to 1995, living standards in Canada fell significantly relative to its neighbor and most important trading partner, the United States. While the U.S. was busy restructuring, streamlining, and privatizing business, reducing tax rates and deregulating many industries, Canada was pretty much doing the opposite. Tax rates were boosted and FDI was discouraged. In some industries, FDI is even prohibited. For example, in bookselling, airlines, banking, and telecommunications, foreign ownership of domestic companies is either prohibited or highly restricted.

In the past few years, however, spurred by the deep recession of the early 1990s, Canada has developed its competitive position in the knowledge-based economy. Corporate and personal tax rates have been reduced and government support of research and education has been enhanced. Canada has a strong technology sector and, since 1996, a relatively strong economy.

Individual Risk-Taking versus Social Cohesiveness

There has been a shift around the world away from the model of social cohesion—the collectivist model encouraged in continental Europe and Japan—towards a model of individual risk-taking, which is most evident in the U.S. But even Europe and Japan today are shifting, moving toward more deregulation and privatization. German Chancellor Gerhard Schröder, for example, has launched a blitzkrieg of reforms since taking office in 1998. He has cut personal and corporate taxes significantly and has proposed the biggest overhaul of the country's generous pension system in 120 years—shrinking government support and encouraging private pensions for the first time ever.

He won the labor unions' support for pension reform by promising—at least for now—that he would not change laws that make it difficult to hire and fire workers. Some believe, however, that he will even take those on in his second term, especially if the jobless rate, which was at 9.3 percent in the spring of 2001, edges downward after the next election, which must occur by the fall of 2002. He has even gone after the arcane discount law, which limits the freedom of retailers to cut prices, and he is streamlining the Bundesbank—the once mighty institution that has been enfeebled by the birth of the European Central Bank.

Other examples of this shift include the creation of the New Labour Party in Britain and the move to the center left (from the farther left) by both the Democratic Party in the U.S. and the Liberal Party in Canada. Most dramatic, of course, was the end of communism in Russia and the Eastern bloc. Even the Communist government in China is relaxing some of its grip on the economy and society, at least on the surface.

At the one extreme is the U.S., which emphasizes the supremacy of the individual. Risk-taking is encouraged and the social welfare system is comparatively minimalist. In many ways, it is a "survival-of-the-fittest," "dog-eat-dog" society, at least in comparison to the social welfare states of continental Europe. Individuals are, in large measure, responsible for themselves, and the role of government is minimized. In the other Anglo-Saxon countries the model applies to a more muted degree. The social welfare system is far more generous in the U.K. and even more so in Canada.

Consistent with the risk-taking mindset is the widespread American ownership of stocks. Big government and big business no longer guarantee lifetime security. The demise of the defined-benefit pension plan in the corporate sector is representative of the growing attitude that individuals should be self-reliant. Americans must, therefore, save for their own retirement security. The popularity of the 401(k) plans and the Individual Retirement Accounts is testimony to this.

In contrast, the continental European model or the Scandinavian model emphasizes the social consensus and takes a more egalitarian approach. Income is redistributed from rich to poor to a far greater degree and the social welfare system is extensive. Governments are more pervasive and regulatory control is tighter. It is accepted that the government knows what is best and regulates the animal instincts of the marketplace. Unbridled capitalism is seen as dangerous and detrimental to the quality of life. So, France and Italy legislate a thirty-five-hour workweek and Germany and Switzerland limit the days and hours that stores can be open.

SOCIETAL AND GOVERNMENTAL MODELS

The IMD delineates further the differences in attitudes and mindset in different regions of the world and their impact on competitiveness. These include the Anglo-Saxon model, the Northern European model, and the Southern European model, as described below.

The Anglo-Saxon Model

Labor and business flexibility, deregulation, and privatization characterize the Anglo-Saxon model. There is a greater tolerance for risk-taking and the society is more individualistic. In the U.S., the U.K., Hong Kong, Singapore, and, to a lesser degree, Canada, the Anglo-Saxon model holds sway. The mindset is less cautious and failure is not seen as the end of the line. In the U.S., there are many examples of businesses and individuals that have risen from the ashes of a downfall. Labor unions are much less powerful than in many other countries in the world and government impediments to business are minimized. There is a can-do mindset—an optimism and a feeling that if you have a dream, pursue it and it will be yours. Build it and they will come. Anybody can do anything if they just try hard enough. All of this may not actually be true, but the sentiment is deeply imbedded in American culture.

This environment fosters entrepreneurial spirit and innovation. It encourages out-of-the-box thinking and creativity. Individualism is a necessary ingredient to breakthrough technological advance. Galileo broke all the rules when he suggested the world was round. So did Kondratieff and Einstein and Newton. A society that fosters this "rebel" mentality is one that will likely excel in the creation of new ideas and processes. It can be quite unstable, however, with a good deal of social upheaval. It is not surprising, as an example, that the U.S. was among the leaders in the liberation of women from traditional family roles.

Within the Anglo-Saxon countries, there are degrees of adaptation to the model. The U.S. is a nation of immigrants. The culture is grounded on the rebellion of the past—the Revolutionary War—when the people, hardened individualists, rose up against the mighty power of the throne. The Declaration of Independence guarantees the rights of life, liberty, and the pursuit of happiness. In contrast, Canadians were the loyalists. They respect government and demand that the state intervene to guarantee a minimum standard of living for all. Their constitution called for peace, order, and good government. Not nearly as individualistic as Americans, Canadians rely on government to protect the poor and to redistribute income. Unions are much more powerful than in the U.S. and labor markets are somewhat less flexible. The glaring divergence between even so closely aligned cultures as the U.S. and Canada is summarized in the following old saw: A cultural icon for the U.S. is the cowboy—independent and rootless—whereas for Canada, it is the Mountie—enforcer of the law.

The Northern European Model

The Northern European model is characterized by a strong emphasis on social consensus, stability, and regulations. Respect for authority, respect for elders, collectivist rules, and homogeneity characterize the cultures of Japan, China, Taiwan, and much of Europe. Unions are very powerful and labor laws are quite strict. As a result, the labor markets are highly inflexible, making it very difficult for companies in Germany and France to restructure. Layoffs are illegal and wage rates within the companies follow a very strict hierarchy. This is why the banks in Germany have shifted their trading operations to London. It was impossible to pay their traders competitive market salaries within the German corporate context. In consequence, the jobless rate in the more flexible economies such as Britain and the U.S. are low, while in Europe they are very high. Ironically, the very policies that were designed to protect workers actually weakened the economy and therefore caused the jobless rate to be higher than in countries with more flexible labor and product markets.

The Northern European model does, however, favor a longer-term perspective. Particularly now that CEOs in the U.S. receive compensation packages that are largely tied to the stock price of their company, the short-term performance of the stock often takes precedence over the longer-term outlook.

While the U.S. is a very heterogeneous society, where everyone is seen to be an immigrant of sorts, countries such as Japan, China, Germany, Switzerland, and, to a somewhat lesser degree, France shun immigration. They do not welcome foreigners into their society. This has been a meaningful disadvantage in the New Economy because their population growth is low and the supply of talent, particularly technical and innovative talent, is limited. The Asian societies encourage conformity. Rote learning is emphasized and government is seen to be good. The best and the brightest students in Japan, Singapore, and China strive to work for the government—similar to what happens in France. In contrast, in the U.S., government bureaucrats are significantly underpaid.

Bureaucracies are large in Japan—in government and in business— and entrepreneurial spirit has not been encouraged in the past. Change is slow and society shifts at a glacial pace. While the expectation of lifetime employment, from graduation to retirement, is now changing, labor markets remain relatively inflexible. Entrepreneurship has only recently been blooming. Social cohesion is most important and societal changes are very slow to reach Japan. The labor force participation rate of married women is still quite low. Only recently has the birth control pill been legalized.

The Southern European Model

Finally, relatively limited infrastructure, business regulation, or social protection characterizes the Southern European model—which includes countries such as Italy, Spain, Portugal, Turkey, Greece, and much of the emerging world. Government is generally weak and often corrupt. Labor costs are low, but so is productivity. This model does favor inventiveness, style, and a certain joie de vivre in some places, but it does not bode well for economic performance in the cyber age.

THE ABILITY TO ADAPT TO CHANGE

Crucial to success and competitiveness in the New Economy is the ability to change rapidly with evolving technology. Countries with the greatest capacity for creative destruction have the greatest advantage. FleetBoston Financial developed a Creative Destruction Index, based on ten measures that predispose a country to profiting from a period of rapid technological change.[12] The measures include government spending as a percentage of GDP, the proportion of the population completing college, personal computer use per household, the rate of job turnover, years of democratic rule, average age of the population, top corporate tax rate, level of corruption, trade barriers, and foreign exchange management.

The U.S. is in the lead, and Singapore and the United Kingdom follow very closely—tied for the number two spot (Table 11.2). Japan and the Euro-11 lag not just the U.S. but also much smaller countries, such as Korea, Brazil, and Denmark. Of course, lumping together all of the eleven European countries is misleading. Certainly Ireland and Finland have

Table 11.2

CREATIVE DESTRUCTION INDEX

WORLD'S MOST INNOVATIVE ECONOMIES: 2000

1. United States	6. Canada
2. Singapore/U.K.	7. Mexico
3. Norway	8. Australia
4. Sweden	9. Korea
5. Switzerland	10. Brazil

Source: Paul Podolsky, *Creative Destruction Index* (FleetBoston Financial Corporation, September 2000).

embraced change relatively well in comparison to Germany, France, and Italy, as we have seen. The demographics in Japan and the large countries of Europe are not conducive to change, as we will explore in the next chapter. They have lower overall labor market turnover, reflective of the reduced level of corporate restructuring and individual willingness to change. In this way, they are predisposed to slower growth than the countries ranking higher on the list. Moreover, lagging Internet penetration rates only exacerbate this situation.

The U.S. not only enjoys the highest proportion of college graduates—followed by Norway, Canada, Singapore, Japan, Russia, Australia, Korea, and the U.K.—but the talent pool is augmented by the inflow of very well-educated people from the rest of the world. To some degree, the U.S. has benefited from outsourcing education investment abroad.

U.S. PROBLEMS

The U.S. is not without its shortcomings, however. These could diminish its lead in the future or at least dampen its long-run growth prospects and should be addressed. The key negatives, as I see it, are low savings rates and/or high debt levels; people problems, including crime, violence, substance abuse, and poor public primary and secondary education; and, to some extent, an overzealous legal system—lawyers run amok.

While many point to the record trade and current account deficits as a sign of significant weakness, I disagree. As elaborated in Chapter 9, the fundamental trade picture of the U.S. is strong and the current account deficit reflects the superior rate of return of American assets as well as the key-currency, superpower, safe-haven characteristics of the U.S. Treasury market. The dollar's strength may well ebb as Europe enjoys stronger relative growth, but the underlying role of the U.S. as a trade powerhouse, especially through its foreign affiliates, is not likely to be supplanted any time soon. Moreover, the U.S. will continue to be investment banker to the world and the only country that can enjoy the seigniorage—the profits and positive benefits—of being the world's sole key currency.

Savings Shortfall

I am more concerned about the low personal savings rate, although it is not as low as the official data suggest. Nevertheless, debt levels are too high in the private sector in the U.S. for both households and businesses. The ratio of gross domestic savings relative to GDP ranks thirty-seventh in the forty-seven-country survey of the IMD. As we saw in 2001, when the economy slows, the debt burden becomes all the more onerous and all the more risky. As capital markets dry up and the banks become far more restrictive in their lending practices, the weakest tumble. Americans, therefore, are too vulnerable to a slowdown, a recession, a stock market rout. Too many live at the edge of insolvency. A wave of layoffs collapses confidence and, worse yet, household balance sheets. The U.S. is too dependent on the inflow of foreign capital to finance its investment and consumption spending—however reliable that inflow might be.

As the population ages, savings rates should rise; but we have been saying that for years. As Boomers reach the age of peak income and investment—which will continue to occur for the next decade—savings rates will likely increase. Budgetary surpluses should help. But the optimistic nature of the American public is a deterrent here, especially for the Boomers. Unlike their parents, they did not experience world war or depression. They are not good savers, which is a competitive disadvantage for the country and a serious problem for many individuals. Continued liberalization of retirement savings plans, increasing the maximum contributions to 401(k) plans and IRAs, should help. The wake-up call of turning fifty with virtually no retirement nest egg might create some sense of urgency.

People Problems

For a country as wealthy as the U.S., considerable problems of poverty and underprivilege remain. The good news is, however, that they are improving, particularly in response to the decade-long expansion in economic activity. As we have seen, labor shortages during the boom caused many businesses to dip to the bottom of the knowledge spectrum for workers. The jobless rate for high-school dropouts fell to a record low of 6 percent in December 1999, and has only edged modestly higher since. This on-the-job training will be invaluable for keeping the formerly hard-core unemployed in the labor force. The proportion of the population on welfare has fallen as well, to a thirty-six-year low, and the violent crime rate has dropped sharply.

This is all great news, but further action needs to be taken. In comparison to other wealthy countries, crime and poverty continue to be problems in the U.S. Moreover, alcohol and drug abuse remain major contributors to crime, especially in the large urban centers. The U.S. ranks very poorly in the IMD survey of substance abuse and its impact on the workplace. Harassment and violence are also reported to seriously destabilize the working environment. Youth unemployment, though down six percentage points since 1992, remains over 13 percent, still too high for complacency.

Education a Critical Issue

Education is another area needing critical attention. While the U.S. has some of the best universities and graduate schools in the world, it ranks poorly in primary and secondary education. Moreover, even at the graduate levels, more must be done to assure that government, the universities, and the business community work together to develop the skilled labor needed to excel in the New Economy. For example, there remain insufficient numbers of graduating scientists and engineers. Universities are notoriously slow in responding to market forces, as each department is reluctant to reduce its resources so that others might grow. Government grants to graduate students in these fields would help. Businesses, too, must help provide the impetus for response. It has worked in the past. Chemical engineering degrees, for example, are the direct outgrowth of the demand emanating from the petrochemical industry.

Local support for lifelong training is also strategically important. The community college system is improving, and mounting opportunities for remote learning—online and on TV—have also helped to improve skills. Children, however, are the keys to the future. Increasingly, the divide between the "haves" and the "have nots" will be knowledge based. Access to computers is essential for learning today. Computer literacy is an important determinant of future workplace success. The wealth of information available online is still accessible only to roughly 65 percent of families with children and to an even smaller proportion of the children. Commitment to science and math education, as well as economic literacy, should be stepped up to the levels of Singapore, a much poorer country.

Much of this requires not just governmental support but parental support. Here we intersect with the issues of family stability and cultural attitudes toward education. Each wave of immigrants into the U.S. has seen the education of their children as a ladder to their advancement. But inner-city poverty, teenage births, substance abuse, and single-parent poverty all deter the basic parental desire for a better life for our children. The problems are particularly difficult in the U.S.—in comparison to the other wealthy countries—as they raise the specter of the racial divide. While African Americans are disproportionately represented in the underprivileged categories, the situation is improving. Crucial will be the widespread availability of good, safe public schools with the appropriate technology and resources. Getting children there and keeping them there will also be a challenge. The colleges and universities have aggressively opened their doors to women and minorities. Scholarship money is available. The key is getting there. The Congress and the Administration are addressing these issues today. Nothing could be more important to the sustainability of growth prospects of the American economy.

Legal System Excesses

Finally, the American legal system, which in its glory assures the rights and freedom of the individual, at its worst mires the system in needless litigation and contentious upset. Companies report that legislation on product and service liability over-restricts business activity. There is no more litigious society in the world, and nowhere are there more lawyers relative to the size of the population. While I am not here to beat up on the lawyers—my dad, my uncle, and my brother-in-law are lawyers and my son talks about going to law school—it is clear that too much of a good thing is not so good.

We saw it with the legal maelstrom during the thirty-six days of presidential-election indecision. Armies of lawyers descended upon the state of Florida, egged on by the twenty-four-hour media frenzy—somehow reminiscent of the O.J. Simpson spectacle. Maybe it was the convoy and the reemergence of all those legal talking heads. There has to be a more productive use for all of those resources. In any event, not to belabor the point, the system would be a lot more efficient if it were somewhat less hidebound by excessive legal wrangling and contentious litigation.

But even with these remaining problems, the U.S. stands to move through the opening decades of the twenty-first century as the global technology leader. While U.S. leadership may narrow, it will not disappear. The advantages of having the most innovative, educated, technologically sophisticated country in the world, coupled with the American can-do mindset and financial-market depth, create too big a breach to close entirely. In addition, as we will see in the next chapter, the U.S. has a strong demographic advantage over virtually all of the wealthiest countries in the world, an advantage that is so crucial in today's knowledge-based economy where talent is such a critical performance indicator.

12

The U.S. Demographic Advantage

The demographic advantage of the United States in relation to the other rich countries of the world is that it has a younger, faster-growing population with a very high labor-force participation rate for women. The U.S. will continue to be a magnet for talent. Immigration laws will be further relaxed to help meet the growing demand for labor and the workforce will be augmented as well by the aging Boomers, many of whom will not feel disposed to full retirement until relatively late in life.

There will be a global surge in the number of older people in the next fifty years, largely reflective of the worldwide improvement in health and life expectancy. But according to the United Nations Population Division, the median age of the U.S. population in 2050 will be forty-one years, compared to thirty-six today. This is markedly younger than for the rest of the West—Europe, North America, Japan, Australia, and New Zealand—which will have a median age of over forty-nine years. Unlike the rest, the U.S. is poised for continued population growth over the coming decades. This factor will be a strong positive for sustained growth and prosperity relative to elsewhere in the developed world.

POSTWAR BABY BOOM

Among the G-7 countries, it was only Canada and the U.S. that enjoyed a postwar baby boom (Figure 12.1). Birth rates rose in the U.K. following World War II, but to nowhere near the degree as in Canada, the U.S., Australia, and New Zealand, as the British were busy recovering from the physical devastation of the massive bombings. Between 1946 and 1965, 8.5 million babies were born in Canada. In 2000, these children-turned-middle-aged adults represented an eye-popping 27 percent of the Canadian population. In the U.S., there are just over 75 million Boomers, also representing 27 percent of the population. The number of births in both countries rose over the course of the boom, peaking in the early

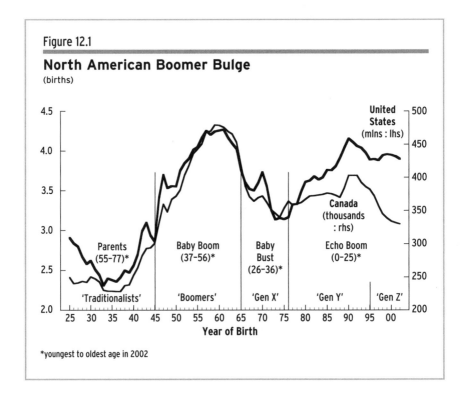

Figure 12.1

North American Boomer Bulge
(births)

*youngest to oldest age in 2002

1960s. So while the oldest Boomers are now in their mid-fifties, the bulk of the generation is still in the neighborhood of forty years old.[1]

For as long as this generation is alive, it will have an important impact on the economic, political, and social fabric of the U.S. and Canada. Child Boomers and their traditional parents created the suburban-consumer culture of the 1950s and 1960s. As teenagers, they led the anti-Vietnam War movement and jammed the colleges and universities. By the 1970s, the leading-edge Boomers were entering the labor force, buying consumer durable goods, and ultimately buying homes. This began the inflation froth of the 1970s and 1980s, as labor force growth surged and so did prices. Women entered the workforce in unprecedented numbers and family formation was postponed. The labor force participation rate of women over the age of sixteen doubled from 32 percent in 1948 to a record 60.5 percent today. The greatest gains in this rate were posted in the late 1960s and 1970s when early-Boomer women swelled the job ranks.

The baby boom was followed by a baby bust. Birth rates peaked in 1957 and fell sharply for about nineteen years. The relatively small age cohort born between 1966 and 1976 is known as Generation X—the group that grew up and entered the job and housing markets in the shadow of the Boomers. These were the first latchkey kids—growing up when divorce was common, moms were at work, and the economy was tough. The birth rate was to resume its upward climb when Boomers began having children in the mid-1970s. This triggered an echo baby boom that began in 1977 and continues today. U.S. birth rates, though down slightly from their 1990 echo-boom peak, remain high today.

A THEORY OF SEX AND THE ECONOMY[2]

The power of demographic forces is considerable, altering the social fabric of nations and driving the longer-term economic trends. The dramatic escalation in birth rates in the United States and Canada, beginning in the 1940s—well before the official start of the baby boom—and lasting until 1960, triggered a gender-related social revolution twenty-five years later. Some social demographers have suggested that the reason for the sexual revolution was *the excess supply of marriageable women*—more women than men in the age range most common for first marriages—no kidding.[3] This led to the significant shift away from traditional family values.

Some believe the "marriage squeeze"—in this case, too few men for the number of marriageable women available—can explain many of the social changes that ensued.[4] These changes include the rise in sexual promiscuity, the postponement of marriage and childbirth, the increase in the divorce rate, the surge in non-family households, and the dramatic uptick in the labor force participation rate of women that began in the 1960s and culminated in the mid-1980s. Some have seen the marriage squeeze as a major contributor to the women's liberation movement in the U.S. between 1960 and 1975.[5] Belinda Tucker and Claudia Mitchell-Kernan, among others, have argued that for female African Americans, the marriage squeeze was particularly severe, which has contributed to the crisis of the African American family.[6] While no single factor can explain social change fully, this one—the marriage squeeze—does provide some provocative insight.

THE SEX RATIO AND ITS IMPLICATIONS

The *sex ratio* is defined by demographers as the number of men per one hundred women for a selected population cohort—in this case, unmarried adults in their twenties. A high sex ratio reflects an excess supply of marriageable men. Colonial America in the seventeenth century and the Frontier West in the nineteenth century were extreme cases. A low sex ratio reflects an excess supply of marriageable women, as evidenced in the U.S. during the period from roughly 1965 to 1985, which is likely to arise once again around 2002 to 2015—twenty-five years after the peak in a period of rising birth rates.

First-time bridegrooms tend to marry women their age or younger. The average age difference is two to three years. This trend has remained constant for decades and is still true. It appears to be unrelated to education or socioeconomic background—women generally marry men their age or older. This is not to say there aren't exceptions, but for first marriages the pattern is quite clear. The pool of marriageable women twenty or twenty-five years after a rapid rise in birth rates exceeds the number of older men. Since nearly every year from 1940 until 1960 saw a larger number of births than the year before, each age group of older men sought partners among a larger group of eligible women. The number of eligible men was too small for the growing group of younger women. According to some social demographers, this had profound effects on the socioeconomic backdrop of the period from 1965 to 1985.

The situation changed dramatically from 1986 through to about 2002, however, as the sex ratio rose sharply and eligible women became relatively scarce. Once the bulk of the Boomers passed through their twenties—which happened in 1985—then the younger remaining Baby Boom men had to begin looking for their female companions within a smaller group from the Baby Bust generation born between 1966 and 1976. The marriage squeeze for females was then over for the Baby Bust—better known as Generation X—females.

Sorry, ladies of my generation; the Boomer females will forever be in excess supply, because middle-aged male Boomers in search of a *new* mate still dip back into the younger age pool, often very far back. This exacerbates the female surplus for Boomers, and the female shortage for Generation Xers, given that significantly older men are often more attractive to young women in the marriage market, providing greater financial security in a still-healthy package, thanks to today's fitness craze. So we see that there are far more unattached Boomer women than men, even as they move through their forties and fifties. In fact, according to Professor Charles Jones of the University of Toronto, the marriage squeeze for women today intensifies with age. Based on the 1996 Canadian census data (similar results will likely be evident in the latest U.S. census data as well, when they are released), there was no marriage squeeze for women in their late twenties in 1996. But the sex ratio falls sharply as female age rises. For women in their late forties and early fifties, there were nearly two marriageable women for every available man. That will come as no surprise to my single Boomer friends, male and female.

Generation Y—born between 1977 and 1995—will have a Boomer-like experience. Thanks to the rising birth rates over much of that period, twenty-five years later, men will be in relatively scarce supply. That means that from roughly 2002 until 2020 we may well see a resurgence of women entering and remaining in the workforce, as many never marry.

THE SOCIAL IMPLICATIONS OF SHIFTS IN THE SEX RATIO

The changing balance of the sexes among first-time marrieds has interesting implications for society, the economy, and business. A number of cultures have long had disproportionately few women relative to men in the marriage pool. These include societies where male babies are especially prized—for example, China, India, Latin America, and Muslim countries. In societies where sex ratios are high—more eligible men than women—young adult women are highly valued for their glamour and beauty when single, and for their skills as a wife and mother when married. Men are in competition to possess the *"best"* wife possible and are willing to make and keep a social and financial commitment to remain with her. When women are scarce, men and women marry younger, as the most "desirable" men attach themselves to the most "desirable" women as early as possible, before the pickings get too slim.

When women are scarce, men attempt to have exclusive possession of a mate, virginity is prized in potential wives, and a double standard exists—males might be promiscuous, but females are expected to be chaste. Women, achieving their satisfaction through traditional roles in the family, have a subjective sense of power and control over their lives because they can choose among a number of men for a marriage partner. They often gain economic mobility through marriage, marrying upward in socioeconomic class. They do not have strong career ambitions, nor do they actively agitate for personal or political rights. With limited exception, this scenario characterized the societies of Canada and the United States from the 1930s until the mid-1960s.

Beginning in the early 1960s, however, the tables turned in North America. The sex ratio began to plunge, and marriageable men were in increasingly short supply until the mid-1980s. As sociologists Paul Secord and Marcia Guttentag pointed out in their 1983 book entitled *Too Many Women? The Sex Ratio Question,*[7] societies with more marriageable women than men exhibit social, cultural, and economic trends opposite to those described above. Sexual libertarianism becomes the prevailing ethos and transient relationships rather than long-term monogamy are prevalent. Men have multiple relationships with women and are in less of a hurry to commit to one woman in marriage. Women have a subjective sense of economic powerlessness and are more likely to be valued as sex objects than as wives and mothers. These women find it difficult to achieve economic mobility through marriage. More men and women remain single or, if they marry, they are more apt to get divorced. Divorce rates surge, but the remarriage rate is high for men only. The number of single-parent families headed by women increases markedly.

Women react to this situation by trying to achieve economic and political independence. Feminism emerges, the average education level of women rises, and more and more women enter the labor force. Men can no longer be counted on to provide economic stability—not even husbands—given the transience of a growing number of marriages. Women demand and gain more sexual freedom. The widespread use of reliable contraception in the 1960s and the legality of abortions reflect these demands. Women delay motherhood to assure that their careers are well anchored, and a growing number have babies out of wedlock when the biological clock runs down to the wire.

But, it all changed once again for Gen X, albeit temporarily, with the return to the traditional values of an earlier era as the sex ratio rose and young women returned to a position of relative scarcity. This transformation began in the late 1980s and was accelerated by the fear of AIDS and other sexually transmitted diseases. It was reflected, as well, in the considerable shift to political conservatism. From 1985 through 2002, the number of family households began to grow faster than the number of non-family households for the first time in twenty years. Birth rates trended upward once again. Divorce rates peaked in 1981 and have trended downward ever since (Figure 12.2). Most telling of all, the labor-force participation rate of young women peaked in late 1989 in the U.S. at over 66 percent and has moved lower ever since.

Similar to the period immediately following World War II, women since 1985 have been leaving the workforce in reasonable numbers when they have children. Many made the choice to stay at home, at least while their children were young. This was a choice that their Boomer sisters often felt they were unable to make without jeopardizing their hard-won career progress and their future financial security. We will never return to the suburban-housewife days of *Ozzie and Harriet, The Donna Reed Show,*

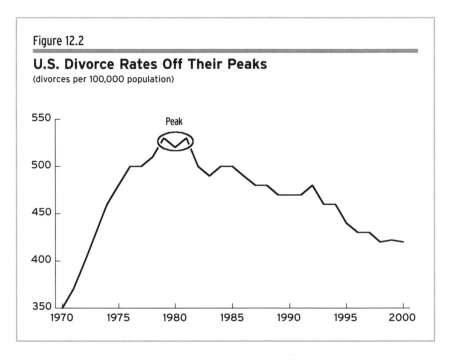

Figure 12.2

U.S. Divorce Rates Off Their Peaks
(divorces per 100,000 population)

Father Knows Best, or *Leave It to Beaver*. Economic reality is such that it often takes two incomes just to maintain a reasonable standard of living for most families. And many women, now having the elder Boomers as role models in business and government, will never want to return to their more traditional roles. In some respects, therefore, it is impossible to turn back the clock in full.

THE LIFE CYCLE OF SPENDING AND INVESTMENT

When the Boomers came of age and began to enter the labor force, the effect on the U.S. and Canadian economies was enormous. By the mid-1970s, household formation boomed and residential real estate values began their upward climb. Labor-force growth surged as well, boosted by the unprecedented influx of women to the working community, and nominal GDP growth escalated. Inflation and real expansion were fueled by the rapid growth in consumption—both for durable consumer goods and for high-end convenience-oriented services. The new households—traditional and nontraditional—had more money than time, and convenience, rather than bargain, was the watchword. Purchases of women's business apparel, sports cars, and restaurant meals surged, just to name a few of the sectors impacted.

The tides began to turn as we moved into the 1980s, however; Boomers were having children and settling down. Home purchases soared and house prices began a multi-year boom that would not end until the late 1980s. As we moved into the 1990s, Boomers—now accompanied by Gen Xers—were strapped with more financial responsibility and became decidedly more value conscious. Families with children, burdened with mortgages and daycare bills, were far less likely to spend a night on the town or buy an expensive sports car. The mass of new entrants to the workforce and the first-time homebuyer's market had dissipated and inflation pressure began to wane. In came the family-friendly SUVs and minivans and out went the two-seater sports coupes—at least until the Boomers became empty nesters.

As the eldest Boomers moved into middle age, the financial and economic climate continued to shift. The peak earning years in the U.S. (and Canada) are generally between ages forty-five and fifty-four. The peak spending years are typically in the late-forties, although that age is probably rising because Boomers had children later than earlier generations. Around age fifty (or thereabouts), household expenditures begin to decline—children leave home and college tuition bills are finally over. This is the time when households commonly become net savers, rather than net debtors, and mountains of money begin to pour into financial assets. For Boomers, the financial asset of choice is the stock market. The surge in stocks since the mid-1990s—even with the lapse in 2000–2001—coincided with the first Boomers turning fifty. Just as Boomers raised the price of houses when they moved into that market, they are raising the price of stocks as they move, once again en masse, into their investment years.

Every seven seconds, a Boomer turns fifty. I know. I recently did that myself. There is nothing like the "Big 5-0" to make people think about retirement saving. And these Boomers are certainly not rolling in excess dough. Many will still be paying college bills, which average more than $8,000 a year in the U.S. for tuition and room and board at a public school. They may also be facing the responsibility of eldercare, as their parents move toward assisted living. Tight as the squeeze might be, however, investment flows will rise and continue very strong for at least the next twenty years. Even beyond age sixty-five, Boomers will remain invested in stocks to garner the higher rates of return.

The net accumulation of wealth generally continues until age sixty-five to seventy, depending on the age of retirement. Given the significant rise in life expectancy that will result from coming medical breakthroughs, many will want to work well into their seventies and even beyond. Moreover, the demand for talent and experience in the workplace will augment this trend, which will be enabled by the use of technology. Telecommuting and more flexible work schedules will be available to many in their fifties, sixties, and seventies. Older workers who choose to remain employed beyond traditional retirement age will be an important augmentation to the growth of the workforce in the U.S. and throughout the developed world.

THE ECHO BOOM

The echo baby boom was much bigger in the U.S. than in Canada, augmented by immigration—particularly the immigration of Hispanics, mostly from Mexico and Cuba, whose birth rates are relatively high. The Canadian echo boom was muted by the plunge in birth rates in Quebec, reflective of the waning influence of the Catholic Church.

Just as important as the Baby Boomers today in the U.S. are the Echo Boomers, the young people born after 1976, comprised of what is commonly referred to as Generation Y (born roughly from 1977 to 1995) and Generation Z (born after 1995).[8] The names "Generation Y and Z" seem to have stuck because marketers are familiar with their older cousins, Gen X. But there are all sorts of more creative monikers floating around: Millennials, the Digital Generation, Echo Boomers, Speeders, the Internet Generation, and Generation Next. In the United States today, Generation Y is more than 71 million strong, with increased immigration making up for the Boomers having slightly fewer children than their parents. Adding in their younger siblings, the total number born since 1977 tops 80 million young people. This is the biggest generation in North American history. There are roughly 30 million teenagers, already spending an estimated $150 billion annually.[9] It is far more ethnically diverse than the Boomer generation, as African Americans and Hispanics represent only 18 percent of middle-aged Americans but 33 percent of the youngsters.[10] That ethnic diversity is likely to increase.

Between 2001 and 2010, the number of non-Hispanic white elementary school students will plunge by just over two million, down over 8 percent. The decline in African American elementary school kids will be smaller—about 400,000. Overall enrollment, however, will be increasing steadily. The spots vacated by the African American and white students will be more than made up for by kids of other racial and ethnic backgrounds. The number of Hispanic children will increase by nearly 25 percent and the number of Asian kids will rise proportionately even more.[11]

The Echo Boomers' families are also diverse. While the "traditional" family structure, with two parents present, is still the most common in the U.S., it has rapidly become less so. In 1970, 87 percent of American children lived with two parents. The number declined steadily until the start of the 1990s and has stabilized since at around 70 percent. Nearly 23 percent of all children lived in 1999 with just their mothers, 4 percent with their fathers, and 4 percent lived with neither parent.[12]

The Digital Generation

For all the problems that remain in American society, the truth is that things are getting better. Teenage pregnancies, drug use, and dropout rates are down. For all the grief over the horrifying shooting tragedy at Columbine high school in Colorado in 1999, students have a higher likelihood of being struck by lightning than being shot at school. Scholastic Aptitude Test (SAT) scores for college entrance are at their highest in a generation, and the number of kids going on to higher education is at a record of nearly 65 percent in the U.S. today. Throughout the developed world, the polls suggest that this is the most optimistic group of teenagers in decades.

More than 65 percent of American households with children have computers with Internet access. Although only 10 percent of American university students graduate with science or engineering degrees, nearly all use e-mail, have access to the Internet, and are very experienced Web surfers. While Gen Xers embraced computers in high school and college,

Gen Ys were introduced to them in primary school. In the case of Gen Z, many will be computer literate even before they get to school. For these kids, multimedia will be as prevalent in the classroom as chalk. Teens today are often the Chief Technology Officer of the family and are more computer literate than their parents—a fundamental achievement for the innovation that is central to the economy.[13] Kids have always been better at something than their parents, but in days gone by it was often in games, music, or sports, not the most important technological breakthrough of the era.

American Echo Boomers are the richest generation in history, the best educated, the healthiest, and they know even less about war, famine, disease, and poverty than their pampered parents. The eldest among them have entered college. They will begin to enter the workforce well before the eldest Boomers start to retire. The Boomers will be the big shadow over their careers, first as the elder statespeople in the workplace and then as the pensioners who threaten to bankrupt the Social Security System. Eventually, the Boomers will be the benefactors who bestow trillions of dollars on their heirs, if they don't spend it all themselves—which is possible.

The Echo Boomers will be a new breed in the workplace, more similar to their Gen X cousins than their Boomer parents. Like Michael Dell, the customized-computer wizard, and Napster genius Shawn Fanning, this generation will not be afraid to innovate, to think outside of the box. They are not even aware that there is a box. Bill Gates was a nineteen-year-old Harvard dropout when he began what was to be Microsoft. Marc Andreessen was twenty-four when he created Netscape, the first commercial Web browser. Whiz kids brought us Yahoo!, eBay, and a plethora of dot-coms. The Internet is the first technology revolution in history that has been led by the young, because the young understand the technology. That is why having the youngest, best-educated population in the G-7 is such an important competitive advantage for the U.S., and it will continue to be an advantage for decades.

American culture is particularly adept at accepting the renovating influence of youth in its business community. It is not nearly as hidebound by tradition as much of Europe, Japan, or China. Never embracing the Confucian reverence for age and tradition, the American spirit is always rife for revolution. The technologically precocious are now starting businesses in their dorm rooms and basements. In a break with tradition, Harvard University has dispensed with a long-standing rule prohibiting student businesses run from dormitories. Prospective students were threatening to go elsewhere unless they could bring their high-school companies with them. Had this been allowed in Bill Gates's day, he might have completed his Harvard degree. To be sure, the swell of euphoria has been dampened by the dot-com debacle of 2000, but the passion of youth will continue to drive much of the coming technology revolution.

This digital generation is particularly well suited to the vagaries of the ever-volatile marketplace. They expect upheaval and churning. They welcome change and unpredictability far more than their parents do. They are looking for an opportunity to learn, not for lifelong employment. They see themselves as consultants or free agents, rather than tethered to the corporate structure. They expect no loyalty from the company and they give none. Their creed is challenge and interesting work. They will continue to job-hop; they are the benefactors of outsourcing and they are entrepreneurial. According to an Opinion Research Council survey, 54 percent of eighteen- to twenty-four-year-olds are interested in starting their own business compared to 36 percent of thirty-five- to sixty-four-year-olds. Mortgages and kids do not yet shackle them—they are risk-taking and thrill-seeking, a boon to innovation and growth.

U.S. IMMIGRATION

The U.S. population has also been augmented in recent years by an influx of immigrants. Thanks to enormous demands for labor and the freeing of trade, Americans have become far less paranoid about the threat of immigration. The U.S. has always been a nation of immigrants, but beginning in the early 1900s—following the huge inflow of workers primarily from Europe—the borders were gradually closed as residents feared the competition for jobs. U.S. immigration fell sharply from 1925 to 1945. It bottomed in the 1930s at an average rate of around 50,000 legal immigrants each year. It has been edging upward ever since.

By the 1990s, the legal average was nearly 700,000 immigrants annually with another 200,000 or so illegal immigrants.[14] Average annual immigration now tops the peak of the great immigration wave at the turn of the twentieth century, although as a percentage of the population it is much smaller. The proportion of foreign-born nationals in the U.S. in 2000 was 10.4 percent, about midway between the high of 15 percent in 1910 and the low of 5 percent in 1970.[15]

The earlier immigration wave was primarily from Europe. Today it is primarily Hispanic and Asian. In 2000, 51 percent of all foreign-born residents were from Latin America, and two-thirds of those were born in Mexico. They are the second-largest immigrant group in American history—the largest when including illegal immigrants. Asians—mostly from China and India—represent 25.5 percent of the foreign-born.

The largest share of new arrivals by far in 1998 was from Mexico, accounting for nearly 20 percent of the 660,000 immigrants legally admitted that year. The next-largest group was from China, at about 6 percent, with another 5.5 percent from India. All European countries combined accounted for roughly 14 percent of the total, with Russia and the U.K. representing the greatest numbers. The European share of America's foreign-born population has dropped sharply over the decades. In 1970, they represented 62 percent of the total, while by 2000, that proportion had dropped to only 15.3 percent, dwarfed by the 51 percent Latinos and 25.5 percent Asians.

The geographical distribution of immigrants is remarkably concentrated in only four states. California, New York, Texas, and Florida account for over half of all immigrants. Adding New Jersey and Illinois raises that proportion to two-thirds. Spanish has become an important second language in all of these states and Spanish-language media and marketing are key factors for economic growth in those regions. Minority experiences have always acted as a powerful force in the creation of the American identity. "The Latinization of America is so profound that no one really sees it," says Kevin Starr, the leading historian of California.[16] When I was a kid growing up in Baltimore in the 1950s, ketchup was preferred to salsa, if salsa even existed in the stores—but there's a good chance salsa outsells ketchup today.

Immigrants bring a new enthusiasm to the U.S. experience, anxious to partake of the American dream. In the workplace, they expand the labor pool at both ends of the knowledge spectrum—the highly skilled and the unskilled. They are among the best- and the worst-educated, overrepresented relative to the population as a whole in the proportion with graduate degrees and the proportion with less than a high-school education. For the native-born population, the proportion with a bachelor's degree or higher was 25.8 percent in 2000, compared to 44.9 percent for Asian and 32.9 percent for European immigrants. Not surprisingly, the Asian and European immigrants had disproportionately higher incomes as well.

At the other end of the knowledge divide, 4.7 percent of native-born Americans over the age of twenty-five had less than a ninth grade education, compared to 34.6 percent of Latin American immigrants. The good news is, though, that Mexican-Americans do not remain mired in poverty. *The Wall Street Journal* cited a recent study by the Thomas Rivera Policy Institute, which found that Hispanics are quickly climbing the economic ladder.[17] While the number of Hispanic households doubled between 1979 and 1998, to 7.5 million, the number of those in the middle class—defined as those having an annual household income of $40,000 or more—increased by 80 percent. Hispanics born in the U.S. are doing better than those newly arrived, a pattern common for all immigrant groups. The reason for the upward mobility is, not surprisingly, education. Nearly 80 percent of Hispanic children born in the U.S. finish high school, while the majority of their parents did not. Still, more improvement is necessary to encourage these kids to stay in school. Only about 15 percent of Hispanics earn a bachelor's degree, half the rate of non-Hispanic whites.

THE REST OF THE DEVELOPED WORLD

The remainder of the developed world, outside of the U.S. and Canada, is for the most part top-heavy, aging, and shrinking in population. Table 12.1 shows that among the G-7 countries, the U.S. and, to a lesser degree, Canada, have the youngest and fastest-growing populations. Japan and Italy are the oldest and most stagnant. While the workforce is forecasted to decline at an average annual rate of roughly 0.3 percent in Japan and Italy, and 0.1 percent in Germany, it will grow by almost 1.0 percent in the U.S. and 0.6 percent in Canada. While all of the developed economies are aging, people over the age of sixty-five will represent only 15.1 percent of

Table 12.1

G-7 Population

	1999-2015 Avg. Ann. Population Growth Rate (percent)	Population Aged 65 and Over* (percent of total)		Labor Force Avg. Ann. Growth Rate (percent)	Female Percent of Labor Force
		1998	2015	1999-2010	1999
Canada	0.6	12.3	15.9	0.6	45.6
France	0.3	15.5	18.1	0.3	44.9
Germany	-0.2	15.7	20.3	-0.1	42.2
Italy	-0.3	17.0	22.5	-0.3	38.3
Japan	-0.1	16.0	24.7	-0.3	41.3
United Kingdom	0.0	15.8	18.9	0.0	43.9
United States	0.8	12.3	15.1	0.9	45.8

*2000 *World Development Indicators*, March 2000, 38–40
Source: *The World Bank, 2001 World Development Indicators*, April 2001, 44–46, 48–50

the population in the U.S. in 2015, compared to 24.7 percent in Japan (a huge problem given their public debt levels), 22.5 percent in Italy, and 20.3 percent in Germany. The aging trends are not as pronounced in France and Britain, but they exceed the U.S.

Developed countries are rightfully worried about how a relatively small proportion of working people in the future will support the enormously generous pension and health care systems. In countries such as Germany, Japan, Spain, and Italy, the population over sixty-five already exceeds those under fifteen, creating a frightening imbalance for the future.

Much of aging Europe has been plagued by relatively high unemployment rates, which disproportionately hurt younger workers. For instance, in 2000, nearly a third of those under age twenty-five in Spain were jobless, and in Italy and France the situation for youth was not much better. It is difficult to imagine that the young could be a driving force in reforming the corporate culture of Europe—as they have been in North America—when they can't even get their foot in the door.

The youth are no less frustrated in Japan. Restrictive labor policies, age-bound traditions of apprenticeship and corporate paternalism, and a bureaucratic culture that is highly reluctant to change hamstring much of continental Europe and Japan. The irony is, however, that their future growth prospects lie in a growing workforce and population base. But, in Japan especially, fertility rates are falling because of the more-than-decade-long economic slump, and the job and financial insecurity that it has generated. In 1999, the fertility rate in Japan fell to 1.48 children per woman per lifetime, the lowest ever recorded there, well below the 2.1 rate in the U.S.

For a developed country, the U.S. fertility levels are remarkably high. With the sole exception of tiny Iceland, the U.S. fertility rate in the 1990s was the highest in the developed world at 2.1, compared to 1.4 for the rest of the grouping. America's changing ethnic composition accounts for only part of this difference; Hispanic Americans now equal African Americans in total numbers, according to the latest census. Non-Hispanic white American women are currently having 1.7 births per lifetime.

THE BABY BOOM IN THE DEVELOPING WORLD

Most of the emerging world is quite young, with rapidly growing populations. The exceptions are the countries of the former Soviet bloc. Their populations are relatively old, more in line with the age distribution of much of continental Europe. According to a recent United Nations Population Division report, Russia is slated for a dramatic, demographically driven decline in its economic clout.[18] Today the Russian Federation has one of the lowest fertility rates in the world, at only 1.14 births per woman. Mortality levels are appalling, currently hovering between those of the Dominican Republic and North Korea. The Russian population is forecast to plunge from 146 million in 2000 to 104 million in 2050, the same level posted in 1950. The working-age population will fall even more precipitously. While Russia today is the sixth most populous country, it would be only number seventeen in 2050—smaller than Vietnam, Iran, or even demographically-challenged Japan; this is only slightly larger than Turkey. While demographics isn't everything, it is hard to imagine that Russia in the next fifty years will regain its former superpower stature.

For countries in the emerging world, the key to future economic prosperity will be their ability to educate their populations and provide them with the technology needed to excel in the New Economy. As we have seen, there have been varying degrees of success thus far, with East Asian countries acting as the leaders and Africa, parts of South Asia, and Latin America the laggards.

The twentieth century was one of unprecedented population growth. In 1950, there were roughly 2.5 billion people on the planet, and that number surged to just over 6 billion by 1999. According to recent projections, the 7 billion mark will be surpassed in 2014, a slowdown from the pace of the previous billion.[19] Most of those babies will be added in the poorest parts of the world, where they can be only minimally nurtured. More than half of the next billion will be born in South Asia (India, Bangladesh, and the like) and sub-Saharan Africa. East Asia and the Pacific will add about 220 million, and the remaining 230 million will be divided mostly between the Middle East and North Africa, Latin America, and the Caribbean. Today's highest-income countries will add a scant 30 million, or 3 percent of the total, over the next fifteen years.

However, there is good news coming for the developing world on the population front. The proportion of the population that is working age is slated to rise 66 percent by 2014, faster than the rise in youth dependents (children under the age of fifteen). It was this very demographic shift that occurred in East Asia years ago, enabling the dramatic improvement in education and living standards. In 1999, a third of the people in the poorest countries were under the age of fifteen, while only a small fraction was aged sixty-five or older. By 2014, young-age dependency is expected to decline to 28 percent, and only a small increase is expected in old-age dependency. The rapid growth in the working-age population in the poorest countries in the world—particularly India and Bangladesh—will provide a window of economic opportunity.

David Bloom and Jeffrey Williamson call this the *demographic gift*—the young-age dependency ratio falls rapidly before the old-age ratio rises.[20] This happened first in East Asia and will be followed in Latin America and then South Asia. Bloom and Williamson estimate that fully one-third of the surge in per capita income growth in some East Asian countries was the direct result of this demographic bonus. Pressures and demands on education systems were reduced, allowing for greater coverage and improvements in quality. These boosts brought increases in savings rates and productivity growth, which, together with the rise in employment, gave enormous impetus to economic expansion.

These positive changes do not come automatically, however. They require concerted government effort to strengthen human capital development and technology usage, as well as to enhance labor market flexibility and attractiveness for foreign direct investment. The challenge is real, but the opportunity remains.

THE GENDER BATTLE

The issues surrounding the role of women in the economy will be of enormous importance for the developing as well as the developed world. Evidence suggests that high fertility is as much a symptom of poverty as a cause. Many of the burdens of poverty fall more heavily on girls and women. In most parts of the emerging world, fewer girls than boys enroll, remain, and learn in schools, with negative implications for future reductions in fertility rates and child mortality. Gender-sensitive investment in health care and education is crucial to the long-term economic development of the emerging world.

But it is no less important in the developed world as well. It is no coincidence that the richest and fastest-growing economy of the past twenty years, the United States, is also the one where the role and opportunities for women in education and the workplace are among the highest. While women still face cultural restrictions and a glass ceiling in the corporate world, it is undeniably true that women have greater opportunity for advancement and accomplishment in the U.S. today than ever before, and in the U.S. in comparison to most of the developed world. Exceptions exist—Sweden, for example, has a highly educated and accomplished female population; but in the main, women are under-represented in business, government, and the professions in much of Europe and Japan.

In the U.S. today, women outnumber men in the colleges and universities and they are more likely than their male counterparts to finish their degrees. They account for nearly half of all medical and law school enrollments and are beginning to make their way to the very top of the corporate ladder in the Fortune 500 companies. Carly Fiorina, CEO of Hewlett-Packard, was recently on the cover of *Business Week* and she is no longer alone in the corporate suites and boardrooms of America. Women entrepreneurs are also taking the country by storm, as the proportion of women owner-operated businesses has surged in the past two decades. In the U.S. today, the girls in a family are just as likely as the boys to be encouraged to get a higher education and to think about their careers and financial security. This trend is augmented by the increasing role of women in the news media. In direct contrast to some countries in the developed world, there has yet to be a female head of state in the U.S., but the likelihood of a woman president in the next decade (or so) has got to be high.

The role of women in American business is having its effect all over the world. American companies are more likely than Canadian, European, or Japanese businesses to be headed by a woman, and only in the U.S. have women now had more than twenty years of corporate experience. It is not surprising, therefore, that in a recent *Wall Street Journal* article featuring the top-ten women business leaders in Europe, three were American, including Margaret Barrett at Merrill Lynch HSBC, Fabiola Arredondo at Yahoo!, and Marjorie Scardino at Pearson Plc.[21] In Canada, American firms have promoted more women to the CEO spot than domestic firms have. Many of the top women business leaders in Canada are running the Canadian subsidiaries of American companies, including General Motors, Home Depot, Kraft, Merrill Lynch, Cisco Systems, and Xerox.

Foreign affiliates have always been an important training ground for American business leadership, so it is not surprising that so many women are now popping up in these spots all over the world. This global infiltration of the American gender mindset is already having an effect.

SOLUTIONS TO THE DEMOGRAPHIC PROBLEMS OF THE DEVELOPED WORLD

As the labor force growth slows with an aging population, especially in continental Europe and Japan, the keys to addressing the pension "time bomb" and other associated problems are as follows:

- Encourage women in the workforce.
- Increase immigration.
- Abolish mandatory retirement.

The Role of Women

The increased role of women in the workforce has been a major source of economic dynamism in the U.S. and Canada for more than twenty years. Additional actions to eliminate cultural and legal impediments to greater educational and workforce participation of women would spur growth throughout the developed world. Technology can be more effectively used to deal with the responsibilities of family and work life. More flexible working arrangements, telecommuting, corporate support for family and home responsibilities, and a more equal sharing of these responsibilities between men and women would all contribute to the improving productivity of half of the world's people—women. Many can and will choose to spend some time outside the workforce when raising children, but it should be a matter of choice, not a matter of cultural stricture as it is today in Japan and much of Europe.

Widely available information technology and workers hoping to balance work and family have generated a strong interest in telecommuting—working at home using IT. This can be full-time or part-time work. It is estimated that as much as 10 percent of the American workforce in 2000 were teleworkers.[22] These arrangements often increase worker satisfaction and productivity. The digital economy generates millions of jobs that can be done in workers' homes either all or part of the workweek. More than two-thirds of all workers use a computer at work every day, according to the John Heldrich Center for Workforce Development. The growth of inexpensive, high-speed, secure Internet connections will assure that telework becomes increasingly more prevalent. The percentage of Internet users with broadband access is expected to triple from just over 7 percent to 21 percent from 2000 to 2003. Not only will this help to assure that retirees and working parents have greater flexibility and access to the labor market, but it is a valuable component to reducing traffic congestion and air pollution, especially in urban centers. Companies that already have formal telework programs include AT&T, Merrill Lynch, Prudential, IBM, Mobil Oil Corporation, United Airlines, Cisco Systems, and Johnson & Johnson.

International Integration

In the U.S., immigration is already a key driver of economic growth. In Europe and Japan it has been a more moderate factor, discouraged in large measure by the intentional homogeneity of the society and the fear of job competition. Particularly in core Europe—Germany, France, and Italy—where the jobless rate remains high, the fear of foreign invasion (except for the most menial jobs) has been an impediment to productivity growth and the fulfillment of the need for technical workers.

A significant argument can be made for the greater integration of richer and poorer neighbors, as their demographic patterns are complementary. For example, Mexico is aging less rapidly than the U.S. The more the economies integrate through capital flows, trade, and foreign direct investment, the more the overall economic growth of the two will be augmented, mitigating the aging problem in the U.S. As we have seen, the U.S. also attracts students from all over the world and many of them choose to stay. This will be a continuing positive for American economic leadership.

Just as Mexico is aging more slowly than the U.S., Turkey is aging more slowly than the European Union. Complementary benefits would arise from further integration there as well. Similarly, Japan would benefit from opening its borders to the talent in Asia; this process will be only slow to start, however, as long as the economy is weak and the jobless rate of Japanese youth remains high (at least by Japanese standards).

Harness Gray Power

Finally, the role of people over the age of sixty-five will change rapidly in the developed world as the need for talent continues to grow and life expectancy rises. No longer is fifty what it used to be; the Boomer mission for eternal youth has seen to that. And an increasing number of seniors are remaining in the workforce, a trend that was enhanced by the mounting labor shortages in the U.S. in the 1990s. While the economy has slowed for now, the underlying trend of more flexible retirement will nevertheless continue.

Prince Otto Von Bismarck, Chancellor of Germany, established the first Old Age pension system in 1889. He initially set the retirement age at seventy, when life expectancy was only forty-five years. Twenty-seven years later, in 1916, Germany lowered the age to sixty-five. When President Roosevelt and the Congress introduced the Social Security System in 1935, they also set the retirement age at sixty-five. In the U.S. at that time, life expectancy averaged sixty-three years. Anyone receiving Social Security was not expected to do so for long. Back then, people aged sixty-five were truly old—already having lived beyond the average life expectancy of the population. Today, that age falls more than a decade shy of full life expectancy, and the gap will widen sharply in the next twenty years. The mindset in the workplace will change rapidly. This is already happening.

Just as youth are playing an increasing role in the business world, at the other end of the age spectrum, seniors are as well. Septuagenarians such as Alan Greenspan at the Fed, Alan "Ace" Greenberg and Wayne Angell at Bear Stearns, Sandy Weill (who is in his late sixties) at Citicorp, Paul Desmarais at Power Corp., and Warren Buffett at Berkshire Hathaway are but a few of the increasingly visible examples of older people remaining in the workforce well beyond traditional retirement age.

Greater flexibility of work-leisure mix will become more common as people in their fifties, sixties, and seventies seek a work–life balance that falls outside of the traditional roles and mores of the past thirty years. As healthful life is extended considerably, many will chose to remain at least partially employed for much longer. Businesses will outsource increasingly to these people. Just as the young workers are willing to be entrepreneurial and to freelance, the older workers will increasingly do the same, providing their services to former employers and to others on a less structured, more innovative basis. Telecommuting will become increasingly common.

Many employees—working moms and near-retirees, among others— are already seeking more flexible working environments and bosses should listen. After a fifteen-year trend toward workplace flexibility, most large employers now offer setups aimed at allowing people to juggle many roles and responsibilities. But allowing people to simply cut back hours to create a good, permanent part-time job has still not happened at most companies. Those who have chosen to reduce hours—voluntary part-timers—slipped to only 13.8 percent of the U.S. workforce in 2000, compared to 14.3 percent in 1994, according to the Bureau of Labor Statistics. Hewitt Associates in Lincolnshire, Illinois, reports that the number of companies offering part-time jobs fell from 50 percent of the total in 1998 to 47 percent in 1999.

According to the surveys of the American Association of Retired Persons, 58 percent of Baby Boomers want to work part-time into their retirement. While there are plenty of low-paying part-time jobs out there—call centers, retailing, and other low-end service jobs—many people who ask to reduce their hours meet strong resistance. Managing a part-time and full-time workforce can be complex and, from the employer's perspective, can entail issues of office space and open-ended work hours that make the definition and compensation of part-time work difficult. However, most of the costs are manageable. Part-timers tend to pay a larger share of their health insurance, while life insurance, pensions, and payroll taxes tend to cost employers less. In addition, a well-managed part-time program can retain top performers and increase productivity. Pfizer, as an example, began such an experiment in 1999. The company created a part-time sales force called Vista Rx for employees who wanted to work 60 percent of full-time, with benefits. They targeted talented high-performing people and their results exceeded projections. The program has been expanded and internal employees are waiting in line to get in. An increasing wave in this direction is likely in the future.

After all, the financial burdens of retirement at sixty-five (or younger) on a society that could well live to nearly one hundred, will be too much for individuals or the government pension plans to bear. A greater utilization of this very productive labor source will be increasingly prevalent in the developed world.

Five

Realizing Your
Potential
in a Rapidly Changing
World

13

Taking
Personal
Responsibility

We are in a rapidly changing world where traditional forms of personal and financial security are disappearing. No longer can anyone be guaranteed a job for life or a pension that will satisfy all needs in old age. Fewer than half of the working-age population in the U.S. and Canada will be covered by a defined-benefit pension plan, the old-fashioned kind that guarantees your annual income in retirement at close to the maximum earned when you worked. Even if you do work for a big corporation or for a government agency that still offers these pensions, the likelihood of staying there for the thirty years needed to garner the maximum payout is much smaller than in the past.

THE TRADITIONALISTS

The fact is there was really only one generation—the Boomers' parents— that benefited from the conventional retirement system and the lifelong jobs of the past. They were the *Traditionalists*, the children of the Depression and the young warriors of World War II. They understood hardship and self-denial. They finished college and entered the workforce and then they created the great Boomer onslaught. They came of age in the days before the pill, abortions on demand, and drugs. They got there first, but they missed all of the fireworks. Getting there first was their greatest strength. They were a relatively small generation, as birth rates fell during the Depression. They didn't confront the school-entrance and job competition faced by their Boomer children. They climbed the corporate ladders in relative ease and relative solitude.[1]

While this generation had it tough in their formative years, they prospered during their early-adult life. This was the generation to marry and parent the earliest. They were the traditional folks that the Boomers rebelled against with alternative lifestyles, anti-war demonstrations, and women in the workforce. But they benefited from the Boomers. They paid their dues, worked for The Establishment, and saved for retirement. Assuring their retirement security wasn't too difficult, as it was augmented meaningfully by the Boomer-induced surge in the value of their homes and their stock and bond portfolios. The Boomers have supported them in retirement, through Social Security and Medicare contributions. Their generation has an enormous Social Security surplus, a legacy the Boomers will never see.

EARLY BOOMERS—A NEW MINDSET

The Boomers certainly had it good as kids, at least the first half of the generation did, born before 1955. They grew up in the suburbs in the nest of old-fashioned parents. For the most part, dad was at work and mom was at home. Role models were traditional and well established. The leading-edge Boomers came of age during the Vietnam War, while their younger siblings had the Watergate period as their generational marker. The older Boomers got there first—like their parents—before the schools, corporate ranks, and housing markets were too clogged to progress easily. This was the group that marched against Vietnam and in favor of civil rights. The effort to avoid service in Vietnam was a more unifying force than the war itself. We burned our bras and our draft cards and shut down university administration buildings. I missed my sophomore year final exams because the college closed in the wake of the Cambodian-invasion demonstrations.

Even with all of this turmoil and pain—the inner-city riots following the murder of Martin Luther King and the Kent State shootings of students by the National Guard—the leading-edge Boomers maintained a sense of optimism and a belief in the possibilities of change. This group was able to outpace their parents in educational and economic achievement, although much of the latter was the result of two-income families. While the "liberation" of women to the workforce was a powerful positive, it was also a strain on the social fabric. Daycare, work–life balance, latchkey kids, and sexual tension in the workplace became enormous burdens on the psyche.

Leading-edge Boomer women are a unique force in society. They battled their fathers' traditions by finishing college in unprecedented numbers and then many went on to professional and graduate schools. This was the last generation of women to go to the famous single-sex colleges—the Seven Sister Schools—the female rendition of the then mostly male Ivy League.[2] Most of these schools abandoned their single-sex roots and admitted men in the late 1980s. But studies since have shown that graduates of these colleges in the late '60s and '70s have disproportionately risen through the corporate and government ranks, providing role models for younger women today. This was the group that was the most impacted by the social revolution of the '60s to '80s—the group most influenced by the falling sex ratio, the excess supply of marriageable women. These are the ones who found it most difficult to partner for life. Disproportionate numbers are single in their forties and fifties compared to men the same age. Career commitment for them often was more than just self-actualization. Economic reality helped to dictate their career orientation.

LATE BOOMERS—NOT AS IDEALISTIC

Those that were part of the birth explosion from 1955 through 1964—the bigger "half" of the generation—have never had it as good as their older brothers and sisters. Rather than being first in line in the booming '50s, they were last in line in the war-ravaged, inflation-prone '60s. The bomb shelters and air-raid drills of early childhood gave way to the Watergate trauma and the resignation of a president in 1974. The '70s was the decade of oil price shocks, stagflation, the Watergate tapes, and Iranian hostages—the beginning of a downwave in the long economic cycle. While the eldest Boomers were turning thirty by the late 1970s, the youngest Boomers were still children and teens. Economic prosperity was no longer assured. Younger Boomers never shared their older siblings' optimism or feelings of power and omnipotence.

GENERATION X—TOUGH START

Even more disillusioned and prone to cynicism were the Gen Xers, the small cohort born in the birth-dearth years from 1966 through 1976. They came into a world that couldn't have been more different than the *Leave-It-to-Beaver* world of the early Boomers. For many, mom was at work and dad often lived somewhere else. These were the kids that suffered as divorce rates headed higher. This generation—like the Boomers— remembers television without cable (although not without color), vinyl records, and life before the PC. They were the first generation to see the world in real time, thanks to CNN. This group understood adversity and diversity. Markers for them were Chernobyl, Tiananmen Square, and the Challenger disaster. The deep recession of the 1980s put their parents out of work and the recession of the early 1990s made it more difficult for them to start their careers.

Xers therefore are inherently more skeptical, pragmatic, and less trusting than the Boomers, particularly the older Boomers. They came of age in the 1990s and many have excelled in the Internet world. More comfortable outside of traditional organizations, they are well suited to the outside-of-the-box world of the Net. Among their stars are Jerry Yang of Yahoo!, Pierre Omidyar of eBay, and Michael Dell of Dell Computers— putting to lie the stereotypical "slacker" moniker they were once pinned with.

I have already discussed the Boomers' kids—the enormous cohort born after 1976. Generation Y is coming of age today in a world where, for many, the computer is ubiquitous and the Net is their medium of choice. The oldest ones are finishing university. The teens, in their huge numbers, will dominate the landscape for some time, and the kids will remain a growing force in the U.S. thanks to continued high fertility rates.

WARP SPEED IN THE ACCELERATION AGE

Technology has altered the business world in a way that will never be undone. Speed is key to success. Information technology provides the data necessary to respond at a pace unheard of in history. The slowdown in economic activity in late 2000 and 2001 was a dramatic example of the degree to which business can and must adjust quickly and forcefully. The just-in-time downturn showed how abruptly and dramatically companies would react to slowing demand. In no time, production was slashed, capital spending plans were shelved, and workers were laid off. If we needed any proof that there was no such thing as long-term job security any longer—not even in the fastest-growing sectors—the economic downturn of 2001 provided it.

But this acceleration in the pace of change is not new—it has been in train for some time. Obsolescence is more rapid, fashions shift more quickly, and the loyalty bonds within institutions, corporations, and families have weakened. More and more of us are nomads, wandering far from our hometowns for school and jobs. Extended families are increasingly dispersed, so children lack the comfort and guidance of multi-generation family caregivers. Marriage is no longer immutable— symbolized by Toffler's "paper wedding gown" in the throwaway economy/society.[3] Career stability—working for a single company for thirty-five years—is increasingly rare. In fact, executive recruiters today will tell you that staying too long in one job doesn't look good on your resumé. It gives a sense of complacency and lack of experience and ambition. The ground is constantly shifting underfoot and people are aware of this. There is no permanence; nothing stays the same.

As Lawrence Friedman, law professor at Stanford University put it: "The Old World suffered through wars, plagues, and vast nomadic movements. But these events took place within a mind-set, a mental framework, of greater fixity and stability than would be true today."[4] While we expect change today and do not see it as necessarily causing instability and insecurity, it does take its toll—psychologically and emotionally and also from an economic perspective. This is the Acceleration Age.

THE DISPOSABLE WORKER

Ever since the economic restructuring of the early 1980s, corporate America has believed that layoffs are a sure and fast way to fight sagging profits. They cut costs, reposition a business, and increase productivity— or so the conventional wisdom goes. It is true that a competitive advantage of the U.S. compared to Europe and Japan is the flexibility of its labor markets, but this does not come without a price. Repeated downsizing and layoffs reduce employee loyalty, as well they should. The only way to survive psychologically in the workforce today is to see yourself as a free agent—a consultant selling your services to the bidder offering the greatest opportunity or compensation. But the corporation and the individual bear the burden of this approach.

Rather than increasing productivity, layoffs can sometimes hurt it by leaving "surviving" workers overburdened and demoralized. It can damage customer relationships, disrupting continuity and reducing the likelihood of a corporate memory. Lessons learned through the experience of departing workers are lost. According to the *Wall Street Journal*, Watson Wyatt Worldwide found that fewer than half of the companies it surveyed after the 1990 recession met profit goals after downsizing. Bain & Co. found that companies that announced mass or repeated layoffs underperformed the market over a three-year period. And Mercer Management Consulting found that 68 percent of the "cost cutters" it studied did not achieve profit growth for five years. True, these might have been a self-selected group of underperforming companies by virtue of the fact that they laid off workers in the first place, but layoffs have now become a routine practice for many large corporations.

The result is that employee loyalty and corporate identification have dramatically waned. You don't engender a sense of shared mission by resorting to layoffs first. Turnover rates rise and often the most productive employees are the ones you lose, while the laggards remain. The costs of finding, replacing, and training new workers are high and the disruption is meaningful. Nevertheless, impermanence in the workforce is a fact of today's economic life and all of us must cope with it.

THE PRESIDENT OF YOUR OWN PERSONAL SERVICES CORPORATION

If it weren't the layoffs during the weak periods that disrupt, it would be the mergers and acquisitions during the strong ones. Churning in the job market is an inherent characteristic of current economic reality. New replaces old, and then new-new replaces new, and the only thing you can count on is that change is unremitting. In this world, each of us must adopt a *"quit-your-job"* mentality.[5] I don't mean you should literally quit your job; most of us can't or don't want to do that. I mean, mentally quit your job so that you no longer think of yourself as an employee, but, instead, as an entrepreneur. You are president of your own personal services corporation. I call mine Me, Inc.

As Tom Peters put it so well, you are a brand.[6] You are an entrepreneur, and as such, you must invest in your company—invest in you. Investing in your own human capital is the most important thing you can do to assure financial security in today's Acceleration Age. That means a commitment to lifelong learning, staying at the top of your field, whatever that may be. If you read only one nonfiction book a year, you are in the minority of college graduates, and if you read one per month, you are in the elite 1 percent of the population. There is too much to read—professional journals, popular media, training journals, studies, reports, analyses abound in every field. The world is changing so rapidly, and the knowledge base is expanding so quickly, that remaining current is no easy matter.

The Internet helps, but it hurts too. The noise on the Net can be overwhelming. Sifting through the chaff is tough, distracting, and time consuming. Training is available now on-the-job, online, and at local colleges and universities. Take advantage of it where and when you need it. The responsibility is yours, and it doesn't get any easier the older you get. You must be more than just computer literate. You must understand the technology enough to let it enhance your productivity.

When you think of yourself as president of your own personal services company, your mindset shifts. Your boss is no longer your boss, but your client. And if your services are terminated, often through no fault of your own, you move on to your next client. You are similar to a professional athlete on contract. You work as hard as you can for your team, but if you are put out on waivers, you move on to the next team. Nothing personal—no harm, no foul. A job title can no longer be a definition of self, as it was in the Old Economy. The organization is no longer an extension of family. As big business long ago gave up the mantle of corporate paternalism—taking care of employees from entry to retirement—you too must shift your loyalties. You are committed to building your brand. And you do that by doing the best job possible on every assignment. But think of your work as assignments or projects, not as a job or career in the traditional sense. That way, you have the sense that nothing is forever. When assignments are completed, you move on to the next thing without your ego being damaged.

YOUR GREATEST TALENTS

We are all consultants in a world of consultants, free agents, and entrepreneurs. And there is no point in doing a great job and having unique talents and not letting anyone know about it. Just like any entrepreneur building a business, you must advertise your capability. Sometimes that means volunteering for tough assignments, masterminding unpopular projects, or joining forces with members of other teams. It certainly means getting involved in sectors outside of your current realm, including community service or social endeavors that broaden your scope and contacts. Networking is key in today's world. We are each, in essence, self-employed, whether we work for a big business, government, or ourselves. And like entrepreneurs or free agents everywhere, we must help each other. Trading in favors is a well-worn method of success and development.

Marketing your talents and capabilities is crucial. There is no room for modesty. You are great at something—many things. What are they? People will value your abilities, talent is key in the fast-paced economy of today. Be clear in your own mind where your talents lie. Doing what you are good at usually means doing what you enjoy. Think about the things you have enjoyed most in life, the times you have felt most fulfilled—gratified, with a true sense of accomplishment. Write those things down. It is tough—most people don't have a clue what they really want, let alone how to get it.

GOALS

Time is precious, it is the currency of life, and it is in short supply. Think of time as a gift, not to be squandered. Don't waste it on people or assignments that demotivate or deenergize you. Let's face it, there are plenty of people who will point out the risks in whatever you are attempting to do. Realistically assessing the downside of any option is smart, but assuming the worst will always happen will paralyze you. This is the difference between contingency planning and sober assessment versus negative thinking and a defeatist attitude. Indeed, a positive can-do attitude is crucial for goal fulfillment. And you must be passionate about your goals. Passion is the wellspring of all achievement.

The keys to accomplishing any goal—no matter how tough—are:

- First—conceive of it.
- Second—believe in it.
- Third—act to achieve it.

This isn't as simple as it sounds. Figuring out what it is you want is no small matter. There are many terrific books in the motivational literature that can help you do it. One of my favorites is *Maximum Achievement* by Brian Tracy.[7] I am a real junkie for these motivational books and tapes, devouring one on every vacation. I find they are feel-good, believe-in-yourself material that make any goal seem achievable. And once you believe in your goal, visualize it, and make it real in your mind, you can work to make it happen methodically, step by step. In fact, the psychological conception and visualization almost assures that you take the steps necessary to make it happen. I have used this method over and over in my life. Just as examples: I used it to lose weight as a fat teenager; to get a Ph.D.; to have a happy marriage; to finally have a child when the doctors said it was impossible; to write two books; and to run my first marathon two weeks before my fiftieth birthday. It works.

MARATHON AS METAPHOR

The marathon, as an example, was a very big deal for me. Although I have been an avid fitness buff for more than a decade, I never considered running a strong suit. In fact, I had injured a ligament in my right leg a year earlier and couldn't run for more than about thirty minutes before it would start hurting. But approaching my fiftieth birthday made me want to do something big—reach a new level of fitness, accomplish something I never imagined I could do. I thought of a marathon; the notion had intrigued me for years.

The first thing I did was to buy five books on marathon training. Researching the subject, getting the gist of how it is done and what is involved, is a good starting point for any new endeavor. It also helps to make it real for you psychologically. Scanning each book, I discovered that there is a real science to marathon training. I started talking to people about my desire to run a marathon, which markedly increased my commitment. It went from being a silly pipe dream to a very real goal; I was on the line.

I tried to find a friend who would train with me, at least for the long runs. But everyone I asked thought it was too time-consuming, too difficult, or just plain excessive. So I hired a trainer. This took some homework; I wanted someone who specialized in marathon training and with whom I could relate—feel a sense of simpatico. I believe that support is important in every endeavor. Having a coach, a mentor, can make all the difference. I heard about Julia through my fitness club. She is a terrific young woman who has run many marathons and successfully completed two Iron Man races. Best yet, after meeting me and running with me, she believed I could do it. That kind of support is invaluable; when my self-doubts surfaced, as they did repeatedly during the months of training, Julia's assurances that I was right on track were highly motivational. We met two mornings a week from late May until the marathon date on October 15—one for speed training and one for the long run. I ran on my own the other three days a week and did some weight training on my "rest days."

I kept a detailed diary of my runs, distances and times, on a month-at-a-glance calendar. Writing things down makes them concrete and impresses the psyche with their importance and tangibility. I planned my running routes with a tape measure and a detailed running map of Toronto—obsessing on the precise distance to be run.

My friends and colleagues were subjected to an ongoing commentary of my training. I seemed to live and breathe the marathon, while still doing my very demanding job. The pace was grueling for me; I travel a great deal on business, and so I had to run on strange terrain, in strange cities. On a business trip through Europe, I got lost running in London, Paris, and Berlin. I was so lost in Berlin that I had to get into a taxi to make my way back to the hotel in time to quickly change and catch a plane. I ran in Boston, Chicago, Philadelphia, New York, and Washington, D.C., as well. On really difficult runs when I was feeling tired, I would visualize the finish line and how I would feel in those last few paces. I'd imagine my sense of accomplishment and achievement.

In the meantime, marathon runners seemed to just fall into my life. Once I began to talk about my goal and my training, people with similar interests just started showing up. It is amazing how many avid marathoners there are, and they seek each other's company. This was an enormous source of support as I made my way through the strains of training—constant soreness, hunger, and fatigue. The highs were incredible, but the disappointments on days when even a mile felt like a long distance could really destroy my confidence. The slightest comment that my training was inappropriate or that my diet wasn't quite right could send me into a tailspin for a few hours or even days. But the vision became very real for me. I stopped being concerned about turning fifty and realized that I had never felt stronger, never been more fit. I read runners magazines and watched running videos to keep my motivation going. The three twenty-mile runs you have to do before the actual 26.2-mile marathon were particularly frightening. Bad weather or dark early mornings were no excuse—time was running out.

A month before my birthday, two weeks before the run, my husband and I sent out invitations to my party—inviting people to a celebration of my birthday and first marathon. I was really exposed to failure now. Imagine my embarrassment if I didn't finish the run. The week before the race, I felt just awful. I could barely run. You are supposed to taper training, but even a twenty-minute run seemed like an eternity to me.

Every inch of me ached, my feet burned, and I was perpetually and ravenously hungry. What was worse, I didn't lose an ounce of weight given how much I was eating—not that I needed to lose much, but it would have been nice. The night before the race I couldn't sleep; I was too excited and anxious.

But on race day, it all came together. All the planning, visualization, and training. I kept telling myself, all along the way, I can do this, I can do this. I wasn't fast, but I was steady. I used the power of my mind to keep me going by ignoring my aches, which were increasingly striking as the miles mounted, and concentrating on other thoughts. I had found during the training that I could really make the time fly by thinking about my work, upcoming speeches or articles I was writing. I could become totally immersed in my thought processes and "forget" that I was running. This proved extremely valuable in the marathon. At about the twenty-mile point I had just finished a long, steep descent, which is actually harder on your legs and feet than a climb at that point in the race. My feet were badly blistered and I was running out of gas—I hit the proverbial "wall" but, I realized, I had only six more miles to go, the length of my short run. I practiced over and over in my mind a speech I was about to give that week. I could see my sixty slides, one by one, and worked my way through the analysis, over and over again. The more I concentrated on the speech, the less my blisters bothered me. The final three miles were uphill and it was pouring rain. I knew I could do it, I knew I would finish. The feeling going into the final few hundred meters is indescribable. The crowds were cheering, my friends and family were applauding, and I burst into tears as I crossed the finish line. The sheer utter joy of it was amazing.

It took me a week to come down from the high. As tired as I was, I couldn't sleep because I was still so excited, so thrilled about what I had done. I will never set any records; I did the Toronto marathon in four hours and twenty-one minutes, but for a first-time, almost fifty-year-old female runner, that was not bad.

I realized throughout the training that the marathon is a metaphor for life. By the end, maybe even in the beginning, it is a head game. It is more psychological than physical in many ways. Accomplishing the goal required a series of steps, each one following on the one before. When the goal itself seemed overwhelming, focussing on just the next step, just the next day's run, made it doable. As it turned out, it was not the marathon itself that was difficult, it was the training—all those dark mornings and cold, rainy afternoons. But visualizing the result and believing it was possible made it happen. I truly believe that any physically able person can do it—anyone, that is, who is willing to believe in the possibility, commit to it, and work for it.

You can achieve any goal you set. All it takes is a positive mindset, perseverance, and commitment. If you think you can, you can.

YOUR GAME PLAN

The first step is for you to discover what your goals truly are. To do that, imagine your life if you could achieve absolutely anything with no risk of failure. Write down what your life would look like in terms of your personal, professional, and spiritual achievements. Remember, no limits, no fear of failure. It is difficult to do this. Next, distill the list to its essential elements—the five things you want to accomplish in the next year and in the next five years. Now trim it down even further, to three things, described in five words or less each. Keep those on a piece of paper at your desk and in your home. Better yet, rewrite them every day. The habit of doing this makes the goals believable and, before you know it, you are consciously and unconsciously doing what it takes to achieve them. Assume you can accomplish what you set your mind to; it is really a matter of brainwashing yourself into believing it. Once you do that, you will naturally, almost effortlessly, take action. The mind is that powerful. Every day you do seemingly small things to get you one day closer to your goal. It is truly quite miraculous.

Once a year, update your list—the one-year and five-year goals. I do it New Year's Day each year and keep the list in my briefcase. I have a file going back many years. It is an interesting history of my life, my aspirations, my successes and failures. Sometimes the failures are just postponements—my timing was off. Sometimes they are the result of my discovering along the way that I really didn't want what I thought I did. The disappointments and failures usually teach me something important and often turn out to be a blessing in disguise, or at least they open up another avenue of possibility.

The main thing is to have a road map, a game plan. After all, if you don't know where you want to go, how do you know if you are on the right path? Most people have no concrete, predetermined goals. Instead they live their life from day to day buffeted about by the random events that shake us all. Sure we all want to be happy and achieve some level of success and security, but we often have no idea what will really get us there. In consequence, everything becomes reactive rather than active. This creates a sense of inefficacy, the feeling of being unable to control our destiny.

We are especially vulnerable to these feelings in today's economy, where change is so swift and volatility so great. Too often, others seem to make our decisions for us. But creating your own goals and focusing on achieving them reduces the risk of losing control. Sure the unexpected will happen, but often enough, if you have a solid plan, it can be worked to your advantage. If you are laid off because your company falls on hard times, you may well be available for an even better assignment. Sometimes being forced to change generates the momentum you need to improve your outlook and take on a new and better challenge. Remember the words of Darwin—it is not the most intelligent or the strongest that survive and excel, it is the most adaptable, "the most responsive to change." The main thing is to understand and expect the volatility in today's world, and prepare for it. Even relish it.

14

The Road to Financial Security

Your financial security is increasingly your responsibility alone. You must take control, set goals, and stick to your plan to assure success in this realm as well as in the rest of your life. In today's world, you must expect volatility in financial markets. It is part of the creative destruction process in a period of rapid technological change. Businesses and individuals will be prone to excesses in both directions—up and down. With life expectancy rising rapidly, you have to be prepared for the good times and the bad. The only way to do that is to live below your means, invest regularly, and set your goals with a mind to the volatility inherent in stock market returns.

LIVE BENEATH YOUR MEANS

Wouldn't it be nice if it were simpler—if there were some magic investment plan that would allow you to amass enough wealth to assure your financial security without having to postpone gratification or exhibit self-discipline? Well, there isn't. It really doesn't matter if the rate of return on your portfolio is 8 percent or 18 percent if you have only $1,200 invested. *Wealth is not what you earn but what you keep.* Some of the highest-paid people are not wealthy because they spend it all and more. We often hear of actors, musicians, and professional athletes who ultimately go broke because of lavish living. That is not to say that you shouldn't enjoy life; all of us need to have fun and splurge a bit. It is certainly no fun to pinch pennies or be overly thrifty or money conscious, but at the same time, unless you win the lottery or inherit a lot of money, there is no way to amass wealth without living below your means.

For each person, that means something different. Thomas Stanley and William Danko in their best-selling book, *The Millionaire Next Door*,[1] describe the 3.5 percent of American households, roughly 3.5 million of them, that have a net worth—defined as the current value of their assets less liabilities[2]—of $1 million or more. About 95 percent of these households had a net worth of between $1 million and $10 million and most of the families in this group were self-made.

Stanley and Danko analyzed the statistical relationship between wealth, income, and age. For working people between the ages of twenty-five and sixty-five with annualized incomes of $50,000 or more, there is an expected level of wealth (or net worth excluding inheritances). Those who have net worth above this level can be considered wealthy relative to others their age with their income. So you don't have to be a millionaire to be wealthy. And having a million-dollar net worth does not qualify you as wealthy if your income and age are sufficient to warrant more. If, for example, Michael Jordan, Barbra Streisand, or Oprah Winfrey had only a $2 million net worth, Stanley and Danko would not consider them wealthy. Wealth is relative, not absolute. What is wealthy for a family earning $50,000 annually is very different from what is wealthy for a family earning three times that. They found that high-net-worth households have a low-consumption lifestyle. They are able to save and invest disproportional to their age and income.

How Wealthy Should You Be?

According to the Stanley-Danko research, your expected net worth (less inheritances) should be:

> Your age times your gross annual household income from all sources (except inheritances) divided by ten.[3]

If you are starting out in your career, it is unlikely you will satisfy this criterion, but once you have been working for an extended period, it is an achievable goal. So if you are a fifty-five-year-old corporate CEO making $525,000 a year and have a net worth of $1 million, you are not considered to have high net worth by Stanley and Danko. You have a high-consumption lifestyle and would not be likely to successfully sustain yourself and your family very long in retirement unless you had an exceptional company pension (unlikely because that would normally be considered a part of your net worth). In this example, the CEO's net worth should have been nearly $2.9 million.

But a couple aged fifty earning $52,000 a year with a net worth of $300,000 is wealthy. The formula shows their net worth should be $260,000. These people know how to save and invest on $52,000 in annual income. The trick to wealth accumulation is spending less than you earn and investing it regularly—plain and simple. Most of the wealthy millionaires in the study were quite frugal—surprisingly so. They often cared more about financial security and wealth accumulation than impressing their friends and neighbors with all of their possessions.

Pay Yourself First

The only way to reliably save money is to consider it a necessity—an expense, in a sense. Have the money automatically deducted from your checking account or paycheck once a month, before you have the chance to spend it. It is like the automatic payroll deduction of your mandatory

Social Security contribution.[4] The money never hits your wallet. It is gone before you can spend it, unless, of course, you are among the many who live above your means, having negative net worth. The only way to do that is to live on credit. Credit card debt is the nemesis of these people and it always catches up with them. Often the only solution becomes personal bankruptcy, which might wipe the slate clean of debt but does not wipe the slate clean. The stigma can stay with you for life and precious years of potential accumulation have been wasted.

Ideally, you should save 15 percent of your gross (before-tax) income. This is not easy. With median family income of roughly $52,000 a year and an average federal tax rate at that income level of about 17 percent,[5] it is tough to save any money at all. But you can begin with your Individual Retirement Account (IRA) contribution of $2,000 a year.[6] That is only $167 a month and it adds up. Moreover, the government pays a good chunk of it. Your marginal federal and state tax rate combined at this income level is roughly 33 percent; so one-third of your IRA contribution each year is covered by the government in deferred taxes. Even if you might have enough in pensions and Social Security to fund your retirement needs, you still need a nest egg. Retirement does not make you immune to emergencies—car disasters, leaky roofs, and furnace breakdowns. In addition, extended illnesses and the need for eldercare can become a huge burden on families.

Learning to save is a critical life lesson for all of us. Like our investments in education, it requires postponing the gratification of our needs. Students in university and graduate school forgo the income of full-time employment while they are in school for the benefit of higher compensation over many years in the future. As we have seen, the investment in education pays off handsomely in this knowledge-driven economy. Similarly, over the course of your working life, you must save for the down payment on a house, your kids' college education, emergencies, and, of course, the maintenance of your lifestyle in retirement. No one wants to substantially reduce their standard of living when they stop working, especially with the real prospect of living decades in retirement. While we may be willing to downsize somewhat, and expenses fall when children are self-sufficient, the mortgage is paid off (or nearly so) and work-related expenses are gone—it is still important to achieve a level of net worth that will allow you to live comfortably and relatively worry-free.

If you can't manage to save 15 percent of your gross income, start with 2 percent or 5 percent and gradually work your way up. The important thing is to start, the sooner the better but it is never too late. The trick is to invest regularly—monthly, so that you can dollar-cost average. Invest when prices are up and when they are down so that you share in the upward trend in the stock and bond markets over long periods of time. Do not try to time markets. No one can do it successfully and consistently for long. If they could, tactical asset allocation mutual funds—the kind that takes bets on varying cash, stock, and bond allocations depending on detailed analytical models—would outperform balanced funds (that have static asset allocation), and they don't. Trying to jump in and jump out at just the right moment only makes your broker and the government rich. You run up meaningful commission bills and, unless your money is in a retirement account, you pay a chunk of your capital gains to Uncle Sam (now 20 percent for investments of more than a year, and your ordinary income tax rate for shorter-term investments[7]). That puts you at a huge disadvantage given that the power of compound returns is what propels the growth of your nest egg. Imagine how the day-traders of the Internet-euphoria days felt when they discovered they owed the government one-third or more of their stock market gains, depending on their income.

COMPOUND RETURNS—HOW THEY WORK

The beauty of saving over a long period of time is that your money works for you. Through reinvestment of your returns, they compound. There is a simple rule of thumb to tell you how fast your money will double—the Rule of 72. Dividing the rate of return on your money into 72 gives you the number of years it takes for your money to double. So, for example, if the rate of return is 7.2 percent annually, your money will double every ten years. For it to double every five years, you would have to earn double the rate of return, or over 14 percent. This rule works in reverse with inflation. Dividing the inflation rate into 72 gives the number of years in which your money will be halved. With a 3 percent rate of inflation, the value of your money declines by 50 percent in twenty-four years.

Of course, in the real world, rates of return are not constant and predetermined—far from it. Financial markets are quite volatile, particularly stock markets, and how the markets behave from year to year matters a great deal to your ultimate savings valuation. Returns come in an unpredictable mix of dazzling gains and rotten losses. Deterministic models of stock market behavior give investors a false sense of security. To capture the uncertainty, many financial planners are now recommending that "probabilistic" models be used to help investors gauge their strategies. Many of these models use so-called Monte Carlo analysis of the probabilities of varying outcomes. Analysts measure the odds by plugging into their computers historical returns and volatility of stocks, bonds, and cash, running hundreds of scenarios. The goal is to find the mix of assets and a withdrawal rate that can pay off for twenty-five years or so in 75 to 95 percent of those market scenarios.

A CAUTIOUS APPROACH TO RETIREMENT SAVING IS WISE

According to Chicago's Ibbotson Associates, U.S. stocks have gained 11 percent a year during the past seventy-five years. Since 1970, the average annual return on the S&P 500 has been around 12 percent. This compares to bond returns of over 9 percent and 7 percent for cash. Since 1980, the average annual stock performance has been an even better 16 percent while bond and cash returns have not changed much.[8] But even if your portfolio enjoyed average returns that approached these levels, you might end up with far less wealth than a deterministic model suggests. A lot depends on the timing of your gains.

If you are saving for retirement, you would rather have the bad markets early in your life, when your nest egg is still relatively small. Conversely, when you stop working, you want great returns early in your retirement, before your spending depletes your portfolio. Run into a bear market soon after you retire and your portfolio may be so mauled that you never get a chance to participate in the next bull market. For example, a retirement account invested 60 percent in stocks, 30 percent in bonds, and 10 percent in cash earned an average annual return of 11.7 percent from 1968 to 1998. This is a payoff that should have easily supported a retiree spending 8.5 percent of his or her portfolio each year for thirty years. But the bear market of 1973–74 reduced the value of stocks by a stunning 40 percent. This coupled with 8.5 percent withdrawals and the high inflation of the 1970s would have depleted the $1 million portfolio in just thirteen years. As this example shows, the sequence of returns is critical when it comes to spending in retirement.

To protect yourself, you have to scale back your spending plans. Indeed, the new consensus from a growing body of research suggests that a "sustainable" withdrawal rate may be no more than 4 percent to 5 percent of the retirement account's initial value, plus adjustments each year for inflation. In other words, you can start off by withdrawing no more than 5 percent in the first year, increasing yearly with the rise in inflation of say, 3 percent, to 5.15 percent the second year, 5.30 percent the third year and so on. This is a far cry from the old rule, which was to reinvest only a small part of the earnings in your portfolio as a hedge against price increases and spend the rest. A moderately aggressive retiree with $1 million invested 60 percent in stocks and 40 percent in cash and bonds could, based on average returns since 1970, expect to earn 12.2 percent a year. Even with some protection against inflation, it was generally believed it would be enough to support a healthy 8 percent rate of withdrawal—$80,000 annually—or even more if the retiree were willing to draw down principal.

Today, however, it is recognized that this conventional wisdom might well be a prescription for running out of money. The new consensus, recommending only a 4 to 5 percent withdrawal rate, says that if you're going to need $80,000 a year in income, you'll need to save not just $1 million, but $1.6 million to $2 million. This will come as quite a shock to many saving Boomers. The further into your retirement you are, the higher your withdrawal rate can safely be. It means you will have less to spend in your early retirement years when you are more active, and more to spend when you are eighty, eighty-five, or ninety, when discretionary income won't be as crucial. This is, of course, the opposite of what most people would wish, which means you need that much more savings to assure the lifestyle you desire in the early retirement years. If you run into a bear market during those years, your golden goose can be cooked if you are forced to sell stock at markedly depressed prices.

This cautious approach also means that the odds are high that you will leave behind a large estate, rather than enjoying the money in your lifetime. For example, starting with $1 million and a 5 percent drawdown rate, you have a 50 percent chance of bequeathing more than $1.4 million. This is money you could have spent on yourself had you been certain of your investment returns. Planners now counsel that you be conservative in the early years of retirement, but once you have reached age seventy, you might want to step up your withdrawal rates if the markets had performed according to plan.

Annuities can help fix this uncertainty by guaranteeing a lifetime income—fixed or variable, depending on the terms. Of course, you pay for the security of a defined income. Guarantees cost money, often more than they are truly worth in hindsight. That's what the insurance company actuaries determine. They are betting on actuarial probabilities about your life expectancy and rates of return on investments. The insurers certainly build into the premiums a margin of safety for themselves. The main drawback is that you could die soon after buying an annuity, not collect much income, and have the bulk of the money end up with your insurance company rather than your heirs. The income from annuities, as well, is only as good as the solvency of the insurer. Be sure to consult an independent financial advisor to help consider the benefits and drawbacks of annuities for you.

THE STOCK MARKET—HIGH RETURN, HIGH RISK SPELLS DISCOMFORT

It is not just the average returns on your portfolio that matter but the timing of those returns, which is inherently unpredictable. The fact is that even though stocks outperform other asset categories over long periods of time, they do not do so on a month-to-month basis. Empirical analysis of monthly total returns from 1970 through 2000 shows that bonds outperformed stocks in 47 percent of the months, while cash did better 43 percent of the time. Further evidence of why stock market investments can be so hair-raising is the volatility on a month-to-month basis. Even since 1980, when average annual returns in stocks have been a stellar 16.3 percent, stocks declined 20 percent or more at an annual rate in 15 percent of the months. There were more moderate declines in another 21 percent of the months, bringing the proportion of losing months to 36 percent.

Even more astonishing, the full capital gain over the thirty-year period occurred in the best 13 percent of the months. In other words, a relatively small number of very large monthly gains dominate the long-run returns in stocks. In the remaining 87 percent, gains offset losses to yield a net return of zero. But you can never know when those best 13 percent of the months will be. The spikes are often dramatic, sudden, and relatively short-lived. No one sends you an e-mail telling you when they will be. You have to be in the market to enjoy them. Frequently, the largest gains occurred in the depths of economic downturns when virtually no one predicted them. The very fact of surprise is needed to move the markets so aggressively. If everyone were expecting a rally, there would be no money left on the sidelines to buy. Five of the top-ten months in equity returns were during recessions, a market-timer's nightmare.

The moral of this story is that you should diversify your overall portfolio between stocks and bonds depending on your age and risk tolerance. Professional advice on the appropriate mix for you is well worth the effort and expense. The younger you are, the larger the stock component should be, but even retirees are now generally recommended to hold roughly 60 percent of their assets in stocks. The stock component should be well diversified and invested for the long run not the short run. Stay invested and don't try to time markets. If you had missed the best ten days of stock market performance in every year since 1996, you would have garnered an average annual loss of 10 percent, rather than the 17 percent gain actually posted. Even during 2000, when stocks fell for the year as a whole, the top-ten days registered a 33 percent gain. No invitations are sent informing you when those great days will be, so you need to ride out the nearly 90 percent of the time when things are just hobbling along. Even ride out the meaningful amount of time when stocks are down sharply. As long as you don't jump in and out, you will benefit from the big up days that will more than offset your losses over long periods of time.

Stocks have a higher expected rate of return than bonds, but they have greater volatility as well. That means that over the long haul, bonds could potentially fall one percentage point below their expected return, while stocks might fall three percentage points below. The bottom line: adding more stocks may boost your portfolio's likely performance; but because there is more volatility in stock returns, it will also increase the risk of earning far less than you expected.

Stocks Lead the Economy

Remember that stocks and bonds lead the economy—up and down. The markets anticipate economic developments. Stocks typically lead the economy by roughly four to six months. And the biggest gains in the stock market often occur when the current economic situation seems dismal. So if you wait for everything you read in the newspapers to be positive—for firms to be hiring, profits to be surging, and production to be rising following a downturn—you could well miss the big rallies. Stocks generally rise nearly 40 percent in the first months prior to a recovery in the economy. The best days occur when you least expect them—by definition. So do the worst days. All of this makes timing the markets all the more difficult. Don't even try.

HOW MUCH DO YOU NEED TO SAVE?

As we have seen, the uncertainty of the pattern of market returns behooves you to take a more cautious stance in planning for retirement. It is far better to be surprised on the high side, and end up with too much money, than to be caught short in the end. The first step is to determine your income needs in retirement. The younger you are, the more difficult that will be, which is why getting into the habit of saving 15 percent of your gross income is such a good idea. It gives you the money needed during your family-formation years for big-ticket items such as a house, cars, and education, while it provides a sound foundation for your retirement security later in life.

Most financial analysts suggest you need roughly 50 percent to 75 percent of your pre-retirement income after you stop working to maintain the equivalent standard of living. You will spend less on work-related items such as business clothes, transportation, and lunches, and you will not need to save for retirement or pay such high tax rates. However, if you have expensive hobbies or like to travel, you might want to err on the high end of the income range.[9]

In making these calculations, keep in mind that the top benefit today for a couple on Social Security is about $32,500 a year.[10] This would be payable to a family earning just under $80,000 (or more) per year before retirement. It would, however, likely maintain the current living standards for a family earning between $43,300 and $65,000 before retirement, depending on their circumstances. If you have other pension income, that is all the better. An increasing number of people, however, are no longer covered by defined-benefit pension plans—the kind that pay you a set income over your retirement years. For many now, retirement savings programs such as 401(k) and IRA plans are their main retirement vehicles.[11]

Given the limits on annual contributions into these plans, they will not be enough for some.[12] You will have to save without the benefit of the tax deferral—you will have to save in after-tax dollars. The good news is, however, that once you begin to spend the money in retirement, you do not pay income tax on the money outside of your retirement account. It is a frightening thought, but for a growing majority of current and future retirees, the skill they show in managing their own assets will make the difference between living well and barely making ends meet.

You can use a relatively simple framework to calculate how much money you will need the day you stop working. Estimate what your before-tax retirement income needs are on an annual basis (50 percent to 75 percent of your pre-retirement gross income, less the amount you will earn from Social Security and elsewhere). At the most cautious and conservative end, multiply that retirement income need (before tax) by twenty-five. This implies a very safe 4 percent annual withdrawal rate that analysts agree give a very high probability that your money will last beyond the twenty-five to thirty years in retirement.

On the other end of the spectrum of reasonable retirement planning, you would multiply your before-tax income need by fifteen. This is the equivalent of a 6.7 percent withdrawal rate, which some still consider to be reasonable. In this case, you would die broke after twenty-five years of retirement (assuming an average annual portfolio return of 8 percent and an inflation rate of 3 percent) as long as the rate of return annually was fairly smooth or front-ended. If, instead, a big stock market selloff were to occur early in your retirement years, you would run out of money sooner, even though the average return over the twenty-five year span was the same. This is a big risk to take. As we saw in 2000, big stock market selloffs can occur even when things seem to be going well. They are likely to recur periodically. Getting caught in one soon after you stop working can be devastating to your future financial security. It is better to use a multiplier of between 20 and 25—implying a drawdown rate of 4 to 5 percent. You can spend the money more aggressively when you have been retired for a number of years and seen the lay of the land. You can always begin paying for your grandchildren's education, fund charitable endeavors, or leave a sizable estate.

So, to do some math: For every $10,000 in pre-tax retirement income, you need between $200,000 and $250,000 in savings the day you stop working. These are huge numbers and clearly show that your commitment to save must be ongoing. The sooner you start the easier it is. Many Boomers, reaching their fiftieth birthdays, will get the big retirement-saving wake-up call. Fifteen years of saving can make the difference between self-reliance in old age and being a burden on your children. Many will choose to augment their retirement savings with part-time employment, and opportunities there will likely be available. Many, as well, will postpone retirement. Boomers will, on average, retire later than their parents as economic reality sets in and as many decide that thirty years of golf and gardening are just too much.

THE FINAL MESSAGE

I am optimistic about the outlook. I believe we are in an upwave in the long cycle and that we will continue to see tremendous technology-driven growth and prosperity on balance over the next twenty years. I also believe, however, that it will be fraught with turbulence and volatility. The pace of change will continue to accelerate. This is the Acceleration Age, where everyone expects transformation—expects the world to move at a pace unprecedented in the history of humankind. The difference between success and failure depends on the speed of adaptation to a changing reality, and that requires the ability to accurately predict the future—the perspective course of public sentiment, preferences, and technological advance. In a world hit daily by random shocks, this is extremely difficult. Businesses must be ever vigilant to keep an eye towards the future, recognizing that it will not move linearly, that expectations are not adaptive, that whole new technologies will regularly change the game. Failures will inevitably occur. Periodic bear markets will as well. But these downturns should not be seen as the end of the upwave or as evidence that the New Economy is dead.

Apple's handheld computer, the Newton, was an unmitigated failure, but the idea had merit. The Palm Pilot and the Blackberry have done what the Newton could not do. Just as many dot-coms in the future will get it right, doing what the failed dot-coms of 2000–2001 had not done. In a world that is changing so rapidly, missteps are an inevitable part of the game. With all the management-information systems out there, we still cannot predict future spending trends with complete certainty. And markets are driven by humans, with all of their occasionally irrational and certainly erratic behavior. Sometimes the smallest things make the biggest difference. A little-noticed devaluation in Thailand in July 1997 triggered the Asian crisis, Russian default, and the demise of Long-Term Capital Management in 1998.

Individuals in this environment run the risk of losing a sense of control. Yet power is in knowledge, in creating your competitive advantage to its fullest and marketing it accordingly. Look at yourself as an ongoing concern, an entrepreneur in the Knowledge Economy where everyone needs help understanding and managing the future. Expect volatility, expect change, and plan for it. But also expect growth, prosperity, and value creation. The pace of change will be head-spinning, sometimes gut-wrenching. There will be overshoots, as we have seen, on the upside, and also on the downside. But the general trend will be positive and the opportunities for your career, your business, your investment, and your children will be immense.

Endnotes

Introduction

1. Alvin Toffler, *Future Shock* (New York: Bantam Books, 1970).
2. Ibid., 12.
3. Sherry Cooper, *The Cooper Files: A Practical Guide to Your Financial Future* (Toronto: Key Porter, 1999).

Chapter 1

1. Capital goods comprise structures like factories and houses, equipment like computers and machine tools, and inventories of finished goods, materials inputs, and goods in process.
2. See, for example, Paul Romer, "The Origins of Endogenous Growth," *The Journal of Economic Perspectives* 8, no.1 (Winter 1994): 3–22. Romer's analysis, included in the body of the New Growth Theory, builds on the work of Joseph Schumpeter, *The Theory of Economic Development* (Cambridge: Harvard University Press, 1934), which emphasized the importance of the innovator—the person who introduced new ideas or ways of doing things—in the growth process. This Schumpeterian notion was lost in the traditional neoclassical growth models of the 1950s created by Robert Solow, *Economic Growth* (Oxford: Oxford University Press, 1970), for which he won the Nobel Prize in economics in 1987. Paul Romer added Schumpeter's innovator to the Neoclassical Model. Many believe that Romer, now only in his early forties, is a strong candidate for the Nobel Prize in coming years.
3. "Bank of America Roundtable on the Soft Revolution: Achieving Growth By Managing Intangibles," Panelists: Paul Romer, Lawrence Perlman, Stan Shih, Michael Volkema, *Journal of Applied Corporate Finance* 11, no. 2 (Summer 1998): 9.
4. Michael E. Porter, "Strategy and the Internet," *Harvard Business Review* (March 2001): 63–78.
5. W. Brian Arthur, *Increasing Returns and Path Dependence in the Economy* (Ann Arbor: University of Michigan Press, 1994); and *The Economy as an Evolving Complex System II* (Reading, Massachusetts: Perseus Books, 1997).

Chapter 2

1. See, for example, Joseph Schumpeter, *Capitalism, Socialism, and Democracy* (New York: Harper, 1947); also *The Theory of Economic Development* (Cambridge: Harvard University Press, 1934).
2. Clayton M. Christensen, *The Innovator's Dilemma* (New York: HarperBusiness, 2000); Clayton Christensen, Thomas Craig, and Stuart Hart, "The Great Disruption," *Foreign Affairs* 80, no. 2 (March/April 2001): 80–95.
3. Christensen et al., "The Great Disruption," 88.
4. Ibid., 91.
5. AMR Research Inc., *2001 Outlook*, 13 February 2001.

Chapter 3

1. Bill Alpert, "Seeing the Light: Optical Switches Will Be the Next Big Thing in Data Transmission," *Barron's*, 4 December 2000, 26.
2. World Wide Web Consortium, "A Little History of the World Wide Web" [online; cited 8 March 2001]; available from www.w3.org/History.html.
3. "Untangling e-conomics," *The Economist*, 23 September 2000, 6.
4. Matthew R. Sanders with Bruce D. Temkin, "Global eCommerce Approaches Hypergrowth," *The Forrester Brief*, 18 April 2000.
5. Jeanette Brown, "Don't Count Pure E-Tailers Out," *Business Week*, 12 February 2001, 14.
6. Robert X. Cringley, *Triumph of the Nerds*, "A History of the Computer," [online, cited 23 January 2001]; available from www.pbs.org/nerds/timeline/elec.html.
7. George Gilder, *Telecosm: How Infinite Bandwidth Will Revolutionize Our World* (New York: The Free Press, 2000).
8. Don Tapscott, "Say Hello to the Hypernet, Which Will Link Everything from Mobile Phones to Your Kitchen Appliances," *R.O.B. Magazine*, November 2000, 41–42.
9. Robert D. Atkinson, "The Revenge of the Disintermediated: How the Middleman is Fighting E-Commerce and Hurting Consumers," Progressive Policy Institute Policy Paper, January 2001.
10. Spencer E. Ante, "Why B2B Is a Scary Place to Be," *Business Week*, 11 September 2000, 34–37.
11. Keith Bradsher, "The Long, Long Wait for Cars," *The New York Times*, 9 May 2000, C1.

Chapter 4

1. The potential development of nanotechnology was first brought to mainstream media attention by Peter Schwartz and Peter Leyden in their July 1997 article in *Wired* magazine, "The Long Boom: A History of the Future, 1980–2020." They expanded on these ideas in a later book: Peter Schwartz, Peter Leyden, and Joel Hyatt, *The Long Boom* (Reading, Massachusetts: Perseus Books, 1999).
2. K. Eric Drexler, *Engines of Creation: The Coming Era of Nanotechnology* (New York: Anchor Books, 1986).
3. This section relies heavily on the work of Marvin Cetron and Owen Davies, *Probable Tomorrows* (New York: St. Martin's Press, 1997), as well as the 2000 Delphi Survey by Professor William E. Halal and his students at George Washington University. Halal and his associates pool the knowledge of the world's best experts in all scientific fields to estimate when roughly one hundred technologies will enter the economic mainstream. His work is available online at www.gwforecast.gwu.edu.
4. See, for example, Peter Schwartz, et al., *The Long Boom*, 171–181; and "Untangling e-conomics," *The Economist*, 23 September 2000.
5. "Squeaky Clean," *The Economist*, 10 February 2001, 17.
6. Jeffrey E. Garten, "*The Mind of the C.E.O.* Book Excerpt," *Business Week*, 5 February 2001, 107.
7. Donella H. Meadows, Dennis L. Meadows, and Jorgen Randers, *The Limits to Growth* (New York: Universe Books, 1972); and *Beyond the Limits* (Post Mills, Vermont: Chelsea Green Publishing, 1992).

8. Meadows et al., *The Limits to Growth*, 23.
9. Those who want to destroy technology for fear it will hurt workers, named after the eighteenth century British textile worker Ned Lud, who destroyed his employer's stocking frame, fearful that it would replace his job. The original Luddite revolt occurred in 1811. English weavers protested the arrival of mechanized looms, viewing them as a threat to their livelihood and way of life.
10. "Falling Through the Net," *The Economist*, 23 September 2000, 34.
11. Wilfred Beckerman, "Economic Growth and the Environment," *World Development* 20, no. 4 (1992): 482.

Chapter 5

1. Thomas L. Friedman, *The Lexus and the Olive Tree* (New York: Anchor Books, 2000).
2. Alan Greenspan, "Challenges for Monetary Policymakers" (speech presented to the 18th Annual Monetary Conference: Monetary Policy in the New Economy, Cato Institute Washington, D.C., 19 October 2000).
3. Dr. Edward Yardeni, chief investment strategist of Deutsche Banc Alex. Brown, first coined this term.
4. All GDP growth rates are in inflation-adjusted annual rate terms.
5. Jed Kolko, James L. McQuivey, and Becky Bermont, "Where the Wired Consumer Lives," *Forrester Technographics Brief*, 25 July 2000.
6. L. Slifman and C. Corrado, "Decomposition of Productivity and Unit Costs," *Occasional Staff Studies*, OSS-1 (Washington, D.C.: Federal Reserve Board, 1996).
7. Dale W. Jorgenson and Kevin J. Stiroh, "Raising the Speed Limit: U.S. Economic Growth in the Information Age," Brookings Papers on Economic Activity, no.1 (2000): 125–235.
8. Steve Liesman, "Further Gains in Productivity Are Predicted," *The Wall Street Journal*, 1 August 2000, A2.
9. Carlos Tejada, "Strong Labor Market May Linger," *The Wall Street Journal*, 11 September 2000, A1.
10. The G-7 countries are the U.S., Canada, the U.K., Germany, Italy, Japan, and France.
11. Jared Bernstein and Ellen Houston, "Crime and Work: What We Can Learn from the Low-Wage Labor Market," *Economic Policy Institute* (July 2000).
12. Jeffrey A. Butts, "Youth Crime Drop," Urban Institute Justice Policy Center (December 2000).
13. A merchandise trade deficit is the excess of the value of imports over exports for goods only. The current account deficit is a broader measure. It includes the merchandise trade deficit, the services balance, investment income, and unilateral transfers. This will be explained in more detail in Chapter 9.
14. Dean M. Maki and Michael G. Palumbo, "Disentangling The Wealth Effect: A Cohort Analysis of Household Saving in the 1990s," Finance and Economics Discussion Series (Washington, D.C.: Federal Reserve Board, April 2001).
15. Robert M. Solow, "We'd Better Watch Out," *New York Times Book Review*, 12 July 1987, 36.

Chapter 6

1. Mark Hyman, "Now That's a Hail Mary Play," *Business Week*, 31 January 2000, 100–101.

2. Dent's books were based on solid fundamentals and the investing public loved them. Harry S. Dent, Jr., *The Great Boom Ahead* (New York: Hyperion, 1993); and *The Roaring 2000s* (New York: Simon & Schuster, 1998).

3. Jonathan R. Laing, "The New Math," *Barron's*, 20 November 2000, 31–36.

4. Robert Shiller, *Irrational Exuberance* (New Jersey: Princeton University Press, 2000), 103.

5. Ibid., 104–111.

6. Charles Amos Dice, *New Levels in the Stock Market* (New York: McGraw-Hill, 1929).

7. Shiller, *Irrational Exuberance*, 111.

8. Jeremy J. Siegel, *Stocks for the Long Run: The Definitive Guide to Financial Market Returns and Long-Term Investment Strategies* (New York: McGraw-Hill, 1998); James K. Glassman and Kevin A. Hassett, *Dow 36,000: The New Strategy for Profiting from the Coming Rise in the Stock Market* (New York: Crown Publishers, 1999). Another such book was David Elias, *Dow 40,000: Strategies for Profiting from the Greatest Bull Market in History* (New York: McGraw-Hill, 1999).

9. James K. Glassman and Kevin A. Hassett, " Stock Prices Are Still Far Too Low," *The Wall Street Journal*, 17 March 1999, A26.

10. Joseph Bulgatz, *Ponzi Schemes, Invaders from Mars, & More Extraordinary Popular Delusions and the Madness of Crowds* (New York: Harmony, 1992).

11. Jeremy J. Siegel, "Big-Cap Tech Stocks Are a Sucker Bet," *The Wall Street Journal*, 14 March 2000, A30.

12. Shiller, *Irrational Exuberance*. See note 4.

13. Jack Willoughby, "Burning Up: Warning: Internet companies are running out of cash—fast," *Barron's*, 20 March 2000, 29.

14. Jim Carlton, "Amazon Stock Sinks After Credit Report," *The Wall Street Journal*, 26 June 2000, A3.

15. Stephen H. Wildstrom, "Why Most of Us Can't Have Broadband," *Business Week*, 4 December 2000, 22.

16. George Gilder and Bret Swanson, "The Broadband Economy Needs a Hero," *The Wall Street Journal*, 23 February 2001, A14.

17. Om Malik, "Telcos Get The Wrong Numbers," *Red Herring*, 16 January 2001 [online, cited 6 March 2001]; available from www.redherring.com.

Chapter 7

1. Michael J. Mandel, *The Coming Internet Depression* (New York: Basic Books, 2000), 71.

2. Ken Brown, "Some Tech Investors Shift Hopes to 2002," *The Wall Street Journal*, 21 February 2001, C2.

3. Alan Greenspan, "Semiannual Monetary Policy Report to the Congress" (testimony before the Committee on Banking, Housing, and Urban Affairs, U.S. Senate, 13 February 2001).

Chapter 8

1. The seminal monograph was written by Nikolai Kondratieff, head of the Moscow Institute for Business Cycle Research, and published in Russian in 1925.

2. Paul M. Romer, "Increasing Returns and Long-Run Growth," *The Journal of Political Economy* 94, no. 5 (October 1986): 1002–37; and "Endogenous Technical Change,"

The Journal of Political Economy 98, no. 5 Part 2 (October 1990): S71–102.

3. Tom Standage, *The Victorian Internet* (New York: Walker & Co., 1998).

4. For a terrific discussion of the application of technology to the oil industry, see Jonathan Rauch, "The New Old Economy: Oil, Computers, and the Reinvention of the Earth," *The Atlantic Monthly*, January 2001, 35–49.

5. *The Economic Report of the President*, transmitted to the Congress, January 2001 (Washington, D.C.: United States Government Printing Office), 28.

6. Robert E. Hall, "Struggling to Understand the Stock Market, The 2001 Ely Lecture," 3 January 2001 [online, cited 30 January 2001]; available from www.stanford.edu/~rehall/.

7. Ibid., 24.

8. Robert E. Hall, "e-Capital: The Link between the Stock Market and the Labor Market in the 1990s," 11 October 2000 [online, cited 30 January 2001]; available from www.stanford.edu/~rehall/, 4.

9. Hall, "Struggling to Understand the Stock Market," 25.

10. Andrew Whinston, "Measuring the Internet Economy," McCombs School of Business, University of Texas at Austin, and Cisco study, January 2001.

11. Ibid.

12. The definition of who is and who is not in the Net Economy is becoming increasingly arbitrary. As the Internet rapidly becomes the infrastructure for all sectors of the economy, there will be no need for measurement distinctions between the Net Economy and the rest. Unfortunately, however, the official government statistical collection processes have not yet caught up with reality. While we have a plethora of data regarding the traditional industrial world, the data are much more limited and sporadic for the tech-driven and Net-driven parts of the economy that are growing so rapidly and increasing in importance. For this reason, private studies—even those funded by the tech industry itself—are often all we have to rely on. Governments are addressing these issues, but it will take time. Similar to the antiquated accounting protocols for businesses, government accounting systems do not yet adequately measure and assess the New Economy.

13. George Gilder, *Telecosm: How Infinite Bandwidth Will Revolutionize Our World* (New York: The Free Press, 2000), 10.

14. Carl E. Van Horn and Duke Storen, "Telework: Coming of Age? Evaluating the Potential Benefits of Telework," *Telework and the New Workplace of the 21st Century*, U.S. Department of Labor, 2000: available from www.dol.gov.

15. David Wessel, "E-Progress Depends on E-Profits," *The Wall Street Journal*, 11 January 2001, A1.

Chapter 9

1. This figure excludes the Federal Reserve's holdings. Including the Fed's holdings, foreign ownership falls to 37 percent.

2. For a useful discussion of this phenomenon, see William Knoke, *Bold New World* (New York: Kodansha America, 1996), 153–155.

3. Joseph P. Quinlan, *Global Engagement* (Chicago: Contemporary Books, 2001), xii.

4. Ibid., xiii.

Chapter 10

1. U.S. Census Bureau, Educational Attainment in the United States (Update), March 2000, issued December 2000.

2. U.S. Census Bureau, Historical Income Tables—Households, Tables H-13 and H-14.

3. For background on skill-based technical change and the impact on wage distribution, see the "Symposium on Wage Inequality," *Journal of Economic Perspectives*, Spring 1997.

4. The theoretical basis for the leveling of income inequality through international trade has been posed by a series of economists since David Ricardo. See, for example, the text by Wilfred Ethier, *Modern International Economics*, 3rd ed. (New York: W.W. Norton, 1997).

5. Product here is measured in terms of its purchasing power in 1998 U.S. dollars.

6. Lant Pritchett, "Divergence, Big Time," *Journal of Economic Perspectives* 11, no. 3 (Summer 1997): 3–17.

7. Robert Summers and Alan Heston, "The World Distribution of Well-being Dissected," in *International and Interarea Comparisons of Income, Output, and Prices*, eds. Alan Heston and Robert E. Lipsey (Chicago: University of Chicago Press, 1999), 479–503.

8. Eli Berman, John Bound, and Stephen Machin, "Implications of Skill-Biased Technological Change: International Evidence," *Quarterly Journal of Economics* (November 1998): 1–40.

9. "Made in China: The Role of U.S. Companies in Denying Human and Worker Rights," National Labor Committee (May 2000).

Chapter 11

1. These are total factor productivity growth differences according to the OECD data reported in "A Survey of the New Economy," *The Economist*, 23 September 2000, 33. The list of countries is in descending order, from largest gain to smallest and from the biggest decline to the smallest.

2. OECD, *OECD Information Technology Outlook 2000: ICTs, E-Commerce and the Information Economy* (Paris: 2000).

3. International Institute for Management Development, *The World Competitiveness Yearbook 2000* (Lausanne, Switzerland, 2000), 445.

4. Ibid., 443.

5. Samuel Kortum and Josh Lerner, "Does Venture Capital Spur Innovation?" *NBER Working Paper* no. 6846 (December 1998): 1–40.

6. IMD, *The World Competitiveness Yearbook 2000*, 406.

7. Nina Hachigian, "China's Cyber-Strategy," *Foreign Affairs* 80, no. 2 (March/April, 2001): 118–33.

8. Jasper Becker, *The Chinese* (New York: The Free Press, 2000).

9. IMD, *The World Competitiveness Yearbook 2001*.

10. IMD, *The World Competitiveness Yearbook 2000*, 48–53.

11. Institute of International Education, *Open Doors 2000*. 54,466 came from China, 46,872 from Japan, 42,337 from India, 41,191 from South Korea, 29,234 from Taiwan, and 23,544 from Canada.

12. Paul Podolsky, *Creative Destruction Index* (FleetBoston Financial Corporation, September 2000).

Chapter 12

1. See Sherry Cooper, *The Cooper Files: A Practical Guide to Your Financial Future* (Toronto: Key Porter, 1999), 97–130, which describes in detail how the eldest Boomers differ socioeconomically from the younger Boomers and the impact of all Boomers on the U.S. and Canadian economies.

2. I am indebted to Professor Charles L. Jones, Senior Fellow in Sociology, Massey College of the University of Toronto, for his excellent review and assistance on the sections regarding the sex ratio and its implications for social change. The views and opinions expressed in these sections, however, are my own and cannot be attributed to Professor Jones.

3. For example, see Zhenchao Qian, "Changes in Assortative Mating: The Impact of Age and Education, 1970–1990," *Demography* (August 1998): 279–292; P.N. Mari Bhat and S. Shiva, "Demography of Brideprice and Dowry: Causes and Consequences of the Indian Marriage Squeeze," *Population Studies* 53, no. 2 (July 1999): 129–148; Robert Schoen and John Baj, "The Impact of the Marriage Squeeze in Five Western Countries," *Sociology and Social Research* 70, no. 1 (October 1985): 8–19; and Jean E. Veevers, "The 'Real' Marriage Squeeze. Mate Selection, Mortality, and the Mating Gradient," *Sociological Perspectives* 31, no. 2 (April 1988): 169–189.

4. For the purposes of this discussion, we use the term marriage to describe both legally married and common-law relationships.

5. David M. Heer and Amyra Grossbard-Shechtmen, "The Impact of the Female Marriage Squeeze and the Contraceptive Revolution on Sex Roles and the Women's Liberation Movement in the United States, 1960 to 1975," *Journal of Marriage and the Family* 43, no. 1 (February 1981): 49–65.

6. Belinda M. Tucker and Claudia Mitchell-Kernan, "Trends in African American Family Formation: A Theoretical and Statistical Overview," in *The Decline in Marriage Among African Americans: Causes, Consequences and Policy Implications*, eds. Belinda M. Tucker and Claudia Mitchell-Kernan (New York: Russell Sage Foundation, 1995), 3–26; and Cynthia M. Cready, Mark A. Fossett, and K. Jill Kiecolt, "Mate Availability and African American Family Structure in the U.S. Nonmetropolitan South, 1960-1990," *Journal of Marriage and the Family* (February 1997): 192–203.

7. Marcia Guttentag and Paul F. Secord, *Too Many Women? The Sex Ratio Question* (Beverly Hills: Sage Publications, 1983).

8. We are using the generation dates set by Diane Crispell in "Where Generations Divide: A Guide," *American Demographics* (May 1993), available from www.americandemographics.com. Wendy Bounds called Generation Y the kids born roughly between 1977 and 1997, in "Buying Gen Y: Rushing to Cash In On The New Baby Boom," *The Wall Street Journal*, 9 August 2000, B1.

9. Bounds, "Buying Gen Y."

10. Todd G. Buchholz, *Market Shock: 9 Economic and Social Upheavals That Will Shake Your Financial Future—and What to do About Them* (New York: HarperBusiness, 1999), 98.

11. Alison Stein Wellner, "Generation Z," *American Demographics* (September 2000); available from www.americandemographics.com.

12. Ibid.

13. For a great discussion of the digital generation, see Don Tapscott, *Growing Up Digital* (New York: McGraw-Hill, 1998).

14. Paul Saffo, "Five Demographic Trends Shaping the Marketplace, 1998 Ten-Year Forecast," Institute for the Future, 52.

15. The U.S. Census Bureau, *The Foreign-Born Population in the United States*, March 2000, available from www.census.gov. Also see Gregory Rodriguez, "The Nation: Mexican-Americans Forging A New Vision of America's Melting Pot," *The New York Times*, 11 February 2001, 1.

16. Rodriguez, "The Nation: Mexican-Americans Forging A New Vision of America's Melting Pot."

17. Eduardo Porter, "U.S. Hispanics Making Economic Strides, But Trend Is Masked by Poor Immigrants," *Wall Street Journal*, 14 February 2001, A4.

18. United Nations Population Division, *World Population Prospects, The 2000 Revision*, 28 February 2001.

19. The World Bank, *2000 World Development Indicators*, March 2000, 33.

20. David E. Bloom and Jeffrey G. Williamson, "Demographic Transitions and Economic Miracles in Emerging Asia," *World Bank Economic Review* 12, no. 3 (September 1998): 419–455.

21. Jo Wrighton, "Europe's 30 Most Influential Businesswomen," *Wall Street Journal Europe*, 1 March 2001, VI.

22. Carl E. Van Horn and Duke Storen, "Telework: Coming of Age? Evaluating the Potential Benefits of Telework," *Telework and the New Workplace of the 21st Century*, U.S. Department of Labor, 2000; available from www.dol.gov.

Chapter 13

1. See Sherry Cooper, *The Cooper Files: A Practical Guide to Your Financial Future* (Toronto: Key Porter, 1999), chapter 6, for details. Also see Susan Mitchell, *American Generations: Who They Are. How They Live. What They Think* (New York: New Strategist Publications, 1998); Cheryl Russell, *The Master Trend: How The Baby Boom Generation is Remaking America* (New York: Plenum Press, 1993); William Strauss and Neil Howe, *Generations: The History of America's Future 1584 to 2069* (New York: HarperTrade, 1992); William Strauss and Neil Howe, *The Fourth Turning: What the Cycles Of History Tell Us About America's Next Rendezvous with Destiny* (New York: Broadway Books, 1997); J. Walker Smith and Ann Clurman, *Rocking the Ages: The Yankelovich Report On Generational Marketing* (New York: HarperCollins, 1997).

2. These colleges included Smith, Wellesley, Vassar, Radcliffe, Bryn Mawr, Mount Holyoke, and Barnard.

3. Alvin Toffler, *Future Shock* (New York: Bantam Books, 1970), 52.

4. Lawrence M. Friedman, *The Horizontal Society* (New Haven: Yale University Press, 1999), 20.

5. This notion was first expressed by Stephen M. Pollan and Mark Levine in *Die Broke* (New York: HarperBusiness, 1997).

6. Tom Peters, "The Brand Called You," *Fast Company* 10 (August 1997): 83.

7. Brian Tracy, *Maximum Achievement: The Proven System of Strategies and Skills That Will Unlock Your Hidden Powers to Succeed* (New York: Simon & Schuster, 1993). See also Wayne W. Dyer, *Manifest Your Destiny: The Nine Spiritual Principles for Getting Everything You Want* (New York: HarperCollins, 1997); Charles J. Givens, *Super Self: Doubling Your Personal Effectiveness* (New York: Simon & Schuster, 1993); Henry Marsh, *The Breakthrough Factor: Creating A Life of Value for Success and Happiness* (New York: Simon & Schuster, 1997); Earl Nightingale, *The Essence of Success* (Illinois: Nightingale-Conant, 1993); Anthony Robbins, *Awaken the Giant Within: How to Take Immediate Control of Your Mental, Emotional, Physical & Financial Destiny!*

(New York: Simon & Schuster, 1991); Jim Rohn, *Leading an Inspired Life* (Illinois: Nightingale-Conant, 1997); Denis Waitley, *Empires of the Mind: Lessons to Lead and Succeed in a Knowledge-Based World* (New York: William Morrow and Company, 1995); Denis Waitley, *The Psychology of Motivation* (Illinois: Nightingale-Conant, 1997).

Chapter 14

1. Thomas J. Stanley and William D. Danko, *The Millionaire Next Door* (Marietta, Georgia: Longstreet Press, 1996).
2. In their definition of net worth, the current value of assets less liabilities, the authors exclude the principal on trust accounts; ibid., 12.
3. Ibid., 13.
4. Or Canada Pension (CP) contribution for Canadians (or QPP for those in Quebec).
5. This assumes that taxpayers earning $52,000 annual income in 2001 are married filing a joint return.
6. IRA contributions will increase with the implementation of the 2001 tax cut. In Canada, you should make your RRSP contribution, which is up to 18 percent of your income to a maximum of $13,500 per year.
7. In Canada, the capital gains tax rate on investment held for more than a year may be even higher. There is no distinction between short- and long-term gains and the rate varies from province to province, but in Ontario, for example, the maximum capital gains tax rate is 23 percent. It would be lower for lower income tax brackets.
8. In Canada, the numbers are somewhat different. Stocks still outperformed bonds, although not by such a wide margin. The average annual return since 1970 for the TSE 300 was 11 percent, compared to 10 percent for bonds and 8 percent for cash. Since 1980, the TSE return fell to 10 percent.
9. For Canadians this is especially important because of the risk of a continued decline in the Canadian-U.S. dollar exchange rate. The currency has been in a secular decline for the better part of twenty-five years. Canadians wishing to spend part of the year in the U.S. in retirement are especially vulnerable to this and should plan accordingly.
10. In Canada, the maximum benefit for a couple on Old Age Security (OAS) and CPP is just under $29,000 per year (all figures in this note are in Canadian dollars), which would be enough to maintain a pre-retirement lifestyle of a middle-class family income of between roughly $38,700 and $58,000 a year, depending on circumstances. If you have other pension income, all the better, but remember that some of your OAS benefit will be clawed back.
11. In Canada, it would be the RRSP.
12. According to the 2001 tax changes, the annual contribution limit for the 401(k) is $10,500 and will rise gradually until it reaches $15,000 in 2006; after that, the maximum increases only to account for inflation. For an IRA it is $2,000 and will rise to $5,000 in 2008; after that, the maximum increases to cover inflation. For a Canadian RRSP, the limit is $13,500 (Canadian). Self-employed people or unincorporated small business owners are eligible for the Keogh Plan, which is more flexible.

Bibliography

Alpert, Bill. "Seeing the Light: Optical Switches Will Be the Next Big Thing in Data Transmission." *Barron's*, 4 December 2000, 26.

Anderson, Clifford. *The Stages of Life: A Groundbreaking Look at How We Mature*. New York: Atlantic Monthly Press, 1995.

Ante, Spencer E. "Why B2B Is a Scary Place to Be." *Business Week*, 11 September 2000, 34-37.

Arthur, W. Brian. *Increasing Returns and Path Dependence in the Economy*. Ann Arbor: University of Michigan Press, 1994.

Arthur, W. Brian. *The Economy as an Evolving Complex System II*. Reading: Perseus Books, 1997.

Atkinson, Robert D. "The Revenge of the Disintermediated: How the Middleman is Fighting E-Commerce and Hurting Consumers." *Policy Paper*, Progressive Policy Institute (January 2001).

BCA Research. *The Bank Credit Analyst*, 52, no. 2. Montreal: BCA Publications Ltd., January 2001.

Bear Stearns Equity Research. *E-volve: Dot-com and Beyond*. New York: Bear Stearns & Co., 2000.

Becker, Jasper. *The Chinese*. New York: The Free Press, 2000.

Beckerman, Wilfred. "Economic Growth and the Environment." *World Development* 20, no. 4, (1992): 481-496.

Belsky, Gary, and Thomas Gilovich. *Why Smart People Make Big Money Mistakes and How to Correct Them*. New York: Simon & Schuster, 1999.

Berman, Eli, John Bound, and Stephen Machin. "Implications of Skill-Biased Technological Change: International Evidence." *Quarterly Journal of Economics*, (November 1998): 1–40.

Bernstein, Jared, and Ellen Houston. "Crime and Work: What We Can Learn From the Low-Wage Labor Market." Washington, The Economic Policy Institute (July 2000).

Berry, Brian J. L. *Long-Wave Rhythms in Economic Development and Political Behavior*. Baltimore: John Hopkins University Press, 1991.

Bhat, P.N. Mari, and S. Shiva. "Demography of Brideprice and Dowry: Causes and Consequences of the Indian Marriage Squeeze." *Population Studies* (Princeton University Office of Population Research) 53, no. 2 (July 1999): 129–148.

Blaug, Mark. *Great Economists Before Keynes: An Introduction to the Lives and Works of the One Hundred Great Economists of the Past*. Brighton: Cambridge University Press, 1989.

Blix, Jacqueline, and David Heitmiller. *Getting a Life: Real Lives Transformed by Your Money or Your Life*. New York: Viking Penguin, 1997.

Bloom, David E., and Jeffrey G. Williamson. "Demographic Transitions and Economic Miracles in Emerging Asia." *World Bank Economic Review* 12, no. 3 (September 1998): 416–455.

Bogle, John C. *Bogle on Mutual Funds: New Perspectives for the Intelligent Investor*. New York: Random House, 1994.

Bounds, Wendy. "Buying Gen Y: Rushing to Cash in on The New Baby Boom." *Wall Street Journal*, 9 August 2000, B1.

Bradsher, Keith. "The Long, Long Wait for Cars." *New York Times*, 9 May 2000, C1.

Brown, Jeanette. "Don't Count Pure E-Tailers Out." *Business Week*, 12 February 2001, 14.

Brown, John Seely. *Seeing Differently: Insights on Innovation*. Boston: Harvard Business School Publishing Corporation, 1997.

Brown, Ken. "Some Tech Investors Shift Hopes to 2002." *Wall Street Journal*, 21 February 2001, C2.

Buchholz, Todd G. *New Ideas from Dead Economists: An Introduction to Modern Economic Thought*. New York: New American Library, 1989.

Buchholz, Todd G. Market Shock: 9 *Economic and Social Upheavals that Will Shake Your Financial Future—and What to Do About Them.* New York: HarperBusiness, 1999.

Bulgatz, Joseph. *Ponzi Schemes, Invaders from Mars, & More Extraordinary Popular Delusions and the Madness of Crowds.* New York: Harmony, 1992.

Burstein, Daniel, and David Kline. *Road Warriors: Dreams and Nightmares Along the Information Highway.* New York: Plume, 1986.

Butts, Jeffrey A. "Youth Crime Drop." *Report*, Justice Policy Center, Urban Institute (December 2000).

Carlton, Jim. "Amazon Stock Sinks After Credit Report." *Wall Street Journal*, 26 June 2000, A3.

Celente, Gerald. *Trends: How to Prepare and Profit from the Changes of the 21st Century.* New York: Warner Books, 1997.

Cetron, Marvin, and Owen Davies. *Probable Tomorrows: How Science and Technology will Transform Our Lives in the Next Twenty Years.* New York: St. Martin's Press, 1997.

Cheung, Edward. *Baby Boomers, Generation X and Social Cycles.* Toronto: Long-Wave Press, 1995.

Chevreau, Johnathan. *The Wealthy Boomer.* Toronto: Key Porter, 1998.

Chilton, David. *Wealthy Barber: The Common Sense Guide to Successful Financial Planning.* Toronto: Stoddart Publishing, 1989.

Christensen, Clayton M. *The Innovator's Dilemma: When New Technologies Cause Great Firms to Fail.* New York: HarperBusiness, 2000.

Christenson, Clayton M., Thomas Craig, and Stuart Hart. "The Great Disruption." *Foreign Affairs* 80, no. 2 (March/April 2001).

Cooper, Sherry. *The Cooper Files: A Practical Guide to Your Financial Future.* Toronto: Key Porter, 1999.

Cork, David. *The Pig and the Python: How to Prosper from the Aging Baby Boom.* Toronto: Stoddart Publishing, 1996.

Cready, Cynthia M., Mark A. Fossett, and K. Jill Kiecolt. "Mate Availability and African American Family Structure in the U.S. Nonmetropolitan South, 1960–1990." *Journal of Marriage and the Family* (February 1997): 192–203.

Cringely, Robert X. "A History of the Computer." *Triumph of the Nerds*, 23 January 2001. Available from www.pbs.org/nerds/timeline/elec.html.

Crispell, Diane. "Where Generations Divide: A Guide." *American Demographics* (May 1993). Available from www.americandemographics.com.

Davidson, James Dale, and Lord William Rees-Mogg. *The Great Reckoning: How The World Will Change in the Depression of the 1990's.* New York: Summit Books, 1991.

Davis, Bob, and David Wessel. *Prosperity: The Coming 20 Year Boom and What it Means to You.* New York: Random House, 1998.

Davis, Stan, and Christopher Meyer. *Blur: The Speed of Change in the Connected Economy.* New York: Warner Books, 1998.

Davis, Stan, and Christopher Meyer. *Future Wealth.* Boston: Harvard Business School Press, 2000.

Dent, Jr., Harry S. *The Great Boom Ahead: Your Comprehensive Guide to Personal and Business Profit in the New Era of Prosperity.* New York: Hyperion, 1993.

Dent, Jr., Harry S. *The Roaring 2000s: Building the Wealth and Lifestyle You Deserve in the Greatest Boom in History.* New York: Simon & Schuster, 1998.

Department of Economic and Social Affairs. *World Population Prospects: The 2000 Revision.* New York: United Nations Population Division, 2001.

Di Matteo, Massimo. "Technological and Social Factors in Long-Term Fluctuations." Lecture Notes in Economics and Mathematical Systems, Springer-Verlag (1989).

Dice, Charles Amos. *New Levels in the Stock Market*. New York: McGraw-Hill, 1929.

Drexler, K. Eric. *Engines of Creation: The Coming Era of Nanotechnology*. New York: Anchor Books, 1986.

Drucker, Peter. *Managing the Future*. New York: Truman Tally Books, 1993.

Drucker, Peter. *Post-Capitalist Society*. New York: HarperCollins, 1993.

Dychtwald, Ken, and Joe Flower. *Age Wave: How the Most Important Trend of Our Time Will Change Your Future*. New York: Bantam Books, 1990.

Dyer, Wayne W. *Manifest Your Destiny: The Nine Spiritual Principles for Getting Everything You Want*. New York: HarperCollins, 1997.

"Economic Report of the President," transmitted to the Congress, January 2001.

Eisenson, Marc, Gerri Detweiler, and Nancy Castleman. *Invest in Yourself: Six Secrets to a Rich Life*. New York: John Wiley & Sons, 1998.

Elias, David. *Dow 40,000: Strategies for Profiting from the Greatest Bull Market in History*. New York: McGraw-Hill, 1999.

Ethier, Wilfred. *Modern International Economics*, 3rd ed. New York: WN. North, 1997.

Evans, Harold. *The American Century*. New York: A. A. Knopf, 1998.

Fischer, David Hackett. *The Great Wave: Price Revolutions and the Rhythm of History*. New York: Oxford University Press, 1996.

Friedman, Lawrence M. *The Horizontal Society*. New Haven: Yale University Press, 1999.

Friedman, Thomas L. *The Lexus and the Olive Tree*. New York: Anchor Books, 2000.

Garten, Jeffrey E. *"The Mind of the CEO."* Book Excerpt. *Business Week* 5 February 2001, 107.

Gates, Bill. *The Road Ahead*. New York: Penguin Books, 1996.

Gates, Bill. *Business @ the Speed of Thought: Using a Digital Nervous System*. New York: Warner Books, 1999.

Genetski, Robert J. *A Nation of Millionaires: Unleashing America's Economic Potential*. Palatine: The Heartland Institute, 1997.

Gilder, George, and Bret Swanson. "The Broadband Economy Needs a Hero." *Wall Street Journal*, 23 February 2001, A14.

Gilder, George. *Telecosm: How Infinite Bandwidth Will Revolutionize Our World*. New York: The Free Press, 2000.

Givens, Charles J. *Super Self: Doubling Your Personal Effectiveness*. New York: Simon & Schuster, 1993.

Glahe, Fred, ed. *Adam Smith's* An Inquiry into the Nature and Causes of the Wealth of Nations. Savage: Rowman & Littlefield, 1993.

Glassman, James K., and Kevin A. Haskett. *Dow 36,000: The New Strategy for Profiting from the Coming Rise in the Stock Market*. New York: Crown Publishers, 1999.

Glassman, James K., and Kevin A. Hassett. "Stock Prices Are Still Far Too Low." *Wall Street Journal*, 17 March 1999, A26.

Gleick, James. *Faster: The Acceleration of Just About Everything*. New York: Random House, 1999.

Global BioTechnology Quarterly. London: S.G. Cowan, July 2000.

Goleman, Daniel. *Working with Emotional Intelligence*. New York: Bantam Books, 1995.

Gould, Stephen J. *Full House: The Spread of Excellence from Plato to Darwin*. New York: Crown Publishers, 1996.

Greenspan, Alan, "Semiannual Monetary Police Report to the Congress," testimony before the Committee on Banking, Housing, and Urban Affairs, U.S. Senate, 13 February 2001.

Greenspan, Alan, "Challenges for Monetary Policy Makers," speech presented to the 18th Annual Monetary Conference: Monetary Policy in the New Economy, Washington Cato Institute, 19 October 2000.

Guttentag, Marcia, and Paul F. Secord. *Too Many Women? The Sex Ratio Question.* Beverly Hills: Sage Publications, 1983.

Hachigian, Nina. "China's Cyber-Strategy." *Foreign Affairs* 80, no. 2, (March/April 2001): 118–133.

Halal, William E., Michael D. Kull, and Ann Leffman. "The GWU Forecast of Emerging Technologies: A Continuous Assessment of the Technology Revolution." Available from www.gwforecast.gwu.edu.

Hall, Robert E. "e-Capital: The Link Between the Stock Market and the Labor Market in the 1990's." 11 October 2000. Available from www.stanford.edu/~rehall/.

Hall, Robert E. "Struggling to Understand the Stock Market, The 2001 Ely Lecture." 3 January 2001. Available from www.stanford.edu/~rehall/.

Handy, Charles et al. *Rethinking the Future.* Naperville: Nicholas Brealey Publishing, 1998.

Heer, David M., and Amyra Grossbard-Shechtmen. "The Impact of the Female Marriage Squeeze and the Contraceptive Revolution on Sex Roles and the Women's Liberation Movement in the United States, 1960 to 1975." *Journal of Marriage and the Family* (National Council of Family Relations) 43, no. 1 (February 1981): 49–65.

Heinzl, Mark. *Stop Buying Mutual Funds.* New York: John Wiley & Sons, 1998.

Henderson, Hael. *Building a Win-Win World: Life Beyond Global Economic Warfare.* San Francisco: Berrett-Koehler Publishers, 1996.

Heston, Alan, and Robert E. Lipsey, eds. *International and Interarea Comparisons of Income, Output, and Prices.* Chicago: University of Chicago Press, 1999.

Hyman, Mark. "Now That's a Hail Mary Play." *Business Week,* 31 January 2000, 100-101.

Johnson, Chalmers. *MITI and the Japanese Miracle.* Stanford: Stanford University Press, 1982.

Jorgenson, Dale, and Kevin Stiroh. "Raising the Speed Limit: U.S. Economic Growth in the Information Age." *Brookings Institution Paper on Economic Activity.* Washington: The Brookings Institute, 1 May 2000.

Judy, Richard W., and Carol D'Amico. *Workforce 2020: Work and Workers in the 21st Century.* Indianapolis: Hudson Institute, 1997.

Kelly, Kevin. *New Rules for the New Economy: 10 Radical Strategies for a Connected World.* New York: Viking Penguin, 1998.

Kiyosaki, Robert T. *Rich Dad, Poor Dad: What the Rich Teach their Kids About Money That the Poor and Middle Class Do Not.* New York: Warner Books, 1998.

Kiyosaki, Robert T. *Rich Dad's Guide to Investing: What the Rich Invest In, That the Poor and Middle Class Do Not.* New York: Warner Books, 2000.

Klazanjian, Kirk. *Wizards of Wall Street: Market-Beating Insights and Strategies from the World's Top-Performing Mutual Fund Managers.* New York: Prentice Hall Press, 2000.

Knoke, William. *Bold New World.* New York: Kodansha America, 1996.

Kolko, Jed, James L. McQuivey, and Becky Bermont. "Where the Wired Consumer Lives." *Forrester Technographics Brief* (25 July 2000): 1–4.

Kortum, Samuel, and Josh Lerner. "Does Venture Capital Spur Innovation?" *Working Paper,* no. 6846. Cambridge: National Bureau of Economic Research, 1998.

Kotkin, Joel. *The New Geography.* New York: Random House, 2000.

Krugman, Paul. *Development, Geography, and Economic Theory.* Cambridge: MIT Press, 1995.

Krugman, Paul. *The Accidental Theorist.* New York: W.W. Norton & Co., 1998.

Krugman, Paul. *Pop Internationalism.* Cambridge: MIT Press, 1998.

Kurtz, Howard. *The Fortune Tellers: Inside Wall Street's Game of Money, Media and Manipulation.* New York: Simon & Schuster, 2000.

Laing, Jonathan R. "The New Math." *Barron's*, 20 November 2000, 31–36.

Lee, Dwight R., and Richard McKenzie. *Getting Rich in America: Eight Simple Rules for Building a Fortune and a Satisfying Life.* New York: HarperCollins, 1999.

Levine, Rick, Christopher Locke, and Doc Searls. *The Cluetrain Manifesto: The End of Business as Usual.* Cambridge: Perseus Books, 2000.

Lewis, Michael. *The New New Thing: A Silicon Valley Story.* New York: W.W. Norton, 2000.

Liesman, Steve. "Further Gains in Productivity are Predicted." *Wall Street Journal*, 1 August 2000, A2.

"Little History of the World Wide Web, A." *World Wide Web Consortium.* 8 March 2001. Available from www.w3.org/History.html.

Luttwak, Edward. *Turbo-Capitalism: Winners and Losers in the Global Economy.* London: Weidenfeld & Nicholson, 1998.

Lynch, Peter, and John Rothchild. *Learn to Earn: A Beginner's Guide to the Basics of Investing and Business.* New York: Fireside Books, 1995.

Made in China: *The Role of U.S. Companies in Denying Human and Worker Rights.* New York: National Labor Committee, May 2000.

Madrick, Jeffrey. *The End Of Affluence: The Causes and Consequences of America's Economic Dilemma.* New York: Random House, 1995.

Maki, Dean M., and Michael G. Palumbo. "Disentangling the Wealth Effect: A Cohort Analysis of Household Saving in the 1990s." *Finance and Economics Discussion Series*, Federal Reserve Board (April 2001).

Malik, Om. "Telcos Get The Wrong Numbers." *Red Herring.* 6 March 2001. Available from www.redherring.com.

Malkiel, Burton G. *A Random Walk Down Wall Street*, rev. ed. New York: W.W. Norton, 1999.

Mandel, Michael J. *The Coming Internet Depression.* New York: Basic Books, 2000.

Marsh, Henry. *The Breakthrough Factor: Creating A Life of Value for Success and Happiness.* New York: Simon & Schuster, 1997.

Matathia, Ira, and Marian Salzman. *Next: Trends for the Near Future.* New York: Overlook Press, 1999.

Meadows, Donella H., Dennis L. Meadows, and Jorgen Randers. *Beyond the Limits.* Post Mills: Chelsea Green Publishing, 1992.

Meadows, Donella H., Dennis L. Meadows, and Jorgen Randers. *The Limits to Growth.* New York: Universe Books, 1972.

Metcalfe, J. S. *Evolutionary Economics and Creative Destruction.* New York: Routledge Press, 1998.

Mitchell, Susan. *American Generations: Who They Are. How They Live. What They Think*, 2nd ed. New York: New Strategist Publications, 1998.

Murray, Alan. *The Wealth of Choices: How the New Economy Puts Power in Your Hands and Money in Your Pocket.* New York: Crown Publishers, 2000.

Naisbitt, John, and Patricia Aburdine. *Megatrends 2000: Ten New Directions for the 1990s.* New York: William Morrow, 1990.

Naisbitt, John. *High Tech High Touch: Technology and Our Search for Meaning.* New York: Broadway Books, 1999.

Nightingale, Earl. *The Essence of Success.* Illinois: Nightingale-Conant, 1993.

OECD Information Technology Outlook 2000: ICTs, E-Commerce and the Information Economy. Paris: OECD, 2000.

"Open Doors on the Web." *Institute of International Education.* 14 February 2001. Available from www.opendoorsweb.org.

Orman, Suze and Linda Mead. *You've Earned It, Don't Lose It.* New York: Newmarket Press, 1998.

Orman, Suze. *The Nine Steps to Financial Freedom.* New York: Crown Publishers, 1997.

O'Shaunessey, Jim. *How to Retire Rich.* New York: Broadway Books, 1998.

Perkins, Anthony B. *The Internet Bubble.* New York: HarperBusiness, 1999.

Peters, Tom. "The Brand Called You." *Fast Company* 10 (August 1997): 83.

Podolsky, Paul, with A. Kostina. "Creative Destruction Index." FleetBoston Financial Corporation (September 2000).

Pollan, Stephen M., and Mark Levine. *Die Broke.* New York: HarperBusiness, 1997.

Pollan, Stephen M., and Mark Levine. *Live Rich.* New York: HarperCollins Publishers, 1998.

Popcorn, Faith. *The Popcorn Report: Faith Popcorn on the Future of Your Company, Your World, Your Life.* New York: Doubleday, 1991.

Popcorn, Faith, and Marigold Lys. *Clicking: 17 Trends That Drive Your Business and Your Life.* New York: HarperCollins, 1997.

Porter, Eduardo. "U.S. Hispanics Making Economic Strides, But Trend is Masked by Poor Immigrants." *Wall Street Journal,* 14 February 2001, A4.

Porter, Michael E. "Strategy and the Internet," *Harvard Business Review* (March 2001): 63-78.

Powers, Richard. *Gain.* New York: Farrar, Strauss & Giroux, 1998.

Prestowitz, Clyde. *Trading Places: How We are Giving Our Future to Japan and How to Reclaim It.* New York: Basic Books, 1989.

Pritchett, Lant. "Divergence, Big Time." *Journal of Economic Perspectives* 11, no. 3, (Summer 1997): 3-17.

Qian, Zhenchao. "Changes in Assortative Mating: The Impact of Age and Education, 1970-1990," *Demography* (August 1998): 279–292.

Quinlan, Joseph P. *Global Engagement.* Chicago: Contemporary Books, 2001.

Rauch, Jonathan. "The New Old Economy: Oil, Computers, and the Reinvention of the Earth." *The Atlantic Monthly* (January 2001): 35–49.

Reich, Robert B. *The Future of Success.* New York: A. A. Knopf, 2000.

Rifkin, Jeremy. *The Biotech Century: Harnessing the Gene and Remaking the World.* New York: Jeremy P. Tarcher/Putnam, 1998.

Robbins, Anthony. *Awakening the Giant Within: How to Take Immediate Control of Your Mental, Emotional, Physical & Financial Destiny!* New York: Simon & Schuster, 1991.

Rodriguez, Gregory. "The Nation: Mexican-Americans Forging A New Vision of America's Melting Pot." *New York Times,* 11 February 2001, 1.

Rohn, Jim. *Leading an Inspired Life.* Illinois: Nightingale-Conant, 1997.

Romer, Paul. "Increasing Returns and Long-Run Growth." *The Journal of Political Economy* 94, no. 5 (October 1986): 1002-37.

Romer, Paul. "Endogenous Technical Change." *The Journal of Political Economy* 98, no. 5, (October 1990): S71-102.

Romer, Paul. "The Origins of Endogenous Growth." *The Journal of Economic Perspectives* 8, no. 1 (Winter 1994): 3–22.

Romer, Paul, et al. "Bank of America Roundtable on the Soft Revolution: Achieving Growth by Managing Intangibles." *Journal of Applied Corporate Finance* 11, no. 2 (Summer 1998): 9.

Rothbard, Murray N. *Classical Economics: An Austrian Pespective on the History of Economic Thought, II.* Northampton: Edward Elgar Publishing Inc., 1995.

Rothschild, Michael. *Bionomics: Economy as Ecosystem.* New York: Henry Holt, 1990.

Russell, Cheryl. *The Master Trend: How the Baby Boom Generation is Remaking America.* New York: Plenum Press, 1993.

Saffo, Paul. "Five Demographic Trends Shaping the Marketplace, 1998 Ten-Year Forecast." Melo Park: Institute for the Future, 1998.

Samuelson, Paul Anthony. *Economics,* 18th ed. Toronto: McGraw-Hill/Ryerson, 2000.

Sanders, Matthew R., with Bruce D. Temkin. "Global eCommerce Approaches Hypergrowth." *The Forrester Brief* (18 April 2000).

Savage, Terry. *The Savage Truth About Money.* New York: John Wiley & Sons, 1999.

Schoen, Robert, and John Baj. "The Impact of the Marriage Squeeze in Five Western Countries." *Sociology and Social Research* 70, no. 1, (October 1985): 8–19.

Schumpeter, Joseph A. *The Theory of Economic Development.* Cambridge: Harvard University Press, 1934.

Schumpeter, Joseph A. *Capitalism, Socialism, and Democracy.* New York: Harper, 1947.

Schwartz, Peter, and Peter Leyden. "The Long Boom: A History of the Future, 1980–2020." *Wired,* July 1997.

Schwartz, Peter, Peter Leyden, and Joel Hyatt. *The Long Boom: A Vision for the Coming Age of Prosperity.* Reading: Perseus Books, 1999.

Schwartz, Peter. *The Art of the Long View: Planning for the Future in an Uncertain World.* New York: Doubleday, 1991.

Shapiro, Carl, and Hal Varian. *Information Rules: A Strategic Guide to the Network Economy.* Boston: Harvard Business School Press, 1998.

Shiller, Robert J. *Irrational Exuberance.* New Jersey: Princeton University Press, 2000.

Shilling, Gary A. *Deflation.* New Jersey: Lakeview Publishing Co., 1998.

Shuman, James, and David Rosenau. *The Kondratieff Wave.* New York: World Publishing, 1972.

Siegel, Jeremy J. "Big-Cap Tech Stocks Are a Sucker Bet." *Wall Street Journal,* 14 March 2000, A30.

Siegel, Jeremy J. *Stocks for the Long Run: The Definitive Guide to Financial Market Returns and Long-Term Investment Strategies.* New York: McGraw-Hill, 1998.

Simon, Julian L. *Ultimate Resource 2.* New Jersey: Princeton University Press, 1996.

Slifman, L., and C. Corrado. "Decomposition of Productivity and Unit Costs." *Occasional Staff Studies, OSS-1,* Federal Reserve Board (1996).

Smith, J. Walker, and Ann S. Clurman. *Rocking The Ages: The Yankelovich Report on Generational Marketing.* New York: HarperCollins, 1997.

Sobel, Robert. *The Pursuit of Wealth: The Incredible Story of Money Throughout the Ages.* New York: McGraw-Hill, 2000.

Solow, Robert M. "We'd Better Watch Out." *New York Times Book Review,* 12 July 1987, C36.

Solow, Robert M. *Economic Growth.* Oxford: Oxford University Press, 1970.

Sowell, Thomas. *Knowledge and Decisions.* New York: Basic Books, 1980.

Sowell, Thomas. *The Economics and Politics of Race.* New York: William Morrow, 1983.

"Squeaky Clean." *The Economist,* 10 February 2000, 17.

Standage, Tom. *The Victorian Internet.* New York: Walker & Co., 1998.

Stanley, Thomas J., and William D. Danko. *The Millionaire Next Door: The Surprising Secrets of America's Wealthy.* Marietta: Longstreet Press, 1996.

Sterling, William, and Steven Waite. *Boomernomics: The Future of Your Money in the Upcoming Generational Warfare.* New York: Ballantine, 1998.

Stewart, Hugh B. *Recollecting the Future: A View of Business, Technology and Innovation in the Next 30 Years.* New York: Dow Jones-Irwin, 1988.

Strauss, William, and Neil Howe. *Generations: The History of America's Future 1584 to 2069.* New York: HarperTrade, 1992.

Strauss, William, and Neil Howe. *The Fourth Turning: What the Cycles of History Tell Us About America's Next Rendezvous with Destiny.* New York: Broadway Books, 1997.

"Survey of Energy, A." *The Economist,* 10 February 2001, 1–24.

"Survey of the New Economy, A." *The Economist,* 23 September 2000, 1–40.

"Symposium on Wage Inequality." *Journal of Economic Perspectives* 11 (Spring 1997): 21–96.

Tapscott, Don. *The Digital Economy: Promise and Peril in the Age of Networked Intelligence.* New York: McGraw-Hill, 1996.

Tapscott, Don. *Growing Up Digital.* New York: McGraw-Hill, 1998.

Tapscott, Don. *Creating Value in the Network Economy.* Boston: Harvard Business School Press, 1999.

Tapscott, Don. "Say Hello to the Hypernet, Which Will Link Everything from Mobile Phones to Your Kitchen Appliances." *R.O.B. Magazine,* November 2000, 41–42.

Tapscott, Don, and Art Caston. *Paradigm Shift: The New Promise of Information Technology.* New York: McGraw-Hill, 1993.

Tapscott, Don, David Ticoll, and Alex Lowy. *Digital Capital: Harnessing the Power of Business Webs.* Boston: Harvard Business School Press, 2000.

Tejada, Carlos. "Strong Labor Market May Linger." *Wall Street Journal,* 11 September 2000, A1.

The Economic Report of the President. Washington: U.S. Government Printing Office, January 2001.

Thurow, Lester. *Building Wealth: The New Rules for Individuals, Companies, and Nations in a Knowledge-Based Economy.* New York: HarperCollins, 1999.

Thurow, Lester. *Head to Head: The Coming Economic Battle Among Japan, Europe and America.* New York: William Morrow, 1992.

Tobias, Andrew. *The Only Investment Guide You'll Ever Need.* Orlando: Harcourt Brace, 1998.

Toffler, Alvin. *Future Shock.* New York: Bantam Books, 1970.

Toffler, Alvin. *Powershift: Knowledge, Wealth, and Violence at the Edge of the 21st Century.* New York: Bantam Books, 1990.

Tracy, Brian. *Maximum Achievement: The Proven System of Strategies and Skills That Will Unlock Your Hidden Powers to Succeed.* New York: Simon & Schuster, 1993.

Tucker, Belinda M., and Claudia Mitchell-Kernan, eds. "Trends in African American Family Formation: A Theoretical and Statistical Overview." *The Decline in Marriage Among African Americans: Causes, Consequences and Policy Implications,* Russell Sage Foundation (1995): 3–26.

2001 Outlook. Boston: AMR Research Inc., 13 February 2001.

U.S. Census Bureau. *Educational Attainment in the United States (Update),* Washington: Department of Commerce, 2000.

U.S. Census Bureau. *The Foreign-Born Population in the United States,* Washington: Department of Commerce, 2000.

U.S. Census Bureau. *Historical Income Tables: Households, Tables H-13 and H-14,* Washington: Department of Commerce, 2000.

Van Horn, Carl E., and Duke Storen. "Telework: Coming of Age? Evaluating the Potential Benefits of Telework." *Telework and the New Workplace of the 21st Century* (2000). Available from www.dol.gov.

Van Wolferens, Karel. *The Enigma of Japanese Power.* New York: A. A. Knopf, 1989.

Vasko, T. "Life Cycles and Long Waves." *Lecture Notes in Economics and Mathematical Systems,* Springer-Verlag (1990).

Veevers, Jean E. "The 'Real' Marriage Squeeze. Mate Selection, Mortality, and the Mating Gradient," *Sociological Perspectives* 31, no. 2 (April 1988): 169–189.

Waitley, Denis. *Empires of the Mind: Lessons to Learn and Succeed in a Knowledge-Based World.* New York: William Morrow, 1995.

Waitley, Denis. *The Psychology of Motivation.* Illinois: Nightingale-Conant, 1997.

Wellner, Alison Stein. "Generation Z." *American Demographics* (September 2000). Available from www.americandemographics.com.

Wesbury, Brian S. *The New Era of Wealth: How Investors Can Profit from the Five Economic Trends Shaping the Future.* New York: McGraw-Hill, 2000.

Wessel, David. "E-Progress Depends on E-Profits." *Wall Street Journal,* 11 January 2001, A1.

Whinston, Andrew. *Measuring the Internet Economy.* Austin: McCombs School of Business, University of Texas, and CISCO, January 2001.

Wilber, Ken. *Sex, Ecology, Spirituality: The Spirit of Evolution.* Boston: Shambhala Publications, 1995.

Wilber, Ken. *A Brief History of Everything.* Boston: Shambhala Publications, 1996.

Wildstrom, Stephen H. "Why Most of Us Can't Have Broadband." *Business Week,* 4 December 2000, 22.

Willoughby, Jack. "Burning Up: Warning: Internet Companies Are Running Out of Cash—Fast." *Barron's,* 20 March 2000, 29.

World Competitiveness Yearbook 2000. Lausanne: IMD, International Institute for Management Development, 2000.

World Competitiveness Yearbook 2001. Lausanne: IMD, International Institute for Management Development, 2001.

World Development Indicators 2000. Washington: The World Bank, March 2000.

World Development Indicators 2001. Washington: The World Bank, April 2001.

World Population Prospects, The 2000 Revision. United Nations Population Division, 28 February 2001.

Worzel, Richard. Facing *The Future: The Seven Forces Revolutionizing Our Lives.* Toronto: Stoddart Publishing, 1994.

Wrighton, Jo. "Europe's 30 Most Influential Businesswomen." *Wall Street Journal Europe,* 1 March 2001, VI.

Yamada, Louise. *Market Magic: Riding the Greatest Bull Market of the Century.* New York: John Wiley & Sons, 1998.

Index

Kondratieff wave, 143
   see also long cycle

L
labor markets, change in, 88–91
LambdaRouter, 53
layoffs, 260–261
leadership in technology revolution
   Anglo-Saxon model, 220–221
   change, adapting to, 223–224
   China, 211–214
   competitiveness, dimensions of, 214–220
   deregulation, 204
   economic flexibility, 206–207
   Europe, 202–203
   fiscal policy, 207–208
   India, 210–211, 214
   Israel, 209–210
   Japan, 202–203
   level playing field, 203
   monetary policy, 207–208
   Northern European model, 221–222
   skilled labor, 208–209
   Southern European model, 222–223
   technology usage, global, 204–205
   United States, 201–203
   U.S. problems, 224–228
Lev, Baruch, 112
Limits of Growth, 68
"lock-in effects," 10
long cycle
   breakthrough technology, 145–146
   controversy of, 143–144
   and Internet, 149–150
   wars and, 146–149
Long-Term Capital Management, 83
Lovins, Amory, 71
Lucent, 21, 23, 53

M
Malthus, T.R., 67–68, 71
Mandel, Michael, 136, 137
"marriage squeeze," 232, 233
Marshall, Alfred, 9
medicine
   artificial organ transplants, 64
   cancer cure, 63

gene therapy, 63
hormone replacement treatment, 63
nanotechnology in, 54
predictions and prevention, 63
in twenty-first century, 62–64
Metcalfe's Law, 10
Mexican-Americans, 243
Mexican War, 147
Mexico, 195, 250
microelectromechanical systems (MEMS), 52, 53–54
Microsoft, 11, 20
Millionaire Next Door (Stanley and Danko), 270
miniature computers, 51–53
mobile Internet, 33–35, 159
"Mobile Net," 34
molecular-size rotors, 53
monetary policy, 151, 207–208
monopoly power, 11
Moore's Law, 33
multinational corporations, 174, 196–199
mutual fund bull market, 110

N
nanotechnology, 34
   carbon nanotubes, 55
   and computing, 54–55
   dark side, 56
   defined, 51
   germ warfare, 56
   internal intelligence, 52
   medicine, 54
   microelectromechanical systems (MEMS), 52, 53–54
   optical switching, 53-54
   ribonucleic acid polymerase (RNA), 52–53
nanoterrorism, 56
Napster, 38, 162
Nasdaq boom
   bursting of bubble, 116–119
   cause of, 106–115
   dot-com *chutzpah*, 107–108
   historical examples, 113–114
   IPO market collapse, 119
   momentum, 115–116
   mutual fund bull market, 110